LOVE IS LOVE IS LOVE

The politics of Broadway musicals matter a great deal more to U.S. American culture than they appear to mean, and they are especially important to mainstream politics surrounding sex, gender, and sexuality. *Love Is Love Is Love* looks to the Broadway musicals of the past decade for help understanding the current state of LGBTQ politics in the United States.

Through analyses of *Promises, Promises, Newsies, Hedwig and the Angry Inch, The Color Purple,* and *Frozen,* this book attempts to move past the question of representational politics and asks us instead to think in more complex ways about LGBTQ identity, what LGBTQ politics are, and the politics of Broadway musicals themselves. Producing new, complex readings of all five of these musicals, author Aaron C. Thomas places each of them within the context of the LGBTQ politics of their day. Some of the issues the book treats are controversies of casting, the closetedness and openness of musical theatre, LGBTQ identities, adaptation from movies into musicals, and the special power of the musical form by examining how these shows differ from the books and movies on which they're based.

Love Is Love Is Love places contemporary LGBTQ political tensions and conversations in a new light, making this an essential companion for students and scholars of contemporary theatre, musical theatre, cultural studies, Queer studies, and gender studies.

Aaron C. Thomas is an assistant professor in the School of Theatre at Florida State University, USA. He is the author of *Sondheim and Wheeler's Sweeney Todd* (Routledge, 2018).

LOVE IS LOVE IS LOVE

Broadway Musicals and LGBTQ Politics, 2010–2020

Aaron C. Thomas

LONDON AND NEW YORK

Designed cover image: Melinda Nagy/Shutterstock

First published 2023
by Routledge
4 Park Square, Milton Park, Abingdon, Oxon OX14 4RN

and by Routledge
605 Third Avenue, New York, NY 10158

Routledge is an imprint of the Taylor & Francis Group, an informa business

© 2023 Aaron C. Thomas

The right of Aaron C. Thomas to be identified as author of this work has been asserted in accordance with sections 77 and 78 of the Copyright, Designs and Patents Act 1988.

All rights reserved. No part of this book may be reprinted or reproduced or utilised in any form or by any electronic, mechanical, or other means, now known or hereafter invented, including photocopying and recording, or in any information storage or retrieval system, without permission in writing from the publishers.

Trademark notice: Product or corporate names may be trademarks or registered trademarks, and are used only for identification and explanation without intent to infringe.

British Library Cataloguing-in-Publication Data
A catalogue record for this book is available from the British Library

Library of Congress Cataloging-in-Publication Data
Names: Thomas, Aaron C., author.
Title: Love is love is love : Broadway musicals and LGBTQ politics, 2010–2020 / Aaron C. Thomas.
Description: Abingdon, Oxon ; New York, NY : Routledge, 2023. | Includes bibliographical references and index.
Identifiers: LCCN 2022047130 (print) | LCCN 2022047131 (ebook) | ISBN 9781032329499 (hardback) | ISBN 9781032329475 (paperback) | ISBN 9781003317470 (ebook)
Subjects: LCSH: Musicals—Political aspects—United States. | Sexual minorities in popular culture—United States.
Classification: LCC ML3918.M87 T65 2023 (print) | LCC ML3918.M87 (ebook) | DDC 782.1/40973—dc23/eng/20221123
LC record available at https://lccn.loc.gov/2022047130
LC ebook record available at https://lccn.loc.gov/2022047131

ISBN: 978-1-03232-949-9 (hbk)
ISBN: 978-1-03232-947-5 (pbk)
ISBN: 978-1-00331-747-0 (ebk)

DOI: 10.4324/9781003317470

Typeset in Bembo
by Apex CoVantage, LLC

CONTENTS

Acknowledgments   *vi*

   Introduction   1

1   Shut Up and Deal   38

2   It Gets Better Than Boyhood   65

3   A Gender of One, a Sexuality of Many   93

4   All My Life I Had to Fight   121

5   Frozen Eleganza   153

Index   *179*

ACKNOWLEDGMENTS

I wrote and conceived of this book during pandemic time, while seeing so many of my former students – musical theatre performers and musical theatre lovers – suddenly bereft of the art form they were used to practicing. In many ways, I wrote this book as a love letter to them, to the power of musical theatre in their lives. It was intended, too, as an homage to musical theatre at Florida State University, where I started working in 2018 and which has an incredible musical theatre program filled with brilliant young people doing great work. I'm proud to teach them.

Love Is Love Is Love was encouraged at all points by Ben Piggott, who pushed me until I wrote, set deadlines he did not expect me to keep, and urged me to keep going. It has been a pleasure to write imagining him as my reader, and this book would not exist without his editing and guidance. I am grateful, too, to George Rodosthenous, Jessica Sternfeld, and Elizabeth Wollman, who edited earlier versions of Chapters 1 and 2, and who gave me license to experiment with thinking queerly about *Newsies* and *Promises*. I was also encouraged by Laura MacDonald and Bryan Vandevender, who invited my ideas about *Frozen* into their working group "Afterlives of Capitalism" at the American Society for Theatre Research.

I have had the great pleasure to work, at the School of Theatre, with Chari Arespacochaga, Jacki Armit, Brad Brock, Colin Cambell, Robert Coleman, Mary Karen Dahl, Michele Diamonti, Michael Fatica, Kate Gelabert, Kevin Grab, Tony Gunn, Kellen Hoxworth, Amy Huang, Yizhou Huang, Dale Jordan, Jean McDaniel Lickson, Jim Lile, Colleen Muscha, Elizabeth Osborne, Tom Ossowski, Kris Salata, Casey Sammarco, and Elliott Turley, and I'm grateful for their comradeship and hard work. I am grateful, too, for my colleagues in other units at FSU, especially Tenley Bick, Malia Bruker, Michael Franklin, Lilian Garcia-Roig, Irvin Gonzalez, Jorge Hernández, Ramiz Kseri, Daniel Luedtke, Preston McLane, Yelena McLane, Christina Owens, Scott Pickett, Dave Rodriguez, Hannah Schwadron, and Allison Spence. Having such a supportive community has made the lonely business of writing much easier.

I am grateful, too, for my support systems in the field, dear friends whom I can count on at any time to talk me through a thorny problem, especially Kate Bredeson, Michelle Liu Carriger, Jessica Del Vecchio, Miriam Felton-Dansky, Jacob Gallagher-Ross, Lindsay Brandon Hunter, Kareem Khubchandani, Patrick McKelvey, and Noe Montez.

The summer I wrapped up this writing, I headed to the Association for Theatre in Higher Education conference, where I was surrounded by support, especially from Donatella Galella, Michelle Cowin-Gibbs, Patricia Ybarra, Chase Bringardner, Laura Edmondson, Detra Payne, Jasmine Mahmoud, Jordan Ealey, Jessica Del Vecchio, Alex Bádue, Julia Listengarten, Jen-Scott Mobley, Michael Stablein Jr., and Dani Snyder-Young. Thank you all for your energy and positivity.

I am so thankful to Lucas Hollister, Lee Hollister, Joseph Cermatori, Daniel Sack, and Alex Ripp, who encouraged me at a key moment in the editing of *Love Is Love Is Love*. And especially the bad team, Katie Hornstein, Jonathan Mullins, yasser elhariry, and Viktor Witkowski, who always have my back.

Julie Evangelista Gil, Arianne Johnson Quinn, Michael Stablein Jr., Patrick McKelvey, and Kellen Hoxworth each agreed to read large sections of the manuscript and give me wise feedback. Meghan Nelson, my graduate assistant in the Spring of 2022, helped me compile resources on *The Color Purple*. And my musical-theatre-loving former students, all now off doing great things, each took the time to read chapters, point out errors, and tell me where my writing was confusing: Lauren Abel, Austin Adams, Carlos Ashby, Colin Brooks, Michael Cleary, Zach Duncan, Tommy Heller, Joey Edward Herr, David Klein, Michelle LoRicco, Jordan Moore, Jonathan Gabriel Mousset, Lauren Muller, Michael Olaribigbe, Jarrett Poore, Nick Richardson, Noah Samotin, Jon-Paul Schaut, Matt Siperstein, Avianna Tato, Jenny Totcky, Benjamin Walton, and Zach Williams. Thank you, thank you.

I'd like to give a special shout-out of appreciation to my dear friends Meredith Lynn, Jason Regnier, Greg Marcks, Tarik Doğru, Leah Hunter, and especially Jason Paul Tate, the people in Tallahassee who made my day-to-day life smooth and kept me sane while I was writing this book – and actually just in general. I also get constant encouragement from my family, and I'm grateful for them every day, especially Dayne Catalano, Deborah Lynn Thomas, Sheila Jorgensen, Hannah Streeter, and Mia Rose Streeter.

INTRODUCTION

At the Tony Awards ceremony in the summer of 2015, Jeanine Tesori and Lisa Kron's musical *Fun Home* emerged triumphant, taking home the trophies for Best Original Score, Best Book, and Best Musical and, perhaps even more importantly, sneaking into the hearts of the viewers at home with a beautiful performance of "Ring of Keys."[1] *Fun Home* is a landmark in lesbian representation on Broadway, and its success during the 2014–2015 season appeared to be a harbinger of good things to come. Kron, one of the original Five Lesbian Brothers, accepted the Tony Award for Best Book of a Musical, and her speech hailed the new future of musicals on Broadway. Kron's speech was not shown during the television broadcast, so I want to begin this book by quoting from it here at length, especially because it is a perfect snapshot of how Broadway understood itself in the summer of 2015:

> For many, many years I have had a recurring dream . . . that I suddenly discover that the apartment I live in has a whole bunch of rooms that I didn't know were there. And I'm like "How did I not know about all these rooms?" And I've been thinking about that dream as I've been thinking about this *amazing* Broadway season, because we all live in this big house, and we've all been sitting in the same one or two main rooms thinking that this was the whole house. And this season, some lights got turned on in some other rooms. And we're all like "Oh my god, this house is *so* much bigger than I thought." . . . You guys, our house is *so* big. Please, let's not just all go back into the living room.[2]

Kron's metaphor is a beautiful one. She asked the assembled audience to recognize that there are many more stories that can be told, that there are many people and ideas that audiences and producers have been ignoring for so long, and that the diversity of the 2014–2015 Broadway season expanded the imaginative possibilities

2   Introduction

for the Broadway musical itself. Kron also noted that "this has been the most successful season in Broadway history," and although she celebrated how far Broadway had come in terms of its representational politics, she also acknowledged the entertainment industry's tendency to go back to business as usual.

But Broadway didn't actually go back. Later that month in the *Hollywood Reporter*, David Rooney hailed the season *after Fun Home* with great excitement, noting that *Hamilton* would soon be opening at the Richard Rodgers Theatre and that it was already an enormous cultural phenomenon. Rooney was energized, as well, by the increased diversity in casting on Broadway, declaring that "Much more so than film or TV, Broadway has long been ahead of the curve in terms of ethnically diverse casting. But this season already is shaping up as one for the record books, across the racial spectrum."[3] As Rooney put it, the 2015–2016 season boasted George Takei, Lea Salonga, and Telly Leung in Jay Kuo and Marc Acito's new musical *Allegiance*, Ana Villafañe, Josh Segarra, and Andréa Burns in Gloria and Emilio Estefan's *On Your Feet!*, and an almost entirely Asian ensemble in the revival of *The King and I*. There would also be the revival of *The Color Purple*, George C. Wolfe's revised version of the Eubie Blake and Noble Sissle classic *Shuffle Along*, and, of course, *Hamilton* to look forward to. All the while, *Fun Home* would still be running at the Circle in the Square Theatre on West 50th Street.[4]

On June 11, the day before the 2016 Tony Awards ceremony, Kristina Rodulfo proclaimed 2016 as the Year of #BroadwaySoDiverse, noting in *Elle* that

> 2015–2016 was a landmark season for diversity on Broadway – of 15 new musicals that premiered, 11 feature racially diverse casts. While 95 percent of Tony nominees have historically been white, 35 percent of this year's acting nomin[ations] went to people of color.[5]

This diversity had again paid off. According to the Broadway League, the new season had topped the previous one, and Broadway "had its best attended and highest grossing season ever" in 2015–2016.[6] For the next day's Tony Awards ceremony, everyone expected *Hamilton* to take home top honors, but audiences also hotly anticipated performances by the casts of *The Color Purple*, *School of Rock*, *Shuffle Along*, *Bright Star*, *Fiddler on the Roof*, *Spring Awakening*, and *On Your Feet!*

Broadway Reckons with Pulse

In the early hours of June 12, 2016, however, a lone gunman killed 49 people and injured 53 others when he opened fire on Latin Night at the gay club Pulse on South Orange Avenue in Orlando, Florida. I will return to the political discourse surrounding the Pulse Massacre a bit later, but here I want simply to note that the attack was, according to the *New York Times*, "the worst mass shooting in United States history."[7] The massacre primarily targeted members of Orlando's queer Latinx community, though early media reports took a different racialized approach to the violence, emphasizing the event as "terrorism." As it happens, the

2016 Pulse Massacre coincided not only with the campaigns of Donald Trump and Hillary Clinton – presidential politics dominated much of the media coverage around the shooting – but also with the 70th annual Tony Awards ceremony, which was televised nationally the night after the killings. This coincidence has long seemed to me an important one, and an analysis of the ceremony and the way Broadway's artists responded to the massacre will begin to illuminate, in miniature, much of what this book is trying to do in its interrogation of the links between LGBTQ politics, queer audiences, and Broadway musicals.

Before noon on the day of June 12, the official Tony Awards Twitter account declared that the ceremony would be dedicated to "the families and friends of those affected" by the "unimaginable tragedy that happened last night in Orlando."[8] And at the morning's rehearsal for the ceremony, the decision was quickly made to cut the prop muskets usually used in the number the *Hamilton* cast would perform.[9] James Corden, the ceremony's host, began the show somberly. Facing a camera upstage with the full house of the Beacon Theatre behind him, he addressed television viewers at home directly:

> Good evening. All around the world, people are trying to come to terms with the horrific events that took place in Orlando this morning. On behalf of the whole theatre community and every person in this room, our hearts go out to all of those affected by this atrocity. All we can say is that you are not on your own right now: your tragedy is our tragedy. Theatre is a place where every race, creed, sexuality, and gender is equal, is embraced, and is loved. Hate will never win. Together, we have to make sure of that. Tonight's show stands as a symbol and a celebration of that principle. This is the Tony Awards.[10]

At these words, the audience behind Corden cheered loudly, and the ceremony began.

Corden's speech declared identity between the Broadway community and the queer community: *your tragedy*, he said, *is our tragedy*. This was not an empty gesture; although Corden identifies as a straight man (more on that in Chapter 1), many in the community of artists who make up Broadway are queer people – including a number of those who would go on to win Tony Awards later that night. Further, Corden specifically addressed a marginalized community that had been attacked. His statement of identity – *your tragedy is our tragedy* – was no ideological pretense that the United States already includes queer people of color in its vision of the future; he was declaring an identity in opposition to, or at least on the margins of, that larger ideological fantasy of national belonging.

The later section of the speech, in which Corden goes on to say that "theatre is a place where every race, creed, sexuality, and gender" is equal, embraced, and loved, is more difficult to understand. *Is* theatre, after all, a place where every race is equal? Where every gender is equal? Where every sexuality is embraced? Where every creed is loved? These questions must decidedly be answered in the negative, both for the industry that the Tony Awards ceremony recognizes and for the musical theatre form as a whole.[11] Corden had undoubtedly moved into fantasy territory.

It is easy, perhaps, to align oneself with the virtues Corden's speech avowed – at least in theory – but it is more difficult to testify to the veracity of the speech's claims about the theatre. Theatre is not a *place* at all, and it is certainly not one of imagined equality or embrace or love – I am not sure that we even would wish it to be. In fact, just a few months later, after Donald Trump became the U.S. President-elect, he tweeted that "The Theater must always be a safe and special place," calling on the cast of *Hamilton* to apologize to Vice President-elect Mike Pence for some imagined rudeness. Theatre practitioners and fans alike were quick to object to Trump's idea of the theatre as a safe place.[12] For those who derided Trump's "safe and special place" but cheered for Corden's "place where every race, creed, sexuality, and gender is equal, is embraced, and is loved," there is no obvious contradiction. To applaud one but denounce the other is really to say nothing about the essential qualities of theatre. Rather, it is, in both cases, to align oneself with a particular politics of acceptance and equality – *with* the LGBTQ and Latinx communities in Orlando and *against* Donald Trump's antigay, anti-immigrant, anti-trans, anti-Mexican, anti-Muslim politics. In either case, theatre (or *The Theater*, as Trump would have it) is an abstraction, a symbol onto which we project our political ideals. Very little of this has anything to do with what theatre actually does.

The big winners at the 2016 Tony Awards were, as expected, Lin-Manuel Miranda and the rest of the team behind *Hamilton: An American Musical*. Miranda also responded to the Pulse massacre during the televised ceremony, reading an original sonnet in lieu of an acceptance speech for his Tony Award for Best Score. June 2016 was a high point in Miranda's popularity, and his sonnet was published in the online version of the *New York Times* by the end of the evening, although Miranda's performance of the poem, which you can watch on YouTube, is much more affecting than the words by themselves:

> My wife's the reason anything gets done;
> She nudges me towards promise by degrees.
> She is a perfect symphony of one;
> Our son is her most beautiful reprise.
> We chase the melodies that seem to find us
> Until they're finished songs and start to play
> When senseless acts of tragedy remind us
> That nothing here is promised, not one day.
> This show is proof that history remembers
> We live through times when hate and fear seem stronger
> We rise and fall and light from dying embers
> Remembrances that hope and love last longer
> And love is love is love is love is love is love is love is love
> Cannot be killed or swept aside.
> I sing Vanessa's symphony, Eliza tells her story.
> Now fill the world with music, love and pride.[13]

Miranda's poem was a sustained performance of connection and mourning, a very public link between the Broadway community, Orlando's LGBTQ residents, and the larger LGBTQ population in the United States. The words *love is love is love* would, in the weeks and months after June 2016, begin to appear on magnets, t-shirts, and other swag, and they'd be reposted on thousands of Instagram and Facebook accounts in a show of solidarity between musical theatre and LGBTQ politics.

Miranda's sonnet offered support and unity; indeed, it claimed a kind of identity – love *is* love – but this was not the same identity with which Corden opened the Tony Awards. Rather, Miranda's sonnet begins with a description of his own *distance* from queer communities; he articulates that difference first, referring to his wife and son and carefully marking his heterosexuality for the audience. The poem also performs the troubling gesture of attempting to transform violence into meaningful value, noting that the "tragedy remind[s] us / that nothing here is promised." Still, the most remarkable section of Miranda's sonnet is the insistent repetition of the phrase *love is love is love*, a mantra he extends for eight metrical feet. This part of the final stanza, one Miranda delivered with intense emotion and a breaking voice, articulates Miranda's clear alignment with LGBTQ politics.

But *which* LGBTQ politics?

Politics and the Pulse Massacre

Although this is a book about Broadway musicals, it is fundamentally also a book about political discourse. I think of *Love Is Love Is Love* as, first and foremost, a historiographical project, one that tells a history of LGBTQ politics across the decade 2010–2020 as illuminated by Broadway musicals. Each chapter takes a single show as its focus – *Promises, Promises, Newsies, Hedwig and the Angry Inch, The Color Purple,* and *Frozen* – but my interest throughout is in the discussions that emerge *around* each of these musicals more than in producing new readings of the shows themselves. My hope is that a careful examination of each of these musicals, their historical connections, and the way they've been taken up by audiences allows us to see more clearly this decade's LGBTQ politics. Holding our focus on the summer of 2016, I turn now to a consideration of some of the political discourse surrounding the Pulse Massacre before coming back to Miranda's repetition of the phrase *love is love is love.*

The morning after the shooting, the *New York Times* called Pulse

> the worst act of terrorism on American soil since Sept. 11, 2001, and the deadliest attack on a gay target in the nation's history, though officials said it was not clear whether some victims had been accidentally shot by law enforcement officers.[14]

In the days and weeks following this violent attack, the motivations of the shooter were analyzed by commentators, although as is clearly evident from the initial *Times* reporting, law enforcement leaned heavily on the "terrorism" motive from the beginning, and the shooter, as early as one day following the massacre, came to be understood as a person who had "proclaim[ed] allegiance to the Islamic State terrorist group, and who had been investigated in the past for possible terrorist ties."[15] From gay men and other users of hookup/dating apps for men who have sex with men, a different story quickly emerged, one in which the shooter lived a life in the closet. It was reported among some queer Orlando men that the shooter, who was married to his second wife, had frequented Pulse, had a hidden life of sexual experiences with men, and had dated more than one Latino man.[16] The national story that crystallized about the Pulse massacre, however, downplayed and even outright denied this possibility, emphasizing instead the shooter's ties with Islamic fundamentalism. Politicians, depending on their leanings, used the violence to call either for stricter gun laws or for more guns on the streets. The massacre, in other words, was immediately politicized, but the way these politics related to race and racism, anti-gay violence and LGBTQ identity, and U.S. American politics of belonging and exclusion were far from clear.

For Donald Trump, who would officially become the Republican candidate for the U.S. presidency a little over a month later, the shooting was a racialized one. This was "terrorism" that targeted U.S. Americans by those hostile to freedom and democracy – an attack on the so-called "West."[17] Trump's was a familiar Islamophobic and Orientalist racialization of West Asian and North African people designed to shore up the military–industrial complex and justify U.S. Imperialism in the "Middle East." But for queer Latinos and other patrons of Upscale Latin Saturdays at Pulse, indeed for many U.S. Americans who identify as LGBTQ, the idea that this was somehow a "foreign" attack on the U.S. way of life immediately rang false. Most of us – queers, people of color, and especially queer people of color – have experienced enough violence, hatred, and exclusion to be well aware that we are in no way symbols of U.S. American freedoms or the U.S. American way of life. For us, a violent attack on hundreds of queer people in a gay nightclub is not the same as a violent attack on "Americans." Legal and extra-legal regulations that govern LGBTQ socialization, movement, behavior, speech, assembly, alcohol consumption, social media content, sexual activity, healthcare, and sex work hamper many of our lives on a daily basis. This was particularly driven home for queer Orlando residents who lined up at OneBlood on June 12 to help victims of the shooting only to be turned away because of the U.S. Food and Drug Administration's ban on blood donations by men who have sex with men.[18] Restrictions such as these, which remind LGBTQ individuals that we are only provisional members of the general population, are especially onerous for queer and trans people of color such as those who made up the majority of the patrons at Pulse on June 11 and 12, 2016.

The attack was about race for many of us too, then, but it wasn't about the typical racialized oppositions offered by Islamophobic news media. As the novelist Justin Torres wrote in a gorgeous piece for the *Washington Post*, the "safe space" of "Latin night at the queer club" means something else for queer people of color:

> Outside, there's a world that politicizes every aspect of your identity. There are preachers, of multiple faiths, mostly self-identified Christians, condemning

you to hell. Outside, they call you an abomination. Outside, there is a news media that acts as if there are two sides to a debate over trans people using public bathrooms. Outside, there is a presidential candidate who has built a platform on erecting a wall between the United States and Mexico – and not only do people believe that crap is possible, they believe it is necessary. Outside, Puerto Rico is still a colony, being allowed to drown in debt, to suffer, without the right to file for bankruptcy, to protect itself. Outside, there are more than 100 bills targeting you, your choices, your people, pending in various states.[19]

The news media's emphasis on the Americanness of the Pulse victims and their framing of the shooting as an attack on the United States, then, worked to cover over the very real way Latinx queer people and other queer people of color are already and consistently excluded from the idea of the nation. This was, in fact, the same time that many, many U.S. Americans were angrily chanting "build the wall."[20] The news media's mobilization of the Pulse shooter's alleged racism worked to mask the United States' own everyday racist hostilities.

News media that framed the massacre as an attack on the United States also covered over the widespread homophobia and transphobia then current in U.S. American political discourse. June 2016 was the summer of the anti-trans "bathroom bills," in which state governments, beginning in North Carolina, began proposing laws that restricted public restroom access to the gender listed on an individual's birth certificate.[21] These explicitly anti-LGBTQ laws were part of a larger, virulent backlash in the wake of the legalization of same-sex marriage by the U.S. Supreme Court in June 2015. That the massacre at Pulse had been motivated by homophobia seemed obvious to many, but any linking of the shooting to *Islamic* homophobia can only be an ideological sleight of hand masking the national discourse of the very *Christian* homophobia that swept through state legislatures, particularly in the southern United States, in the summer of 2016.

As I have been carefully noting, however, the political analysis I've staked out here is not the mainstream view of the events of June 12, 2016. Different political analyses than the ones I've described are conceivable. It is possible, for example, to see the anti-trans discourse of that summer as unrelated to the same-sex marriage decision in 2015; pro-gay-marriage advocates certainly made little mention of trans politics as part of their activism. It is possible, too, to decouple anti-trans rhetoric in North Carolina and elsewhere from anti-gay violence in Florida. One might even consider the homophobic position – taking up the theory that the Pulse shooter's violence was motivated by internalized homophobia – that this violence was somehow internal to the LGBTQ community. There is, in other words, a range of ways of making sense of the politics surrounding the Pulse massacre. To complicate matters further, after the shooting, some queer people in the United States echoed the racism of politicians like Donald Trump, attempting to exclude queer Muslims from vigils and spouting Islamophobic rhetoric.[22]

It is essential that we understand that LGBTQ identity is no predictor of politics, and in fact, that there is no LGBTQ identity as such (it is the rare person indeed who is L, G, B, T, *and* Q). As a coalitional identity, the acronym LGBTQ signifies the interests of a community that includes lesbians, gay men, bisexuals, asexuals, pansexuals, trans people, two-spirit individuals, and other queer people, including nonbinary folks, those who enjoy BDSM, intersex people, and many others. These very different groups occasionally have politics that align, and they apparently share a politics that opposes heteronormativity, but this is an alliance of political goals that often differ widely. Queer theorist Stephen Dillon, for example, urges us to recognize that many of the privileges we experience in our own lives are conditioned by "the purging of imprisoned queer and trans people from 'the community.'"[23] Dillon challenges us to consider that:

> As some seek safety and security under the racially gendered state and corporate power, what quotidian deaths will make such shelter possible? . . . What bodies and lives will be constructed as disposable or even unimaginable by a movement for inclusion? Whose doors will continue to be kicked down?

Whose lives need to be made unsafe so that others can experience freedom? As the Justin Torres essay I quoted earlier similarly hints, the political stance of the "LGBTQ community" when it comes to racism, xenophobia, anti-colonialism, and border politics is far from clear or settled, and the acronym itself covers over *all* racial differences, hinting toward the possibility of a queer, post-race society but more often than not demonstrating the biases of white queer folks, who both consciously and unconsciously steer LGBTQ activism toward the political issues that most affect upper- and middle-class white people.[24]

In addition to a renewed Islamophobia that appeared within the LGBTQ community following Pulse, I want to give another example of the unpredictability of LGBTQ politics that the Pulse massacre illuminated. As I have noted, pro-gun and anti-gun politicians had their typical (opposing) responses to the shooting, advocating, respectively, more guns on the streets or stricter gun regulations. In February 2018 – a year and a half in the future and 200 miles to the south – The Marjory Stoneman Douglas High School shooting would reinvigorate anti-gun politics in Florida and mobilize many young Floridians to fight for stricter gun regulations in the state. The 2016 Pulse massacre, however, had no such catalytic effect: local responses to the shooting in relation to firearms were mostly muted, but *NBC News* reported that the Pink Pistols, "an international LGBT self-defense organization" saw a 300% increase in its membership in the week after the massacre.[25] In a press release, Pink Pistols spokesperson Gwendolyn Patton argued that we should "not reach for the low-hanging fruit of blaming the killer's guns. Let us stay focused on the fact that someone hated gay people so much they were ready to kill or injure so many." Remobilizing the National Rifle Association's oft-repeated phrase, Patton said that "GUNS did not do this. A human being did."[26] So, although large national organizations such as the Human Rights Campaign and the Gay and Lesbian Alliance Against Defamation "support commonsense gun violence prevention measures," more marginal LGBTQ organizations such as the Pink Pistols see things very differently.[27]

We should not make assumptions about the stances people are going to take or the reactions they're going to have, even if they proudly claim LGBTQ identity; the "community" is simply too diverse for that. It is by no means clear what politics will follow from a declaration of solidarity with LGBTQ people or even from a claim of LGBTQ identity. As the poet Rosario Morales argued 40 years ago in the groundbreaking collection *This Bridge Called My Back: Writings by Radical Women of Color*:

> We know different things / some very much more unpleasant things if we've been women poor black or lesbian or all of those / we know different things depending on what sex / what color / what lives we live / where we grew up / What schooling / what beatings / with or without shoes / steak or beans / but what politics each of us is going to be and do is anybody's guess.[28]

What "LGBTQ politics" is, in other words, is far from clear.

Equations of Love

When Miranda used the phrase *love is love is love* at the 2016 Tony Awards, he mobilized a slogan used during the fight for marriage equality in the lead-up to the 2015 decision by the U.S. Supreme Court that made same-sex marriage legal nationally.[29] This phrase, along with the Human Rights Campaign's equal-sign logo, was designed to argue in favor of equality – that is, equality *under the law* – maintaining that gay couples deserved the same right to marry that straight couples already possessed. For practical political reasons, the equation *love is love* deliberately downplays sex and sexuality, attempting to grant gay couples the same privilege of de-sexualization that heterosexual marriages are usually afforded.[30] The phrase, quite pointedly, does not claim that *sex is sex* or that heterosexual desire is equivalent to homosexual desire. Instead, the phrase attempts to change the minds of those hostile to same-sex marriage by asking them to make up their minds based on the question of love *rather* than that of sex.

Although *love is love is love*, in the days and weeks after Pulse and the Tonys, became a popular rallying cry, Miranda's reworking of a phrase that advocated marriage equality as a response to the killings of members of the queer Latinx community is, in many ways, a decidedly strange one. *Love is love is love* is intriguing because it advocates a more general equality of love rather than advocating sex positivity or what anthropologist Gayle Rubin has called "a pluralistic sexual ethics" based on "a concept of benign sexual variation."[31] Miranda's sonnet erases sex and sexuality almost completely, substituting in its place reproductive marriage and the family – with his own wife and son as his central example. Further, the phrase *love is love is love* performs the same conceptual move in regard to the queer Latinx community in Orlando that critics had frequently accused the larger politics of marriage equality of making – an erasure of specific issues related to queer and trans people of color in favor of a politics that largely benefited middle-class white folks. The sonnet mentions neither queer sexuality nor Latinidad.

By no means do I wish to imply that Lin-Manuel Miranda had a duty to articulate a sex-positive LGBTQ politics at the Tony Awards; in truth, it wasn't even his job to respond meaningfully to the Pulse massacre, and he had the right to accept his award and react to the killings in whatever way he felt moved to do so.[32] I am interested rather – and this is a theme that runs through the book as a whole – in the way Miranda's sonnet was taken up by audiences, queer and straight, and in the way its key phrase came to articulate a larger response to the massacre. I am interested in the way that we choose to see ourselves in the ideas Broadway musicals offer us. I am interested, too, in the popularity of the response *love is love is love* over the other options available. Miranda's sonnet, then, is notable not so much for its goals or its failings but for its spectacular reception.

This poem carried the power to influence a larger set of public ideas about queerness, politics, and the place of lesbian, gay, bisexual, and transgender people in the national imaginary. What I want to examine here is the Broadway musical as a form with the power to impact LGBTQ politics on a national scale, with stars who can influence important public issues related to queerness and sexuality, and songs with which queer audiences learn to sing our very subjectivities. Queer and queer-friendly audiences picked up Miranda's sonnet and made things with it – memes, social media posts, hashtags, pins – and this productive, *creative* response demonstrated the power Broadway, especially the Broadway musical, has within LGBTQ culture in the United States. *Love Is Love Is Love* looks to Broadway musicals for help understanding the recent history and current state of LGBTQ politics in the United States. Although Broadway no longer has the enormous influence it once had on mainstream "gay culture" and LGBTQ people in the United States, the queer stars of Broadway are still asked frequently to articulate LGBTQ politics to mainstream U.S. American culture writ large, and this book documents numerous ways that Broadway stars engaged in U.S. politics over the second decade of the twenty-first century. The politics of Broadway musicals, in other words, matter a great deal more to U.S. American culture than they might seem to mean, and Broadway musicals are especially important to mainstream politics surrounding sex, gender, and sexuality.

One final note on Miranda's sonnet will further illustrate the project of this book. As Miranda performed the poem on the stage of the Beacon Theatre, he said the sentence "we live through times when hate and fear seem stronger." As it was reproduced in the *New York Times*, however, Miranda's sonnet took on the air of having *already survived* these difficult times and having come out on the other, brighter side. The *Times* reported the sonnet's text as "we *lived* through times when hate and fear *seemed* stronger."[33] This switch to the past tense gives a different shade of meaning to Miranda's poem, reframing *Hamilton*'s victory at the Tonys as a kind of culmination or final victory over racism and homophobia. The *New York Times* was not the only publication to frame *Hamilton*'s triumph at the Tonys in this way. During the 2016 Tonys performance itself, Corden quipped, "Think of tonight as the Oscars but with diversity,"³⁴ and Chris Jones, the longtime theatre critic for the *Chicago Tribune*, wrote an entire book – *Rise Up! Broadway and American Society from Angels in America to Hamilton* – that frames *Hamilton* as the result of decades of impactful political theatre on Broadway. Both, in other words, behaved as if Broadway were already diverse, already equitable, already politically progressive.

There is a typical story about the relationship between Broadway musicals and LGBTQ politics: it moves us from coded figures of the 1950s and queer readings in the 1960s, to the "out" musicals like *La Cage aux Folles* and *Falsettos*, toward the queer representations we see on Broadway today in *A Strange Loop*, *The Prom*, and *Priscilla, Queen of the Desert*. In many ways, this traditional story is a tale of representational politics, one that sees achievements like *Fun Home*, *The Color Purple*, and *Head over Heels* in the twenty-first century as expanding still further the visibility of queer and gender-nonconforming people in Broadway musicals. It is this story that Jones's *Rise Up!* (intentionally) and the *New York Times*'s misprinted sonnet (unintentionally) tell – a narrative of greater and greater acceptance and an increasing range of representations, one in which "bad" or harmful stereotypes and racist portrayals have become relics of a disavowed past. It is this story that was in operation when Corden opened the 2016 Tonys with the fantasy that "theatre is a place where every race, creed, sexuality, and gender is equal, is embraced, and is loved."

In the final paragraph of *Rise Up!*, Jones offers that "even Broadway, even *Hamilton*, had been forced to pick a side."³⁵ Jones is referring to the incredibly polarized electoral politics in the United States in the second decade of the twenty-first century and to the incident I noted earlier in which Donald Trump demanded that the *Hamilton* cast apologize to Mike Pence. Jones's position is that Broadway and *Hamilton* chose firmly to stand on the side of love (or the side of the Democratic Party, if you'd prefer). I find this point of view both reductive and deceptive. It is reductive because it assumes a consensus in the Broadway community around issues of racism, sexism, and homophobia – a consensus that does not exist – and it is deceptive because it assumes that we all know and agree about what LGBTQ politics are.

Rather than telling the story of greater and greater acceptance that Broadway tells itself *about* itself, *Love Is Love Is Love* refuses to take for granted the content of Broadway's LGBTQ politics. This book asks instead: which politics do we mean when we speak about Broadway musicals and their politics? What, in other words, might be left out of the *love is love is love* formulation? What does LGBTQ representation via Broadway musicals and their performers actually look like? How are these representations sexualized, racialized, gendered? How are they eroticized, demonized, or neutered? Who is absent? What hierarchies are present? *Which* LGBTQ politics, after all, has the Broadway musical embraced? And rather than thinking about Broadway as having been forced to choose one of two sides – the side of love over the side of hate and fear – how might we reconsider LGBTQ politics themselves as more complicated than the simple binary of right and left given to us, on the one hand, by politicians, and, on the other, by acceptance-speech sonnets transformed into memes?

Experiencing Broadway Musicals

This book covers the period from 2010 to 2020. In Broadway musical terms, this decade stretches from *The Addams Family, American Idiot, The Scottsboro Boys*, and *Women on the Verge of a Nervous Breakdown* to the closings of *Tootsie, Frozen*, and *Mean Girls* in 2020. In LGBTQ political terms, this decade saw the founding of the It Gets Better Project in 2010, the repeal of Don't Ask Don't Tell in December of the same year, Chelsea Manning's leak of the so-called Iraq War Logs to the website WikiLeaks, the founding of Trans Lifeline in 2014, the legalization of same-sex marriage in the United States in 2015, the Obama administration's public support of transgender students in 2016, the Pulse Massacre later in the year, the repeal of many of the Obama administration's pro-LGBTQ policies under the Trump administration beginning in 2017, and the outbreak of the SARS-COV-2 pandemic in 2020. Ongoing issues affecting the politics of this decade, too, were the extraordinary crisis of prisons in the United States, in which Black Americans continue to be incarcerated nationally at rates that far exceed white Americans and other people of color,[36] the horrific national rise in murders of trans people, especially Black trans women, over the course of the decade,[37] and the continued destruction of Black life throughout the United States at the hands of violent police forces, vigilante actors, and white supremacist, settler colonialist government policies.

I began this introduction in the middle of the decade with Lisa Kron, the 2016 Tony Awards, and the Pulse killings because the attachment of LGBTQ politics to Broadway musicals seemed to me most colorable in that summer of 2016, especially when the Broadway cast of *Fun Home* performed the show in a concert version for a (largely queer) Orlando audience as a fundraiser for victims of the Pulse shooting and the organization Equality Florida.[38] It seemed to me then – and seems to me now – that the Broadway musical is not only tied to LGBTQ politics but also impacting them in important and lasting ways, steering conversations, changing the way we think about issues, and refashioning our ideas about sex, gender, sexuality, and identity. Further, because of how linked these shows are to LGBTQ cultures, to LGBTQ performers, producers, directors, composers, and librettists, and to LGBTQ audiences, close examination of Broadway musicals is often able to illuminate U.S. LGBTQ history *tout court*, creating intriguing portraits of an always-changing set of dynamics within U.S. American culture. Because of all of these important links between LGBTQ creators and consumers, these shows and the discourses surrounding them also communicate LGBTQ issues and ideas not only to queer communities across the United States but also to the larger heteronormative world within which queer communities must operate.

Our current moment – at the beginning of the third decade of the twenty-first century – has seen an extraordinary rise in the popularity of musicals, especially on film, with USA *Today* pronouncing, in 2021, that "we may be in a new golden age of movie musicals."[39] With high-profile filmed productions of *Annie, Cinderella, Come from Away, Cyrano, Dear Evan Hansen, Diana: The Musical, Everybody's Talking about Jamie, In the Heights, Tick, Tick . . . Boom!*, and *West Side Story*, and original movie musicals *Annette, Encanto*, and *Respect*, to say nothing of *Sing 2*, all appearing in 2021 alone, we are certainly in a new period of musical theatre's popularity. The 2022 Golden Globes saw nominations for the musical performances of Anthony Ramos, Peter Dinklage, Andrew Garfield, Rachel Zegler, Ariana DeBose, and Marion Cotillard – a stunning number of performances in musicals to generate end-of-year awards buzz. We stream musicals into our homes via Netflix, Hulu, and Disney+, and audiences celebrate great musical performances or imagine different casts for their favorite shows (opining about Ariana Grande's casting in the upcoming *Wicked* film, for example, or taking James Corden to task for his performance in *The Prom*). Musical theatre is again in the national conversation.

I've treated the five central case studies in this book – *Promises, Promises, Newsies, Hedwig and the Angry Inch, The Color Purple,* and *Frozen* – as documents taking part in a larger LGBTQ culture as well, examining each show for the conversations, reactions, press, and other paratheatrical activity surrounding them. I have not always aimed to produce queer readings of these musicals, nor have I worked to isolate the ideas a show contains from the way a show has been taken up by audiences and critics. Instead, I am attempting to examine an entire complex of ideas surrounding these five shows, public reception of them, news media coverage, debates on the Internet, and queer readings produced by audiences that have loved (or hated) these shows. I have fundamentally adopted performance scholar Sarah Bay-Cheng's proposal in "Theater Is Media" that

> performance itself functions not as a discrete event but as a network of interrelated components, both on- and offline, both overtly mediated and immediate to various and dispersed recipients. What we encounter in performance (and what we may seek to historicize later) is a network of constitutive parts.[40]

At least since the 1990s, it has been held by scholars of musical theatre that the musical's form is an open one. In his important book *Unfinished Show Business*, Bruce Kirle noted that musicals "thrive on ambiguity and openness." He argued that "By overprivileging the text in such a collaborative form, historians tend to ignore what makes musical theatre so vital to American popular culture; its complex relationship to its historical moment of creation and performance."[41] A musical, Kirle argues, is "an open text that takes on new meanings depending on its production, reception, and cultural moment."[42] I am in complete agreement with Kirle on this point, but surely the same can be said of *all* theatre and not just musicals: whether shows have songs or not, they take on new meanings depending on when we are, what a producer does with the show, and what is happening in the world. Indeed, the task of generating new meanings by making different production choices has been the major function of theatre directors for nearly a century and a half.[43] I have often wondered, while reading pronouncements such as Kirle's – about musical theatre's especial openness – what is *different* about this form's openness. Is a musical any more "unfinished" than a play by William Shakespeare or Alice Childress? Is the form of musical theatre open in a way that is different somehow from theatre without songs?

Musical theatre scholar Stacy Wolf's answer to this question is that we should conceive of this form "not as an object or cultural artifact (as much musical theatre scholarship does), but as a social practice, a doing, a live, visceral experience of creating, watching, listening."[44] Musical theatre, as Wolf's *Beyond Broadway* makes very clear, is a creative activity, in which many, many people across the United States are participating all the time. I only wish to press on Wolf's privileging of the *live*, primarily because most of our interactions with musical theatre – and many of those described in *Beyond Broadway* – are digitally mediated.[45] In this regard, Bay-Cheng's "Theater Is Media" has been inspirational for me as I've turned my attention to the theatre pieces and paratheatrical activity in this book. If we use it to help us think about Broadway musicals, Bay-Cheng's essay offers the idea that we encounter these shows through media long before we encounter them onstage. Any musical theatre fan will have streamed a show's cast recording long before she attends the show in a Broadway theatre, if indeed she attends it there at all. She will have read interviews, followed the show's stars on social media, and watched bootleg performances on YouTube or Instagram; she may even have performed in the show herself on a high school, university, or community theatre stage. (Accordingly, all of the shows in *Love Is Love Is Love* are, in some way, revivals, citations – more on this in a bit.) To be sure, not all audiences for Broadway musicals encounter a show in all of these ways, but many, many audiences do, especially – as scholars such as John Clum have shown – queer audiences.[46] And *all* audiences encounter these shows in *some* mediated ways before the curtain rises at 8:00 pm at the Nederlander or the Bernard B. Jacobs.

Indeed, audiences for Broadway musicals *continue* to encounter the shows they see after they leave the theatre. This is true not only because of possible purchases of show merchandise but also because musicals are eminently more quotable than plays without music. The form itself aims to be sung *again*, hoping audiences will hum the tunes or connect with the lyrics and leave the theatre whistling or singing or dancing.[47] Musicals are designed, in D.A. Miller's words,

> to be . . . "infectious": to be caught and reproduced by the spectators who at a certain moment cease to be simply watching it . . ., and begin, like the orchestra conductor who rises on tiptoe for a dramatic high note, or flings his arms out with a sudden expansion of sonority, *to imitate it*.[48]

And then there are original cast recordings, revival recordings, film adaptations (and *their* audio-recordings), as well as further performances when these shows go on tour or move into the musical theatre repertoire, where they will be performed across the country in regional theatres, community theatres, and other theatres far from Manhattan. Even the phrase "Broadway musical" operates as a fictional shorthand – in this book as elsewhere – and I mostly use the phrase to refer to *form* rather than actual location. As Wolf has noted, we should think of "Broadway" as "a globally recognized brand," rather than the place where most musical theatre performance happens.[49]

The fact that these performances continue long after "the show" is over is extraordinarily important for thinking about musical theatre, because, as Bay-Cheng argues, "Our digital tools are not transparent guides but actively participate as coactors (to paraphrase Latour) to shape our findings within them and thus become part of the performance itself."[50] For Bay-Cheng, historians must respond to this reframing of a performance's duration by designing a way of writing, and of doing history, that "actively attends to the processes by which a performance constitutes, mediates, and is mediated by networks of digital exchange and to trace our own engagement within those networks."[51] These ideas have the ability to change utterly the way we make sense of the history of musical theatre.

If the Broadway musical is more capable of revision and openness than other theatre, one reason might simply be that many, many people are familiar with it as a repertory of songs.[52] Consider, for example, the Instagram account @letshearitforthechoice, maintained by Jimmy Larkin, which collects and posts videos of musical theatre performers making atypical choices as they sing songs from the Broadway musical repertoire.[53] The account features singers like Bea Arthur, Andrew Feldman, and Nikisha Williams as well as (as yet) unknown high schoolers singing songs we know well but singing them *differently*. The performers in these videos, simply put, *make choices* that change the show – even stop the show – and thereby demonstrate the openness of the form. These choices, however, are remarkable only because we are already familiar with other performances, other recordings. In this way, @letshearitforthechoice is dependent on a digital archive of recorded media *that we have already played and accessed*. The performers featured by the account riff on previous versions of the show, and their choices are captured on video and shared with the account's followers, who recognize and applaud the changes that the singer makes. On the one hand, this is an extraordinary example of what Wolf calls musical theatre as social practice; on the other, what this account demonstrates so well is that these live performances (which we experience and re-experience in recorded form via this social medium) are themselves dependent on the digital. These performances are further evidence that the activities of listening to recordings, singing along, and memorizing lyrics ought better to be considered as an extension of the performance experience. And if we avoid privileging the concept of the live here, we can see the choices on @letshearitforthechoice as *expanding the possibilities* that reside within the show itself. We experience these performances via social media, but these small snippets of songs interpret anew, reread, rework, and ask us to think differently about a show we thought we knew.

Love Is Love Is Love takes seriously, as one of its tasks, Bay-Cheng's challenge to write theatre history by engaging with the digital archives, recordings, and reperformances of a piece of theatre. This means writing the history of a show by turning our attention to performances of "the original" show or – as in this book – its revival, while also remembering that "the performance" is "not a privileged site of temporary encounter but instead yet another form of mediated interaction with the text, contexts, and artifacts."[54] The histories in this book are stories of mediated interactions, online kerfuffles, social media fanfiction, repurposed characters, and digital reproduction.⁵⁵ In our own historical moment, it is important that we consider these discourses and performances as the very stuff we must use to write musical theatre history.

Audience Practices

As a musical is revived or reimagined, producers and performers make something new with the show, but more importantly, it is the audiences who change, and audiences who *do something* with the shows, responding creatively and actively to the musical. Much analysis of musical theatre – and indeed theatrical performance in general – focuses on the meanings produced by the shows themselves. The great exceptions to this in musical theatre scholarship have been gay and lesbian authors writing about their experiences as audience members while recognizing their attractions and desires toward specific musicals and to the form in general. I've already cited most of them, but D.A. Miller's *Place for Us*, Stacy Wolf's *A Problem Like Maria*, John Clum's *Something for the Boys*, and, especially, Wayne Koestenbaum's *The Queen's Throat* have all been extraordinarily influential in my thinking about this form. As Scott McMillin has said:

> All three books [Clum's, Wolf's, and Miller's] are also about growing up gay – the appeal of double-coding in the subversive format of musicals is a powerful draw. Everyone who is drawn to the musical should listen to these books, for they are urgent accounts that can tell anyone what lies at the heart of the illegitimate theatre itself: it is not the gayness, or not only the gayness; it is the double-coding and the subversion and the repetition.⁵⁶

These books focus a great deal on meanings produced by the shows themselves but slide constantly into talking about affect, hunches, and gossip. In much of this analysis, these personal feelings, desiring operations, and identificatory experiences seem to me much *more* important than what is ostensibly happening onstage during the show. Or rather, both become stronger and more meaningful when audience experience and representational analysis are spoken about together; separately, musical theatre simply makes less sense.

One of the richest pieces about audience response in recent musical theatre scholarship is Donatella Galella's article "Feeling Yellow," in which she interrogates her own emotional responses to white supremacist production choices and offers ways for audiences to think through identification, interpellation, and (dis)pleasure while watching musical theatre.⁵⁷ What I love about Galella's piece is her attention to how the shows function and the choices made by producers, as well as a simultaneous inquiry into audience responses, without taking for granted what those responses will be or should be. "Feeling Yellow," in fact, proposes new possible audience responses to racist texts and production choices.

Audiences, as Galella reminds us (even though we really ought not to have forgotten), are different from one another. Our responses to what we watch are not going to be the same. Generalizations about audience responses are a bad idea as a rule, but I want again to note specifically that it is also dangerous to generalize in our attempts to describe queer audience responses. Queer audiences are different from each other too, and LGBTQ responses to musical theatre, just like LGBTQ politics, need not be – indeed will not be – identical.[58] It is important that we try to avoid the tendency to make large-scale pronouncements about musical theatre audiences and their reactions. If I take seriously the idea that LGBTQ audience responses differ from one another, I should not trust that my own reception can stand in for LGBTQ audience responses in general or even for those of most gay white men. I want, then, to avoid reading back into the shows themselves my own personal feelings or ways of watching. What Galella does so skillfully in "Feeling Yellow" is to *interrogate* herself and her feelings rather than taking them for granted – while also analyzing what the show purports to be saying. *Love Is Love Is Love* attempts to attend both to the meanings intended or produced by these Broadway musicals and to the ways *some* audience members have taken up those meanings and produced new ones.

In an age in which social media platforms are readily available for audience members to share opinions, ideas, fanfiction, theories, and other responses, theatre historians can much more easily track how audiences respond creatively to the shows they watch. We can see the various new meanings (queer) audiences make for themselves and others. This is especially important with a popular form such as the Broadway musical, since it invites audience participation before audiences even see the show – as cast recordings and choreography tutorials are often used as part of a show's promotional materials – and because responses to these shows via social media are readily available to affect others long before most of us will actually go to the theatre.

The Fiction of Identity

A consideration of audience practices and experiences prompts analysis of how audience members *identify* with the characters in a musical and how desire and identification intertwine for musical theatre audiences. These are questions sketched, in many ways, by Wolf's *A Problem Like Maria*, and they are central to this book.[59] How does desire function as we watch characters onstage in a musical? Do we wish to *be* the performer? Do we wish to be beautiful, talented, and famous *like* the performer? Do we wish to possess the performer? to be loved by the performer? or simply to sing and dance ourselves? We need not disaggregate these different desiring operations as we think about how musical theatre works, but it is frequently intriguing to notice that when a show doesn't work – or is perceived not to work – it is often because of a failure of desire and identification to do the work they were intended to do. Identification, in turn, is central to an important strand of LGBTQ politics, one that asks audiences to identify with queer people, to put themselves in our shoes, and to begin to understand that LGBTQ freedoms affect freedoms for everyone.

In *Love Is Love Is Love*, I use the word *identity* to mean *sameness*. The phrase "love is love is love," as I noted earlier, is itself a statement of identity: one love is the same as another love. I recognize, however, that many others use *identity* to mean something like *subjectivity* or *the self* or as a way to speak about who one is (as in the phrases *personal identity* or *identity theft*).[60] As with the word *performative*, use of the word *identity* always prompts a question for me: how does this scholar mean this word?[61] Does she mean a kind of individual concept of personhood, or are we speaking about an experience or process of recognition and sameness? In *Love Is Love Is Love*, I will not use *identity* to mean *subjectivity*, but I do find the gradual transformation of a term that means *sameness* into a word that stands in for an individual self to be a fascinating slippage. Indeed, I find that thinking about sameness is surprisingly productive for thinking about selfhood or subjectivity.

First, in order to understand who we are, we often need to make sense of different aspects of ourselves, learning to incorporate them into an image of the self that is the same. We disavow parts of ourselves that we dislike or that don't fit in with the self we imagine, and then we make sense of the rest of these parts, incorporating them into a concept of a self to which we hold tight. I'm a Pisces; I'm a good person; I'm a Hufflepuff; I'm a bookkeeper; I'm a writer; I'm an influencer. Or as Usher in *A Strange Loop* might put it, "the second-wave feminist in me / Is at war with the / Dick-sucking Black gay man."[62] I tell myself that all of these different aspects of me *are* me: this is the language of identity/sameness applied to parts of the self. So, when we speak about identity, we can also think about the work it takes to make sense of the self as a kind of whole.

Second, we fashion who we are and learn about ourselves through identificatory practices; we make sense of the self by finding identity *with* others – frequently through mediated representations such as those onstage or on various screens. This is to say that I understand whatever we think of as *individual* subjectivity as always already relational, formed through a process of identity/sameness. In his groundbreaking book *Disidentifications: Queers of Color and the Performance of Politics*, José Muñoz uses the word similarly. "The fiction of identity," he argues,

> is one that is accessed with relative ease by most majoritarian subjects. Minoritarian subjects need to interface with different subcultural fields to activate their own senses of self. This is not to say that majoritarian subjects have no recourse to disidentification or that their own formation as subjects is not structured through multiple and sometimes conflicting sites of identification.[63]

In Muñoz's understanding, subject formation happens through multiple sites of identification, but the process of identification is more complicated for minoritarian subjects because the possible representations available for identificatory practices are more limited for people of color, queer people, and queer people of color than they are for white people and straight people.

The term *identity* is useful, then, because it prompts us to think about how we form our subjectivities both through a concept of sameness applied to ourselves (all of these parts of me *are* me) and relationally with others (through identification and disidentification). There are numerous political ideas related to identity that musical theatre prompts us to consider. The case studies in this book will illuminate many facets of this subject, but I want, here, to articulate two ways in which musical theatre as a form holds particular possibilities that might help us think through some of the thorniest problems of audience identification, identity (especially LGBTQ identities), and difference. These questions of identity and difference are political problems related to how Broadway musicals work and how they manage to hail queer audiences while also representing queerness for straight audiences.

In the first place, the question of a musical's "integration" is a question of identity. In other words, an argument that this or that musical is "integrated" is an argument that one part of a musical is identical to all of its other parts: elements that appear to be different are in fact one central thing, an integrated musical. Is this piece of the musical integrated with the whole of the musical as such? The theory of the integrated musical says *yes*; all of the parts contribute to the whole. This theory of integration has dominated conversations about musical theatre, and scholars and practitioners have found it so attractive and compelling that the idea of a "concept musical" needed to be developed apparently for the sole purpose of explaining how we might include obviously disjointed musicals like *Cabaret* and *Company* under the rubric of "integration."

A few theorists have fought long and hard to point out that there is no such thing as an integrated musical. This is a central argument of Bruce Kirle's *Unfinished Show Business*, and it is the main foundation on which Scott McMillin's masterful book *The Musical as Drama* rests. McMillin tells us in the first few pages of the book that:

> When a musical is working well, I feel the crackle of difference, not the smoothness of unity, even when the numbers dovetail with the book. It takes things different from one another to be thought of as integrated in the first place, and I find that the musical depends more on the differences that make the close fit interesting than on the suppression of difference in a seamless whole.[64]

For McMillin,

> the important feature [of musical theatre] is the incongruity between book and number, between what I describe as two orders of time, the progressive time of plot and the repetitive time of music, yet the theory that usually attends the musical would iron out this incongruity in the name of integration.[65]

I don't want to repeat more of McMillin's arguments here – mostly because I find them convincing and conclusive – but I think it's important to note that what

McMillin is articulating here is similar to the work of identity that we do on ourselves in order to make sense of our subjectivities. We examine parts of ourselves that are obviously different from one another – our eyes, our hair, our nipples; our religions, our politics, our sexual proclivities – and we say that these aspects of the self possess identity, share a sameness. We say to ourselves that we are an integrated self.

Why do we tell ourselves that musicals are integrated when we know they are not? We might ask the same question about ourselves.

In his excellent study *Melodrama*, queer theorist Jonathan Goldberg argues that the music of the melodrama, indeed the entire idea of melodrama, reminds us that identity (our idea of a self that is the same) is a fiction.[66] The music of melodrama, Goldberg says, "intimates that alongside the everyday world there is another."[67] The promise of this music is the reminder that the subject is not a stable one, that we might choose to be – or be even without choosing – something else. A little later in the book Goldberg says that "Melodramas may convey the message that 'you can't escape what you are,' but what you are is not one thing."[68] This thread runs through his book, and Goldberg argues convincingly that although the melodramatic form might, for example, tell stories about the impossibility of true love succeeding across class boundaries or racial divisions, it is more important to understand that:

> Coupling is impossible because no one is single, each one is divided. But it also is in division that coupling resides. . . . Every one is two. And every couple cannot be one. Differences that can be marked as if they are the effect of social divisions (of race, of class, of gender, of age, of sexuality) are the effect of divisions that don't originate in the social: this is the impossible situation of melodrama.[69]

Goldberg's analysis applies perfectly to the form of Broadway musicals. The melodramatic situations that divide these characters – Tony and Maria, Nellie and Emile, Porgy and Bess, Nina and Benny – mark divisions in these characters' very selves, divided loyalties that refuse easy understandings of subjectivity as singular.

It is this division within the self that prompts characters to sing. As McMillin argues,

> Characters like Billy Bigelow and Julie Jordan in *Carousel* have numbers that seem specific to their characters, but the effect of the numbers is not so much to advance characterization as to *double characterization*, by turning Billy Bigelow and Julie Jordan into new versions of themselves, musical versions.[70]

For McMillin, the very form of a musical creates multiple versions of a self. The self is not singular in a musical because there is the Celie who speaks the lines of the libretto and then there is the Celie who sings songs – something Celie would never have done in Alice Walker's novel or Steven Spielberg's film. In the musical *The Color Purple*, there are always already two Celies. The musical's form prompts us to understand the self in a way that we don't normally think of it, as containing more than one aspect or possibility, as *unintegrated*, not possessing the apparent identity that our names seem to promise.

Broadway musicals are not integrated, and it is fundamental that we understand this because the theory of identification maintains the pretense that *characters* in musical theatre are integrated when precisely the opposite is true. Characters have a tendency to burst into song and then to return suddenly to speaking; whenever they do this, they demonstrate that there is more than one someone up there onstage or on screen – not just an actor and a character but an actor, a character, and *another* version of the character, one who sings and (sometimes) dances.

Musical theatre scholar Bradley Rogers puts this another way in his book *The Song Is You*. He argues that the concept of "integration also denies the identifications made possible by the musical form, suggesting instead not only a sophisticated model of authorial and spectatorial control but also a stable subject."[71] Rogers' perspective prompts another line of thinking about identity and Broadway musicals. Like McMillin, he acknowledges the instability of the characters in musical theatre, but his focus here is on the possibilities for audience identification that are opened up by that instability.

In the second place, then, the term *identity* helps us think about how we watch musical theatre and how it is that we *identify* as we watch. I noted earlier how writers such as Donatella Galella, Wayne Koestenbaum, and Stacy Wolf have analyzed their experiences while watching (and listening), but one of the things I am most curious about as I focus on audience practices is how we experience identification with the characters in a musical. How might we think of performances in musical theatre as opening up identificatory possibilities for audiences? How are the pleasures of musical theatre related to impersonation and identificatory practices?[72] In what ways might musical theatre performance confuse the desire to become someone else and the desire to possess someone else? "I knew that to love Julie Andrews placed me, however vaguely, in heterosexuality's domain," says Wayne Koestenbaum in *The Queen's Throat*, "but to identify with Julie Andrews, to want to be the star of *Star!*, placed me under suspicion."[73] And Stacy Wolf reports that a lesbian friend "at once finds Andrews beautiful (is attracted to her) and wants to be *like* her and wants to be *with* her."[74] How does musical theatre make space for multiple modes of queer identification? And how might these descriptions of audience identification with musical theatre characters both help us to examine contemporary LGBTQ politics and to prompt an LGBTQ politics that might be different or new?

As we listen to musical theatre, we often sing along, that is play *as* the characters, copy, identify with them. Not everyone does this, of course, but as I noted earlier and many others have noted before me, the shows are designed to prompt such impersonations.[75] As Rogers argues,

> the chains of impersonation fuel the chains of desire that set the musical in motion. The desire at the center of musical theatre is precisely the creation of complex relationships across bodies, through impersonation and projection –

as modeled in the cross-gender, cross-racial, and cross-ethnic performances that relentlessly populate the genre.[76]

One of the main arguments of Rogers' book is that musical theatre is filled with characters who are trying on the behaviors, melodies, costumes, and genders of people different from themselves, and in this way, characters model their identificatory practices for us.

Characters in musicals cannot contain themselves, and they attempt to deal with the multiplicity inside themselves by trying on the performances of others. In so doing, they prompt us – and the form itself invites us – to copy these identificatory practices, performing the songs of others in order to make sense of ourselves. McMillin, relatedly, refers to:

> the strange business of watching people pretend to be other people and engage in made-up stories for hours at a time. That odd desire lies behind all theatre, the desire to see actors take on new characters, and it multiplies in musical theatre, when the new characters break out in song and dance, adding musical selves to their book selves. They become doubly other, more than one person certainly, even more than two.[77]

What both Rogers and McMillin are exploring are the ways that the multiplicity of characters in musicals – their undecidedness and their refusal to be *one* – allows for an even more complicated, exciting, and pleasurable identificatory experience for the audience, who can experiment with identification,

> try[ing] on a dizzying *series* of bodies in such rapid and incoherent fashion as to undermine the idea of identity. This is crucial, as the musical, with its endless predilection for bursting into song and dance, is constantly asking spectators to associate not just with one other body but with *many* other bodies.[78]

For spectators having trouble making sense of themselves or seeing themselves in the representations provided to them by mainstream society – like young people, like queer people – Broadway musicals can offer a different set of identificatory and disidentificatory possibilities. This is the promise or possibility that you, like Walt Whitman, might contain multitudes. It's musical proof for audiences that inside of the person who is barely getting through the day is another person who is doing great, with a different voice and a different way of singing about what she wants.

Queerness as Unfixed

The chapters that follow approach, in different ways, some of the questions about LGBTQ identity, identification, political commitment, and representation that I've outlined. I have chosen five musicals that don't sit particularly well together or relate to one another in obvious ways. The case studies in this book have interested me because of the problems for LGBTQ politics that each of them has prompted in popular culture. I've chosen five shows that seemed to me to cause enough controversy and generate enough discourse around queerness that they functioned as excellent portraits of LGBTQ politics in this decade. It is likely, however, that I have not chosen the five musicals others would choose were they to write about LGBTQ politics and Broadway musicals in this decade – three of these musicals don't even (apparently) have queer characters! Indeed, *none* of the characters in the shows explicitly identifies as queer or trans. Even characters whom we might understand as queer or trans from an audience perspective – Celie, Shug, Hedwig, Yitzhak – don't claim specific LGBTQ identities. Part of what I'm working with here, though, is the idea that queer audiences and queer performers – what they say about the shows and what they do with the shows – are more important or more interesting than any of a show's own ideas about queerness. Further, as many scholars have demonstrated, a Broadway musical doesn't need to mention queerness for it to have things to say about queer desire, queer spectatorship, and queer reception.

Rather than attaching to homosexuality, bisexuality, or transgender as identity positions, each of the shows in *Love Is Love Is Love* reimagines an earlier form of queerness now eclipsed by our current concepts of "queer," "trans," and "LGBTQ." I've chosen five musicals in which no characters explicitly identify as L, G, B, T, or Q in order to draw attention to the ways that we as audiences do the work of identification, projecting our own subject positions onto these characters and interpreting their (fictional) sexualities as a method for making sense of our own. In each chapter, I take time to discuss older ways of understanding queer desires and identifications. I do this in order to make our own LGBTQ moment seem strange. This is a fundamentally Foucauldian practice, one that, as Cathy Cohen has put it, "focuses on and makes central not only the socially constructed nature of sexuality and sexual categories, but also the varying degrees and multiple sites of power distributed within all categories of sexuality, including the normative category of heterosexuality."[79] Examining understandings of queerness that seem outdated can help us better interrogate our seemingly settled ideas about ourselves.

This queer studies approach also moves us away from the question of whether a show contains "good" or "bad" representations of LGBTQ characters. The work of evaluating bad representations, praising good ones, and criticizing stereotypes has been a preoccupation of many musical theatre scholars, primarily John Clum and more recently James Lovelock and Sarah Whitfield.[80] But *all* representations are available for the work of audience identification and disidentification; representations are *productive* in a Foucauldian sense, despite the value judgments of scholars or activists deeming them positive or negative, authentic or stereotyped. *Frozen*, for example, contains a "bad" representation of an apparently queer character, but that hasn't stopped queer audiences from responding to her in ways many of us would deem "good." It is my hope that by avoiding such value judgments, we can explore more complex connections between representations and audiences.

24 Introduction

Indeed, the politics of representation are only an *aspect* of LGBTQ politics. Let me say again that the identity "LGBTQ" covers over many differences, and a production may be "good" representation for (say) upper-middle-class white gay men while simultaneously offering representation that is harmful for (say) working-class Asian American lesbians. Similarly, a production may be a wonderfully celebratory representation of LGBTQ love without stereotypes while extolling imperialist, reactionary political positions. Instead, I take as fundamental that LGBTQ identity is tenuous, that LGBTQ politics are unpredictable, and that all representations are available for the work of LGBTQ identification and disidentification. Because of this, there is no easy way to evaluate or judge a particular show. What I have attempted to do instead is to situate these performances within their multiple, complicated histories, including histories of sexuality.

Those histories are richer and more complex than they might at first seem. *Promises, Promises* (Chapter 1) was originally written for the 1968 Broadway season, and it marks a time just before Stonewall, before the Broadway musical came out of the closet. This chapter is concerned with how the closet still looms large in our own time, how the legacies of the closet persist, not only in 2010, when *Promises* was revived on Broadway, but also a decade later when Ryan Murphy's film adaptation of *The Prom* premiered on Netflix. *Newsies* (Chapter 2) is set at the turn of the twentieth century, near the time of the invention of homosexuality as a category. But as historian George Chauncey makes clear in *Gay New York*, in the period before men having sex with men came to understand themselves as identical to one another, they understood their desires through the frame of *gender* rather than (homo)sexuality.

Hedwig and the Angry Inch (Chapter 3) continues this interrogation of sexuality through a gendered frame by examining the period of the show's original run in the late 1990s – before the term *transgender* came into widespread use. *Hedwig* does not explicitly formulate any theories about what we understand as transgender, but it has much to say about gender as such, although audiences have (perhaps rightly) seen it as an unhelpful and even damaging representation of a trans woman. *Hedwig* has a further outdated image of queer desire in its reperformance of Plato's *Symposium* from the fourth century BCE. In this way, *Hedwig's* version of love is rooted in and repurposes ancient Athenian modes of queer relationality that have the capacity to make our own LGBTQ identities look very strange indeed.

The Color Purple (Chapter 4) is a story about the southern United States in the early twentieth century, again before the rubric of sexuality began to dominate understandings of sexual desire. The modes of desire the characters articulate in this musical remain outside of this rubric, and Celie and Shug, the narrative's two central queer characters, avoid labels of sexuality. Celie quite clearly enjoys and desires sex with Shug, and she doesn't enjoy sex with men, but the closest she gets to labeling that desire in the novel is to tell Mr. _____ in letter 84 that "men look like frogs" when they take off their pants. "No matter how you kiss 'em, as far as I'm concern, frogs is what they stay."[81] This is, of course, a clever reference to the German fairy tale "The Frog Prince," published in 1812 by the Brothers Grimm, which tells the queer story of a young woman in an intimate relationship with an amphibian, but it is not a claim of lesbian identity. *Frozen* (Chapter 5) is an updated version of a different fairy tale, one imagined by the nineteenth-century fabulist Hans Christian Andersen, whose own queer sexuality has resisted definition by confused biographers. Andersen's snow queen has long been the subject of discussion by literary critics as a figure for queer sexuality as such, although the queen never places a label of sexuality on herself. Her citation in *Frozen* means that we are able to look back at the queerness already at work in the 1844 text of Andersen's fairy tale and examine its influence on queer representation in the twenty-first century.

In this way, all five of these musicals bear the traces of queer identities that existed before the invention of LGBTQ identity and often before the invention of homosexuality as such. This is a queer historiographical practice, one that refuses to take for granted that it knows what the terms lesbian, gay, bisexual, and transgender signify.[82] Each of the case studies in *Love Is Love Is Love* puts at least one apparently outdated form of queerness in conversation with the LGBTQ politics of the second decade of the twenty-first century.[83] An examination of older modes of queerness has the ability to disturb our own seemingly settled ideas about sexuality and our current ways of understanding ourselves. As we think about how far we appear to have come in terms of LGBTQ representation and LGBTQ political victories, these Broadway musicals remind us to look back, to situate our current ideas about LGBTQ identity within queer histories. And as these musicals and – most crucially – their audiences reimagine those histories, they write new ones. These five shows and the ways their audiences took them up describe a provocative portrait of twenty-first-century LGBTQ issues and articulate a potential LGBTQ politics of the future.

Sing It Back to Me

Each of the shows addressed in this book revives a film and a previous musical. These shows, like queer subjectivities, make reference to earlier musicals and other works, redefining previous ways of thinking and refashioning them into something new. But citation is also everywhere in musical theatre. Citation is what's happening on Instagram at @letshearitforthechoice; it's what the performers and producers in *Beyond Broadway* are doing around the country; and it's what the industry does as it develops shows based on previously published material such as *Waitress*, *Jagged Little Pill*, or *Ain't Too Proud: The Life and Times of the Temptations*. The musical theatre industry has always been invested in citation: much older shows like *Show Boat*, *Oklahoma!*, and *Porgy and Bess* were also based on previously published material.

One of the central insights of musical theatre historian Ethan Mordden's *Anything Goes* is that citation is essential to the form as such.[84] Like reality television, almost any animated series, *Saturday Night Live*, or a film by Pedro Almodóvar, musical theatre does much of what it does by citing material it assumes its audiences know and love (or sometimes hate). In this way, musical theatre is formally using what performance theorist Richard Schechner has termed twice-behaved behavior or "behavioral strips."[85] We can take for granted that citation and repetition are essential to performance, but musical theatre repeats more and repeats differently than other theatrical forms. Musical theatre's strips of behavior always mean *something else* or always mean *in addition*.

Musical theatre works differently because of the appearance of the song within the action of the drama. As McMillan notes,

> The song inserts a lyrical moment into the cause-and-effect progress of the plot, a moment that suspends book time in favor of lyric time, time organized not by cause and effect (which is how book time works) but by principles of repetition (which is how numbers work).[86]

Musical theatre time is time spent repeating. Certainly, a song's chorus repeats – and often repeats again – but even the verses of a song repeat, melodically if not lyrically. Such repetition would be irritating, as McMillin points out, in a show without music, but it is pleasurable in a song. If we are listening at home, we may even skip back to the beginning and play it to ourselves again. McMillin tells us that as we listen to a song:

> You are taking pleasure in repetition, and you aren't progressing toward any destination beyond the performance of repetition itself. You may be thinking of some other destination, especially if you are a lover, but you won't go there until the song is ended or you break it off.[87]

The song dwells on something or *in* something; its repetition keeps us from moving on or moving forward. It is impossible for me not to hear in McMillin's words an echo of queer theorist Lee Edelman's claim in *No Future: Queer Theory and the Death Drive* that

> queerness exposes sexuality's inevitable coloration by the drive: its insistence on repetition, its stubborn denial of teleology, its resistance to determinations of meaning (except insofar as it means this refusal to admit such determinations of meaning), and, above all, its rejection of spiritualization through marriage to reproductive futurism.[88]

Edelman understands repetition as a queer practice, a refusal to resolve, a refusal to grow up. Musical theatre's songs take pleasure in repetition, and in this way, they figure queerness itself.[89]

More than the formal properties of repetition within a song or show, this book focuses on the idea of citation more generally. I want to follow yet another of McMillin's provocations in *The Musical as Drama*: citing John Hollander, McMillin says that "in addition to being repeated itself, refrain bears a memory of its own repetition."[90] It is this memory of its own repetition that interests me in *Love Is Love*

Is Love as we think about revival. A revival cites a version of itself that came before. It places itself in relation to a previous iteration, doing things differently or devotedly attempting to recreate a beloved original.

Revivals are especially important for thinking through LGBTQ politics on Broadway because of the way these politics change over time. As we will see in the first case study on *Promises, Promises*, sexual politics and ideas about masculinity shifted widely from 1960 to 2010. Enormous shifts over a 50-year span are certainly no surprise, but careful attention to tiny changes in details and ideas between, say, the film of *Newsies* in 1992 and the Broadway production of *Newsies the Musical* in 2012, or 2013's *Frozen* and its 2018 iteration onstage, can illuminate the shifting ways that we think about LGBTQ issues and LGBTQ politics. As I've said, the musicals themselves aren't always central to the inquiry of *Love Is Love Is Love*, so often what we'll find ourselves able to see by looking at different productions or variations of the same text are the changing politics that audiences bring to these Broadway musicals – and how a show sings those politics back to us.

Revivals are themselves citations, and each of the musicals in this book cites more than just its original Broadway run or a feature film. In their revivals, each of these shows has also worked to *pass on* these shows to others. As we will see with *Newsies* and *The Color Purple*, performers and other artists' identifications with characters and performances are often motivating forces behind revival itself, prompting artists to want to do the show again and differently, to share a musical with new audience members. In many ways – particularly for LGBTQ performers and theatre artists – revival can be a way to pass down or pass on LGBTQ cultures, remaking them and speaking in new ways to new LGBTQ audiences. I outline the arguments and structures of each of my chapters in what follows, but I also note the ways each of these musicals cites other texts, layering new meanings onto old understandings of queerness, old feelings, and seemingly antiquated ways of thinking about our pasts.

Chapter 1, "Shut Up and Deal," examines the 2010 revival (its first) of Burt Bacharach, Hal David, and Neil Simon's 1968 musical *Promises, Promises*, a show based on I.A.L. Diamond and Billy Wilder's Oscar-winning 1960 film *The Apartment*. The revival starred Sean Hayes and Kristin Chenoweth, and though it cited the show's original production (starring Jerry Orbach and Jill O'Hara) and *The Apartment* (starring Jack Lemmon and Shirley MacLaine), it also quoted the Bacharach–David catalog more broadly. The 2010 production added two Bacharach–David numbers – "I Say a Little Prayer" and "A House Is Not a Home" – which were written not for *Promises, Promises* but for Dionne Warwick. These two songs have their own long histories in the popular imagination. Indeed, to sing "I Say a Little Prayer" is also to cite Aretha Franklin's well-known 1968 version of the song, as well as the popular rendition by Rupert Everett in the 1998 film *My Best Friend's Wedding*. "A House Is Not a Home" is now best recognized from its 1981 recording by the inimitable Luther Vandross, a version that was named by *Essence* as #8 on a list of the "25 Best Slow Jams of All Time."[91] *Promises, Promises* in 2010, then, intriguingly harked back to the other voices who sang its songs (two of them

28 Introduction

gay men), but it also found itself in a controversy troubled by the very history it expected its audience to carry with it into the theatre, a complex citation of the NBC sitcom *Will & Grace*.

Chapter 1 charts the history of what I call the Straight Jacket Affair, the 2010 media fracas surrounding a *Newsweek* article that declared that Sean Hayes was too gay to play the central character in *Promises*. This chapter explores the legacy of the closet from 1960 to 2010, a legacy complicated by the question of authenticity in queer performance – who should get to perform which characters and why certain performances make us feel uncomfortable. I attempt to complicate the idea of "playing gay" and "playing straight," asking what we mean when we use those phrases to talk about what actors do. I also place the audience's judgment about the sexualities of the characters in *Promises, Promises* in the context of the larger culture of surveillance explored by the film *The Apartment*. Finally, I place the Straight Jacket Affair beside a second media fracas a decade later that surrounded James Corden's performance as a gay character in the 2020 film *The Prom*.

Chapter 2, "It Gets Better Than Boyhood," situates Alan Menken, Jack Feldman, and Harvey Fierstein's 2011 show *Newsies* in the context of the It Gets Better campaign, a movement designed to combat the suicides of bullied queer teenagers by asking them to turn their attention toward the future. I demonstrate that the 2012 Broadway show alters the content from the original 1992 movie musical, emphasizing the particular LGBTQ political preoccupations of the early part of the decade – queer families and a focus on the future. This chapter attends, as well, to the way *Newsies* refigures a range of gender performances for its young audiences, demonstrating revised versions of masculinity and femininity that are available for identificatory processes. This reworking of masculinity and femininity is also haunted by gender-variant and queer ghosts, those of early twentieth-century stars Mae West and Aida Overton Walker, as well as the ghosts of the fairies of turn-of-the-century New York City and that of Billy Lucas, a bullied 15-year-old in Indiana who committed suicide and moved Dan Savage to utter the phrase *it gets better*. I close with the 2020 revision of *Newsies* for young performers, *Newsies JR.*, and a queer disability studies approach, arguing that the musical's revised, assimilationist gender politics eclipse its oppositional queer politics and illuminate the neoliberal forces already at work in the It Gets Better campaign.

In the book's third chapter, "A Gender of One, a Sexuality of Many," I discuss the 2014 Broadway run of Stephen Trask and John Cameron Mitchell's *Hedwig and the Angry Inch*, a musical which originally ran off-Broadway in 1998. The revival cited both the show's original production and the 2001 film version (directed by Mitchell), but it also – as a way to explain Hedwig's presence at the Belasco Theatre – cited Kathryn Bigelow's 2009 film *The Hurt Locker*. Hedwig quotes and cites numerous rock musicians and asks us to consider their styles and performances of gender as she tells us the story of her own search. As a more complicated intertext, *Hedwig* also refers repeatedly to – and musically retells – the famous Aristophanes passage from Plato's *Symposium*. In this way, *Hedwig* not only considers queer gender and queer desire through the history of rock and roll but also takes us back to antiquity.

Citation got even trickier in *Hedwig*, as Neil Patrick Harris, the revival's star, was replaced by a series of famous performers for shorter runs, including Mitchell himself, in the role he created. This chapter investigates the way audiences (both queer and not) identify with the character of Hedwig by examining interviews given by the famous performers who worked on *Hedwig and the Angry Inch* as they speak about their own identifications. I also contextualize the *Hedwig* revival within a larger history of gay–trans identity politics by placing the musical alongside what news media had begun calling "the transgender tipping point." I am fascinated, especially, by academic affection for and apparent identification with *Hedwig*, and this chapter uses *Hedwig* to think through identity: both the possibilities of gay–trans political identity and a larger concept of inclusion without identity that I elaborate via *Hedwig*'s "gender of one."

Chapter 4, "All My Life I Had to Fight," discusses the 2015 production of Brenda Russell, Allee Willis, Stephen Bray, and Marsha Norman's *The Color Purple*, a revival of the original 2004 musical, which was itself a version of Alice Walker's 1982 novel and its 1985 film version. This chapter takes as inspiration a 2020 audiobook performance of *The Color Purple* and its many characters by lesbian actress Samira Wiley. Wiley has spoken about the power of finding one's voice and the way that the book called to her from the page as a reader; in her performance, she uses her voice to call to a different generation of readers and also to perform some of the novel's ideas and revisions of old ways of encountering and citing the Christian Bible and Christian theology.[92] In this epistolary novel, the difference between what is written, what is spoken, and what is sung matters a great deal, and the chapter is about different ways of citing this novel and musical, the inspirational power of *The Color Purple*, and the way that it prompts audiences, readers, and listeners to use our own voices in protest, activism, and queer worldmaking practices.

This chapter is structured by responses to anti-Black police violence in the United States by two different members of *The Color Purple*'s cast – Heather Headley and Cynthia Erivo. I describe these performers' responses as a way to illuminate the 2015 revival's engagement with the Black church, *The Color Purple*'s treatment of god and religion, the novel and film's vexed relationship with Black men and violence, and LGBTQ engagement in the Black Lives Matter movement. I also link Alice Walker's ethics of forgiveness to potential political positions in the United States, especially concerning prison abolition and police defunding. The chapter closes by considering "I'm Here" both in context and out of context, examining separate performances of the song by Jennifer Hudson and Cynthia Erivo and describing the song's identificatory and political possibilities.

The book's final chapter, "Frozen Eleganza," explores the universe of Disney's *Frozen* both on screen and onstage, most specifically the 2018 Broadway production of Kristen Anderson-Lopez, Robert Lopez, and Jennifer Lee's *Frozen the Musical*, which managed to cite both the 2013 film *Frozen* and its 2019 sequel *Frozen II* (both directed by Lee and Chris Buck). The film and musical are ostensibly based on Hans Christian Andersen's 1844 fairy tale *The Snow Queen*, and in this way, *Frozen* also partially revisits C.S. Lewis's rewriting of Andersen's tale in his 1950 novel

The Lion, the Witch and the Wardrobe. *Frozen* is an extraordinarily self-referential text, and citations proliferate in *Frozen the Musical* because the *Frozen* franchise keeps generating content, including numerous short films, a YouTube series, a video game, and an unbelievable amount of *Frozen*-themed merchandise.

The chapter argues that Elsa is represented not as a lesbian but specifically as a *closeted* lesbian. I also see in *Frozen*, however, an extraordinary interaction with queer audiences, and this chapter describes performances on *Saturday Night Live* and *RuPaul's Drag Race* to chart queer audience creativity around *Frozen*'s characters. I contrast this, especially, with Disney artists' own attempts to contain queer politics while simultaneously extolling LGBTQ identification. One of the central claims of this chapter is that mainstream versions of queerness move, at the end of the decade, to re-contain queer and gender nonconforming children within the bounds of the biological family – in stark contrast with the earlier part of the decade's investment in chosen family. Finally, this chapter turns to a consideration of the queer potential embedded in Olaf, *Frozen*'s quirky snowchild. I argue that Olaf's particular awareness of his own bodily (dis)identity and his apparently dangerous identificatory practices offer especial possibilities for queer and trans audiences. My focus at the end of this chapter is on the child – that always important symbol of the future – and in this way, the final chapter directs our attention toward queer possibilities and queer subjectivities that we have not yet been able to imagine.

Notes

1 The Tony Awards, "Fun Home Performance Tony Awards 2015."
2 The Tony Awards, "Acceptance Speech: Lisa Kron (2015)." Emphasis in original.
3 Rooney, "Broadway's New Season Takes Shape as Game-Changing Musical *Hamilton* Charges In."
4 *Fun Home* closed in September 2016.
5 Rodulfo, "2016 Is the Year of #BroadwaySoDiverse." The hashtag was a riff on the hashtag #OscarsSoWhite, which appeared after the January 2015 Oscar nominations.
6 Dziemianowicz, "Broadway's 2015–2016 Season Sets Record for Attendance and Grosses."
7 Alvarez and Pérez-Peña, "Praising Isis, Gunman Attacks Gay Nightclub, Leaving 50 Dead in Worst Shooting on U.S. Soil," A1.
8 Gioia, "Tony Awards Dedicates Tonight's Ceremony to Orlando Victims."
9 Paulson, "Tonys Hail *Hamilton* and Denounce Hate," C1.
10 CBS News, "James Corden Pays Tribute to Orlando in Tony's Opener."
11 See, as just one example, Hoffman, *The Great White Way*.
12 See Grady, "Trump's Hamilton Outburst Ignores the Theater's History as a Place for Political Protest."
13 This version, which differs from that published in the *Times*, comes from a magnet of the sonnet in his own handwriting that Miranda promoted for the website Tee Rico. See Tee Rico, "Lin-Manuel Handwritten Love Is Love Sonnet – 5"x7" Magnet." For Miranda's performance of the sonnet, see BroadwayInHD, "Acceptance Speech – Best Score: Lin-Manuel Miranda (2016)." See also Miranda, "My Sonnet . . . ."
14 Alvarez and Pérez-Peña, "Praising Isis, Gunman Attacks Gay Nightclub, Leaving 50 Dead in Worst Shooting on U.S. Soil," A12.
15 Alvarez and Pérez-Peña, "Praising Isis, Gunman Attacks Gay Nightclub, Leaving 50 Dead in Worst Shooting on U.S. Soil," A1.

Introduction **31**

16 See Lotan, Brinkmann, and Stutzman, "Witness: Omar Mateen Had Been at Orlando Gay Nightclub Many Times"; Sandoval, Marcius, and Otis, "Orlando Shooter Was Regular at Pulse Gay Club; Former Classmate Says Omar Mateen Was Homosexual"; and CBS New York, "Omar Mateen's Alleged Male Lover: 'He Did It for Revenge' Against Latino Men."
17 Frizell, "Donald Trump Faces Backlash for Tweets About Orlando Shooting."
18 Thomas, "My Father's Pulse."
19 Torres, "In Praise of Latin Night at the Queer Club." See also Rivera-Servera, "Quotidian Utopias."
20 Larimer, "Middle Schoolers Chant 'Build the Wall' During Lunch in Aftermath of Trump Win."
21 Michaels, "We Tracked Down the Lawyers Behind the Recent Wave of Anti-Trans Bathroom Bills."
22 Graham, "The Complicated Pain of America's Queer Muslims."
23 Dillon, "The Only Freedom I Can See," 207.
24 See, for example, Johnson, "'Quare' Studies."
25 Chance, "LGBT Gun Rights Group Sees Membership Spike After Orlando Shooting."
26 Pink Pistols, "Pink Pistols Saddened by Attack on Orlando Club."
27 Human Rights Campaign, "Gun Violence Prevention." See also Okma, "GLAAD Slams the Trump Administration for Pandering to the NRA Instead of Addressing the Crisis of Gun Violence."
28 Morales, "We're All in the Same Boat," 93. Cf. Cedric Robinson's challenge in *The Panthers Can't Save Us Now*, especially 142; see also Cohen, "Punks, Bulldaggers, and Welfare Queens."
29 Human Rights Campaign, "The Journey to Marriage Equality in the United States."
30 Most heterosexual marriages are not looked at primarily as sexual arrangements.
31 Rubin, "Thinking Sex," 283.
32 Seriously. No shade. In 2022, while raising money for an organization designed to help fund Latinx nonprofits, Miranda explicitly linked Florida's anti-gay politics with the Pulse massacre. See Gamboa, "Lin-Manuel Miranda Helps Launch Latinx LGBTQ Support Program."
33 "Lin-Manuel Miranda's Sonnet From the Tony Awards." My emphasis.
34 Paulson, "Tonys Hail *Hamilton* and Denounce Hate," C2.
35 Jones, *Rise Up!*, 215.
36 Rezal, "The Racial Makeup of America's Prisons."
37 Oladipo, "2021 on Pace to Be Deadliest Yet for Trans and Gender Non-Conforming Americans."
38 Dudenhoefer, "Broadway's *Fun Home* Comes to Orlando's Dr. Phillips Center for Some Healing."
39 Ryan, "The Best Movie Musicals of 2021, Ranked."
40 Bay-Cheng, "Theater Is Media," 35.
41 Kirle, *Unfinished Show Business*, xxii. One hears echoes, here, of the objections Dwight Conquergood made in the late 1990s in regard to the discipline of performance studies. See Conquergood, "Beyond the Text."
42 Kirle, *Unfinished Show Business*, 20.
43 The director Jonathan Miller makes just such an argument about Shakespeare in performance, arguing that "A script tells us nothing about the gestures, the stance, the facial expressions, the dress, the weight, or the grouping or the movements. So although the text is a necessary condition for the performance it is by no means a sufficient one. It is short of all these accessories which are, in a sense, the *essence* of performance." Miller, *Subsequent Performances*, 34.
44 Wolf, *Beyond Broadway*, 5. Note the strange aspersions cast toward "much musical theatre scholarship" here. They are identical to the criticisms Kirle made 15 years earlier about "overprivileging the text."
45 See Wolf, *Beyond Broadway*, 140.

32 Introduction

46 Clum, *Something for the Boys,* especially 39–47.
47 As David Savran says, "No theatre form is as single-mindedly devoted to producing pleasure, inspiring spectators to tap their feet, sing along, or otherwise be carried away. This utopian – and mimetic – dimension of the musical (linked to its relentless reflexivity) makes it into a kind of hothouse for the manufacture of theatrical seduction and the ideological positions to which mass audiences can be seduced." See Savran, "Toward a Historiography of the Popular," 216.
48 Miller, *Place for Us,* 86–87.
49 Wolf, *Beyond Broadway,* 4.
50 Bay-Cheng, "Theater Is Media," 38.
51 Bay-Cheng, "Theater Is Media," 40.
52 See Hoffman, *The Great White Way,* 15–16.
53 Larkin, "Let's Hear It for the Choice."
54 Bay-Cheng, "Theater Is Media," 33.
55 For one of my inspirations for this scholarly approach, see Kessler, "'Trash Talk and Visual Protests.'"
56 McMillin, *The Musical as Drama,* 181.
57 Galella, "Feeling Yellow."
58 See also Forsgren, "*The Wiz* Redux," 332.
59 Wolf argues that lesbian reception of musicals involves both identification *and* desire. See Wolf, *A Problem Like Maria,* 211.
60 Raymond Knapp's two-volume history *The American Musical* uses the word in multiple ways throughout but especially in the phrase "personal identity." See Knapp, *The American Musical and the Formation of National Identity* and Knapp, *The American Musical and the Performance of Personal Identity.*
61 See Thomas, "Infelicities."
62 Jackson, *A Strange Loop,* 42.
63 Muñoz, *Disidentifications,* 5.
64 McMillin, *The Musical as Drama,* 2.
65 McMillin, *The Musical as Drama,* x. A number of scholars still use the concept of integration to make sense of musicals. McMillin's ideas, which now perhaps seem commonplace, have not fully been accepted by musical theatre scholars. See, for example, Wolf, *Changed for Good,* 26, 57.
66 Note, too, that in the passage I quote from Muñoz above, he refers to "the fiction of identity."
67 Goldberg, *Melodrama,* 4.
68 Goldberg, *Melodrama,* 25. His quotation is from Halliday, *Sirk on Sirk,* 130.
69 Goldberg, *Melodrama,* 52–53.
70 McMillin, *The Musical as Drama,* 20–21, my emphasis.
71 Rogers, *The Song Is You,* 20.
72 See Wolf, *Changed for Good,* 233.
73 Koestenbaum, *The Queen's Throat,* 18.
74 Wolf, *A Problem Like Maria,* 211.
75 Wolf says that "spectatorship of musicals is literally active," and Raymond Knapp argues that musicals "have given people, in a visceral way, a sense of what it *feels* like to embody whatever alternatives that musicals might offer to their own life circumstances and choices." See Wolf, *A Problem Like Maria,* 33, and Knapp, *The American Musical and the Formation of National Identity,* 283.
76 Rogers, *The Song Is You,* 7.
77 McMillin, *The Musical as Drama,* 179.
78 Rogers, *The Song Is You,* 19.
79 Cohen, "Punks, Bulldaggers, and Welfare Queens," 439.
80 See Clum, *Something for the Boys,* 106, 188, 209, 248; Clum, "'A Little More Mascara'"; Lovelock, "'What About Love?'"; Whitfield, "A Space Has Been Made."

81   Walker, *The Color Purple*, 215.
82   Musical theatre scholarship has not often looked kindly on queer theory or critical theory in general, often explicitly criticizing it and preferring to treat homosexuality, lesbianism, bisexuality, transgender, and even Blackness as essential and avoiding the questions critical theory would ask about the histories and epistemologies of these subjectivities. See Clum, *Something for the Boys*, 19, 46, 51, 275; Wolf, *Changed for Good*, 165.
83   See Love, *Feeling Backward*, especially 23.
84   Mordden, *Anything Goes*.
85   Note that Schechner's metaphor for the single unit of performance is filmic. Schechner, *Between Theater & Anthropology*, 35–36.
86   McMillin, *The Musical as Drama*, 9.
87   McMillin, *The Musical as Drama*, 37.
88   Edelman, *No Future*, 27.
89   Musical theatre scholar Sarah Taylor Ellis makes the argument that "Most musical numbers . . . step outside a linear conception of time to elaborate on and indulge in a given present moment." For Taylor Ellis, "It is possible to locate queer modes of relationality in the genre's musical numbers, which stop time to dream about the open possibilities of the present." In my own argument (following Edelman), I see repetition and its indulgence in the present as figuring queerness and refusing futurity. See Taylor Ellis, "Let's Do the Time Warp Again."
90   McMillin, *The Musical as Drama*, 110.
91   Essence, "25 Best Slow Jams of All Time."
92   Audible, "Behind the Scenes With Samira Wiley, Narrator of The Color Purple | Audible."

References for Introduction

Alvarez, Lizette, and Richard Pérez-Peña. "Praising Isis, Gunman Attacks Gay Nightclub, Leaving 50 Dead in Worst Shooting on U.S. Soil." *New York Times*. 13 June 2016 (A1–A12).
Audible. "Behind the Scenes With Samira Wiley, Narrator of The Color Purple | Audible." *YouTube*. 19 May 2020. www.youtube.com/watch?v=ZfkEmyTS_cw. Accessed 17 December 2021.
Bay-Cheng, Sarah. "Theater Is Media: Some Principles for a Digital Historiography of Performance." *Theater* 42.2: 26–41, 2012.
BroadwayInHD. "Acceptance Speech – Best Score: Lin-Manuel Miranda (2016)." *YouTube*. 24 October 2016. www.youtube.com/watch?v=6jehrbUGdlE. Accessed 4 July 2022.
CBS New York. "Omar Mateen's Alleged Male Lover: 'He Did It for Revenge' Against Latino Men." *CBS New York*. 21 June 2016. newyork.cbslocal.com/2016/06/21/omar-mateen-gay-lover/. Accessed 6 November 2021.
CBS News. "James Corden Pays Tribute to Orlando in Tony's Opener." *CBS News*. 12 June 2016. www.cbsnews.com/video/james-corden-pays-tribute-to-orlando-in-tonys-opener/. Accessed 4 July 2022.
Chance, Bradleigh Miranda. "LGBT Gun Rights Group Sees Membership Spike After Orlando Shooting." *NBC News*. 18 June 2016. www.nbcnews.com/storyline/orlando-nightclub-massacre/lgbt-gun-rights-group-sees-membership-spike-after-orlando-shooting-n594701. Accessed 7 November 2021.
Clum, John M. "'A Little More Mascara': Drag and the Broadway Musical From *La Cage aux Folles* to *Kinky Boots*." In *The Routledge Companion to the Contemporary Musical*. Edited by Jessica Sternfeld, and Elizabeth L. Wollman. London: Routledge, 173–181, 2020.
Clum, John M. *Something for the Boys: Musical Theater and Gay Culture*. New York: St. Martin's Press, 1999.

Cohen, Cathy J. "Punks, Bulldaggers, and Welfare Queens: The Radical Potential of Queer Politics?" GLQ: *A Journal of Lesbian and Gay Studies* 3.4: 437–465, 1997.

Conquergood, Dwight. "Beyond the Text: Toward a Performative Cultural Politics." In *The Future of Performance Studies: Visions and Revisions*. Edited by Sheron J. Dailey. Annandale: National Communications Association, 25–36, 1998.

Dillon, Stephen. "The Only Freedom I Can See: Imprisoned Queer Writing and the Politics of the Unimaginable." In *Captive Genders: Trans Embodiment and the Prison Industrial Complex*. Edited by Eric A. Stanley, and Nat Smith (2nd ed). Edinburgh: AK Press, 195–210, 2015.

Dudenhoefer, Nicole. "Broadway's Fun Home Comes to Orlando's Dr. Phillips Center for Some Healing." *Watermark*. 14 July 2016. watermarkonline.com/2016/07/14/broadways-fun-home-comes-to-orlandos-dr-phillips-center-for-some-healing/. Accessed 24 November 2021.

Dziemianowicz, Joe. "Broadway's 2015–2016 Season Sets Record for Attendance and Grosses." *New York Daily News*. 23 May 2016. www.nydailynews.com/entertainment/theater-arts/broadway-2015-16-season-sets-record-attendance-grosses-article-1.2647260. Accessed 5 July 2022.

Essence. "25 Best Slow Jams of All Time." *Essence*. 29 October 2020. www.essence.com/news/25-best-slow-jams-all-time/. Accessed 16 December 2021.

Forsgren, La Donna L. "*The Wiz* Redux: Or, Why Queer Black Feminist Spectatorship and Politically Engaged Popular Entertainment Continue to Matter." *Theatre Survey* 60.3: 325–354, 2019.

Frizell, Sam. "Donald Trump Faces Backlash for Tweets About Orlando Shooting." *Time*. 12 June 2016. time.com/4365411/orlando-shooting-donald-trump-tweet-congrats/. Accessed 7 November 2021.

Galella, Donatella. "Feeling Yellow: Responding to Contemporary Yellowface in Musical Performance." *Journal of Dramatic Theory and Criticism* 32.2: 67–77, 2018.

Gamboa, Glenn. "Lin-Manuel Miranda Helps Launch Latinx LGBTQ Support Program." *Associated Press*. 14 June 2022. apnews.com/article/politics-entertainment-florida-lin-manuel-miranda-hispanics-ccc2fadd9cb2f2c82c4a8868ec383993. Accessed 6 July 2022.

Gioia, Michael. "Tony Awards Dedicates Tonight's Ceremony to Orlando Victims." *Playbill*. 12 June 2016, www.playbill.com/article/tony-awards-dedicates-tonights-ceremony-to-orlando-victims. Accessed 7 November 2021.

Goldberg, Jonathan. *Melodrama: An Aesthetics of Impossibility*. Durham: Duke University Press, 2016.

Grady, Constance. "Trump's Hamilton Outburst Ignores the Theater's History as a Place for Political Protest." *Vox*. 21 November 2016. www.vox.com/culture/2016/11/21/13691468/trump-hamilton-outburst-theaters-history-place-political-protest. Accessed 7 November 2021.

Graham, David A. "The Complicated Pain of America's Queer Muslims." *Atlantic*. 14 June 2016. www.theatlantic.com/politics/archive/2016/06/lgbt-muslims-orlando/486923/. Accessed 6 July 2022.

Halliday, Jon. *Sirk on Sirk*. New York: Viking, 1972.

Hoffman, Warren. *The Great White Way: Race and the Broadway Musical* (2nd ed). New Brunswick: Rutgers University Press, 2000.

Human Rights Campaign. "Gun Violence Prevention." *Human Rights Campaign*. 8 October 2021. www.hrc.org/resources/gun-violence-prevention. Accessed 7 November 2021.

Human Rights Campaign. "The Journey to Marriage Equality in the United States." *Human Rights Campaign*. www.hrc.org/our-work/stories/the-journey-to-marriage-equality-in-the-united-states. Accessed 8 November 2021.

Jackson, Michael R. *A Strange Loop*. New York: Theatre Communications Group, 2020.

Johnson, E. Patrick. "'Quare' Studies, or (Almost) Everything I Know About Queer Studies I Learned From My Grandmother." *Text and Performance Quarterly* 21.1: 1–25, 2001.
Jones, Chris. *Rise Up! Broadway and American Society from Angels in America to Hamilton*. London: Methuen Drama, 2019.
Kessler, Kelly. "'Trash Talk and Visual Protests': The Musical Genre's Personal and Political Interactivity in the Age of Social Media." In *The Routledge Companion to the Contemporary Musical*. Edited by Jessica Sternfeld, and Elizabeth L. Wollman. London: Routledge, 335–344, 2020.
Kirle, Bruce. *Unfinished Show Business: Broadway Musicals as Works-in-Process*. Carbondale: Southern Illinois University Press, 2005.
Knapp, Raymond. *The American Musical and the Formation of National Identity*. Princeton: Princeton University Press, 2005.
Knapp, Raymond. *The American Musical and the Performance of Personal Identity*. Princeton: Princeton University Press, 2006.
Koestenbaum, Wayne. *The Queen's Throat: Opera, Homosexuality, and the Mystery of Desire*. Boston: Da Capo Press, 2001.
Larimer, Sarah. "Middle Schoolers Chant 'Build the Wall' During Lunch in Aftermath of Trump Win." *Washington Post*. 10 November 2016. www.washingtonpost.com/news/education/wp/2016/11/10/middle-schoolers-chant-build-that-wall-during-lunch-in-aftermath-of-trump-win/. Accessed 3 January 2022.
Larkin, Jimmy. "Let's Hear It for the Choice." *Instagram*. www.instagram.com/letshearitforthechoice/. Accessed 4 July 2022
"Lin-Manuel Miranda's Sonnet from the Tony Awards." *New York Times*. 12 June 2016. www.nytimes.com/2016/06/13/theater/lin-manuel-mirandas-sonnet-from-the-tony-awards.html. Accessed 7 November 2021.
Lotan, Gal Tziperman, Paul Brinkmann, and Rene Stutzman. "Witness: Omar Mateen Had Been at Orlando Gay Nightclub Many Times." *Orlando Sentinel*. 13 June 2016. www.orlandosentinel.com/news/pulse-orlando-nightclub-shooting/os-orlando-nightclub-omar-mateen-profile-20160613-story.html. Accessed 6 November 2021.
Love, Heather. *Feeling Backward: Loss and the Politics of Queer History*. Cambridge: Harvard University Press, 2007.
Lovelock, James. "'What About Love?': Claiming and Reclaiming LGBTQ+ Spaces in Twenty-first Century Musical Theatre." In *Reframing the Musical: Race, Culture, and Identity*. Edited by Sarah K. Whitfield. London: Red Globe Press, 187–209, 2019.
McMillin, Scott. *The Musical as Drama: A Study of the Principles and Conventions Behind Musical Shows From Kern to Sondheim*. Princeton: Princeton University Press, 2006.
Michaels, Samantha. "We Tracked Down the Lawyers Behind the Recent Wave of Anti-Trans Bathroom Bills." *Mother Jones*. 15 April 2016. www.motherjones.com/politics/2016/04/alliance-defending-freedom-lobbies-anti-lgbt-bathroom-bills/. Accessed 7 November 2021.
Miller, D.A. *Place for Us: Essay on the Broadway Musical*. Cambridge: Harvard University Press, 1998.
Miller, Jonathan. *Subsequent Performances*. London: Faber and Faber, 1986.
Miranda, Lin-Manuel. "My Sonnet . . ." *Twitter*. 13 November 2016. twitter.com/lin_manuel/status/797846138669805569. Accessed 4 July 2022.
Morales, Rosario. "We're All in the Same Boat." In *This Bridge Called My Back: Writings by Radical Women of Color*. Edited by Cherríe Moraga, and Gloria Anzaldúa (2nd ed). New York: Kitchen Table, 91–93, 1983.
Mordden, Ethan. *Anything Goes: A History of American Musical Theatre*. New York: Oxford University Press, 2013.
Muñoz, José Esteban. *Disidentifications: Queers of Color and the Performance of Politics*. Minneapolis: University of Minnesota Press, 1999.

Okma, MJ. "GLAAD Slams the Trump Administration for Pandering to the NRA Instead of Addressing the Crisis of Gun Violence." *GLAAD*. 4 May 2018. www.glaad.org/blog/glaad-slams-trump-administration-pandering-nra-instead-addressing-crisis-gun-violence. Accessed 7 November 2021.

Oladipo, Gloria. "2021 on Pace to Be Deadliest Yet for Trans and Gender Non-Conforming Americans." *Guardian*. 14 June 2021. www.theguardian.com/world/2021/jun/14/us-trans-transgender-deaths-2021. Accessed 24 November 2021.

Paulson, Michael. "Tonys Hail Hamilton and Denounce Hate." *New York Times*. 13 June 2016. (C1-C2).

Pink Pistols. "Pink Pistols Saddened by Attack on Orlando Club." *Pink Pistols*. 12 June 2016. www.pinkpistols.org/2016/06/12/pink-pistols-saddened-by-attack-on-orlando-club/. Accessed 7 November 2021.

Rezal, Adriana. "The Racial Makeup of America's Prisons." *U.S. News & World Report*. 13 October 2021. www.usnews.com/news/best-states/articles/2021-10-13/report-highlights-staggering-racial-disparities-in-us-incarceration-rates. Accessed 24 November 2021.

Rivera-Servera, Ramón. "Quotidian Utopias: Latina/o Queer Choreographies." In *Performing Queer Latinidad: Dance, Sexuality, Politics*. Ann Arbor: University of Michigan Press, 134–167, 2013.

Robinson, Cedric. *The Panthers Can't Save Us Now: Debating Left Politics and Black Lives Matter*. London: Verso, 2022.

Rodulfo, Kristina. "2016 Is the Year of #BroadwaySoDiverse," *Elle*. 11 June 2015. www.elle.com/culture/a36982/broadway-diversity/. Accessed 5 July 2022.

Rogers, Bradley. *The Song Is You: Musical Theatre and the Politics of Bursting Into Song and Dance*. Iowa City: University of Iowa Press, 2020.

Rooney, David. "Broadway's New Season Takes Shape as Game-Changing Musical *Hamilton* Charges In." *Hollywood Reporter*. 13 July 2015. www.hollywoodreporter.com/lifestyle/arts/broadways-new-season-takes-shape-808233/. Accessed 5 July 2022.

Rubin, Gayle. "Thinking Sex: Notes for a Radical Theory of the Politics of Sexuality." In *Pleasure and Danger: Exploring Female Sexuality*. Edited by Carole S. Vance. Boston: Routledge and Kegan Paul, 267–319, 1984.

Ryan, Patrick. "The Best Movie Musicals of 2021, Ranked (Including Peter Dinklage's Cyrano)." *USA Today*. 28 September 2021. www.usatoday.com/story/entertainment/movies/2021/09/28/movie-musicals-2021-ranked-dear-evan-hansen-west-side-story/5808525001/. Accessed 3 January 2022.

Sandoval, Edgar, Chelsia Rose Marcius, and Ginger Adams Otis. "Orlando Shooter Was Regular at Pulse Gay Club; Former Classmate Says Omar Mateen Was Homosexual." *New York Daily News*. 13 June 2016. www.nydailynews.com/news/national/orlando-shooter-reported-pulse-club-regular-patrons-article-1.2672445. Accessed 6 November 2021.

Savran, David. "Toward a Historiography of the Popular." *Theatre Survey* 45.2: 211–217, 2004.

Schechner, Richard. *Between Theater & Anthropology*. Philadelphia: University of Pennsylvania Press, 1985.

Taylor Ellis, Sarah. "Let's Do the Time Warp Again: Performing Time, Genre, and Spectatorship." In *The Routledge Companion to the Contemporary Musical*. Edited by Jessica Sternfeld, and Elizabeth L. Wollman. London: Routledge, 273–282, 2020.

Tee Rico. "Lin-Manuel Handwritten Love Is Love Sonnet – 5"x7" Magnet." *Tee Rico*. 13 November 2016. www.teerico.com/product/lin-manuel-handwritten-sonnet-5x7-magnet/. Accessed 12 November 2021.

The Tony Awards. "Acceptance Speech: Lisa Kron (2015)." *YouTube*. 7 July 2015. www.youtube.com/watch?v=AejUt7TdexI. Accessed 5 July 2022.

The Tony Awards. "Fun Home Performance Tony Awards 2015." *YouTube*. 18 July 2015. www.youtube.com/watch?v=pMAuesRJm1E. Accessed 6 July 2022.

Thomas, Aaron C. "Infelicities." *Journal of Dramatic Theory and Criticism* 35.2: 13–25, 2021.

Thomas, Aaron C. "My Father's Pulse." QED: *A Journal in GLBTQ Worldmaking* 3.3: 168–170, 2016.

Torres, Justin. "In Praise of Latin Night at the Queer Club." *Washington Post*. 13 June 2016. www.washingtonpost.com/opinions/in-praise-of-latin-night-at-the-queer-club/2016/06/13/e841867e-317b-11e6-95c0-2a6873031302_story.html. Accessed 6 November 2021.

Walker, Alice. *The Color Purple*. New York: Harcourt Brace Jovanovich, 1982.

Whitfield, Sarah K. "A Space Has Been Made: Bisexual+ Stories in Musical Theatre." *Theatre Topics Online Content*. July 2020. jhuptheatre.org/theatre-topics/online-content/issue/volume-30-issue-2-july-2020/space-has-been-made-bisexual. Accessed 7 August 2022.

Wolf, Stacy. *A Problem Like Maria: Gender and Sexuality in the American Musical*. Ann Arbor: University of Michigan Press, 2002.

Wolf, Stacy. *Beyond Broadway: The Pleasure and Promise of Musical Theatre across America*. New York: Oxford University Press, 2020.

1
SHUT UP AND DEAL

The day after the revival of *Promises, Promises* opened on April 25, 2010, *Newsweek* posted an article on its website titled "Straight Jacket" that began with the following provocation: "The reviews for the Broadway revival of *Promises, Promises* were negative enough, even though most of the critics ignored the real problem – the big pink elephant in the room."[1] As the author, pop culture critic Ramin Setoodeh, saw it, the problem everyone was ignoring about the revival was that Sean Hayes, the actor playing *Promises*' lead role, was unconvincing in the part because he is an out gay man.[2] Setoodeh reminds readers that Hayes is "best known as the queeny Jack on *Will & Grace*" and that the actor's "sexual orientation is part of who he is." Thus, he complains, "it's weird seeing Hayes play straight. He comes off as wooden and insincere, as if he's trying to hide something, which of course he is."[3] Setoodeh then describes a different gay actor's performance on a primetime television show as "more like your average theater queen" than a convincing love interest for a girl, but he returns to the topic of *Promises* to describe Hayes as someone who "tips off even your grandmother's gaydar."[4] The piece's ostensible purpose is to discuss the difficulties of being an out gay or lesbian actor, but the short article is neither a careful critique of *Promises* nor coherently argumentative. Rather, Setoodeh's article is more of a set of musings – about gay actors playing both gay and straight roles and how successfully they pull that off – prompted by his attendance at the *Promises* revival and his dislike of the show and its central performance.

These post-show ruminations caused rather a stir. On the gay culture website AfterElton (now NewNowNext), editor-in-chief Michael Jensen posted a scathing response in which he described Setoodeh's opinions as "shockingly retroactive" and accused the critic of reiterating "the tired gay-obsessions of the far right."[5] For Jensen, the crux of the matter was that Setoodeh's critiques damaged the gay community as a whole. Jensen noted that Setoodeh is *himself* an out gay man, and he argued that "It's already difficult enough for actors to brave any possible backlash by coming out. Having another gay man say he doesn't think gay men can convincingly play straight doesn't make it any easier." A few days later, Sean Hayes was nominated for a Tony Award as best actor in a musical, but the *Newsweek* media fracas had only just begun.

Hayes's *Promises* co-star Kristin Chenoweth was the next to weigh in on the topic publicly, calling the *Newsweek* piece "horrendously homophobic" and describing it as a "bigoted, factually inaccurate article that tells people who deviate from heterosexual norms that they can't be open about who they are and still achieve their dreams."[6] In the first weeks of May, responses to Setoodeh's article proliferated. Television producer Ryan Murphy called for a boycott of *Newsweek* (more on Murphy later), and Oscar-winning screenwriter Dustin Lance Black penned an op-ed for the *Hollywood Reporter* with Jarrett Barrios, then-president of the Gay & Lesbian Alliance Against Defamation. The men attacked Setoodeh directly, saying that his piece "seems to raise more questions about his own internalized biases than what the 'public' actually perceives" and that the article "leans away from reality and tilts toward openly gay Setoodeh's own issues with sexuality and femininity."[7] A few critics came to *Newsweek*'s defense. Alongside Barrios and Black's vituperative *ad hominem* attacks, the *Hollywood Reporter* ran a well-reasoned dissent by Andrew Wallenstein.[8] In a piece for the *Huffington Post* entitled "Now That You Mention It, Rock Hudson Did Seem Gay," playwright and screenwriter Aaron Sorkin defended *Newsweek*, joking, "This is a sentence I never thought I would type: I'm coming to the defense of a theatre critic."[9]

In late May, CBS announced that Hayes – a popular television star, after all – would host the annual Tony Awards, but the theatre industry apparently remained unsettled by the Straight Jacket affair. At the ceremony in mid-June, Hayes and Chenoweth opened the evening by sharing what the *New York Times*' Patrick Healy described as "a long, open-mouthed kiss."[10] This performance of heterosexuality, believable or not, succeeded, for a time at least, at putting the Straight Jacket affair to rest. The controversy only flared up again in January 2011 because Setoodeh himself revisited the issue in an article in the *Daily Beast*.[11] Naturally, this garnered furious responses from AfterElton as well as GLAAD, but by this time, *Promises* was no longer the focus of the criticism – the discussion had transformed into one about whether or not gay actors have the ability to play straight characters.[12]

The enduring point of contention for most of the people commenting on the topic was a question of casting – who should get to play what roles and what it means to perform "authentically" – and this question repeatedly appeared throughout the second decade of the twenty-first century.[13] In fact, although the Straight Jacket affair seemed all but forgotten by the end of the decade, the problems it presented were not: a strikingly similar kerfuffle appeared in 2020 when gay critic Richard Lawson reviewed a movie adaptation of a different musical for *Vanity Fair* under the headline "James Corden Should Have Been Banned from *The Prom*."[14] Lawson took director Ryan Murphy – one of the people who led the charge against Setoodeh and *Newsweek* – to task for lacking sincerity and turning LGBTQ content into "marketing talking points rather than actual ideas," but he more thoroughly excoriated Corden for his "somehow both appalling and terminally bland" performance as (fictional) Broadway actor Barry Glickman. Lawson's is a smart and careful read of *The Prom*, and it winds up with the critic deciding, with tongue in cheek, that we should have "No more straight actors playing gay men until the sins of *The Prom* are properly atoned for."

Most responses to the *Newsweek* piece in 2010 became personal attacks on Setoodeh, and most responses to the *Vanity Fair* piece in 2020 were in agreement with Lawson, but these two small controversies, one at each end of the decade, give us a rich portrait of the politics surrounding musical theatre performance, and acting in general, in the second decade of the twenty-first century. *Promises, Promises* and the Straight Jacket affair may now be forgotten blips in Broadway history, but examining them closely yields fascinating results. Straight actors will continue, of course, to play gay characters, and gay actors will continue to play straight characters, so it would be valuable for all of us to be more intentional about what we mean when we say *gay* or *straight* and how our ideas about sexuality and the politics of its representation have shifted in recent years.

This chapter makes several arguments about these representational politics, audience responses, and citations. First, I want to examine Setoodeh's reception of *Promises'* Broadway revival and what that might illuminate about the closet. I argue that *Promises* is itself a show about the closet, and Setoodeh's perception of the closet onstage is colored by the history of both Broadway and Hollywood musicals and their various deployments of masculinity. I examine *The Apartment*, the source material for *Promises*, and cover the distance between that 1960 film, the musical's Broadway debut in 1968, and its revival in 2010. Second, I want to parse more carefully what it might mean to "play gay" or "play straight": our beliefs about the ability to perform as one or the other have much to say about what we think about gayness itself (and sexuality as such). Complicating this second argument is the deeply vexed question of outing, a divisive political tactic from the 1980s and '90s that haunts the Straight Jacket affair in peculiar ways and resurges repeatedly throughout the decade. My exploration of outing, a practice fundamentally about queer identity and the ways queer people speak to and about other queer people, will lead us, finally, back to the 2020 film of *The Prom* and the question of "authentic" representation of sexuality.

I've taken as the title for this chapter the memorable final line from *The Apartment*, "Shut up and deal."[15] Neil Simon did not use this line in the original Broadway production of *Promises*, rephrasing it so that Miss Kubelik said "Shut up and play cards" instead.[16] Rob Ashford, the director of the 2010 revival, restored the iconic "original" for his production, but I'm interested in the little phrase that remained constant in all of these versions: *shut up*. In many ways, I see the Straight Jacket affair and the Corden–Glickman drama that followed it as controversies about silences and articulations. In his *Newsweek* article, Setoodeh claimed that he was speaking up about something everyone else wished to keep in the closet ("most of the critics ignored the real problem – the big pink elephant in the room"), and then as Setoodeh's critics responded to him, they attempted to shame him into silence, saying more and more about something they wished had never been said in the first place. Not only, then, is the closet a helpful metaphor for understanding *Promises, Promises*; the closet, moreover, persists as one of the technologies that audiences use to watch and enjoy musical theatre. One might imagine that "shutting up" is impossible in a musical, but one can always speak or sing about one thing while being silent about another, and as I argued in the introduction, the very structure of musical theatre demands that everyone is hiding something, no character is single, every one is more than one.

The Sissy Figure on Stage and Screen

Although Chenoweth, GLAAD, Murphy, and many others called the *Newsweek* piece offensive or inappropriate for suggesting that gay people can't play straight people, this was not really what Setoodeh said. Such a statement would, in fact, have been manifestly nonsensical. As Derek Thompson noted at the *Atlantic*, "Gay actors play straight all the time," and this is as true of the out gay actors Thompson cites – "Neil Patrick Harris in *How I Met Your Mother*, David Hyde Pierce in *Frasier*, Ian McKellen in *Lord of the Rings*, and *X-Men*, and everything" – as it is of the (let's just say) dozens of gay, lesbian, and bisexual actors who discreetly keep their sexual preferences out of the public eye or actively mislead the press.[17] In other words, not only do gay actors play straight all the time, many of them are also good enough at it that audiences don't question their portrayals. But the critic never made this argument in the first place. Although most of the commentators in the Straight Jacket affair concern themselves with this topic, Setoodeh did not say that gay actors shouldn't play straight characters; he simply found Sean Hayes unconvincing as Chuck Baxter.

Rather than attacking the critic for homophobia or self-hatred, I want to turn to his observations as an explanation. In the original *Newsweek* piece, Setoodeh says that he found Hayes "wooden and insincere, as if he's trying to hide something, which of course he is."[18] The critic interpreted Hayes's awkwardness as him trying to hide his *gayness* from the audience, but one might just as easily attribute what Setoodeh read as Hayes's insincerity to an attempt to hide something else. More likely, Hayes was trying to shed the persona of Jack McFarland, the sitcom character that made him famous and with whom he is identified in the popular imagination. Most of *Promises*' critics, in fact, found themselves unable to forget Sean Hayes's earlier television performance. *Daily News* critic Joe Dziemianowicz noted that the role of Chuck Baxter calls for "a slapstick clown and a standup comic, so it's inevitable that [Hayes] recalls Jack from *Will & Grace*"; indeed, every single review of *Promises* mentions *Will & Grace*.[19] Even the *Hollywood Reporter*'s Frank Scheck, who enjoyed the show more than most critics, remarks on Hayes's ability to *shed* Jack McFarland as an indication of his skill, writing that he "shows no traces of his familiar persona from TV's *Will & Grace* and delivers a winning, low-key turn."[20] Like the *Harry Potter* franchise has for Daniel Radcliffe since the early 2000s and *The Count of Monte Cristo* did for James O'Neill in the nineteenth century, *Will & Grace* certainly haunts Hayes. As recently as 2016, a *Times* reporter annoyed Hayes with a question about shedding his Jack McFarland persona. "I gave up caring about that a long time ago," Hayes replied.[21] But it has seemingly been difficult for many audience members to see Hayes as anyone other than Jack, and critics continue to have this same problem.[22]

Will & Grace's Jack McFarland wasn't simply the zany next-door neighbor on a television sitcom. He was understood as a particular *kind* of silly neighbor. In an interview for National Public Radio in 2010, Hayes said that the character was more a product of audience and critical reception than his own intentions:

> At the beginning of *Will & Grace*, I played Jack as the funny next-door-neighbor type, as we've seen in the past. And I thought that was my role. I didn't really play into the gay part as much – the stereotypical gay part. And I have to say, the critics . . . pegged Jack as the flamboyant, extremely gay character because they didn't know what else to call him.[23]

Not only mainstream publications read Hayes's performance like this; the gay press saw him this way, as well. Hayes was "*Will & Grace*'s queeny, über-homo Jack McFarland,"[24] "the flamboyantly out-and-proud Jack."[25] Whether Hayes wanted him to or not, Jack McFarland stepped into the shoes of a powerful and seemingly inescapable comedic type, the silly figure that film historian Vito Russo catalogs so comprehensively in the first chapter of *The Celluloid Closet*.[26] To put it another way, Hayes's performance in *Promises* was haunted not only by Jack McFarland but by the entire history of the effeminate sissy on stage and screen, a history that taught audiences how they were supposed to look at Sean Hayes long before he appeared on *Will & Grace* in the late 1990s or on Broadway in 2010.

It is important to point out one of the particular functions served by the sissy figure in pre-Stonewall representations of (queer) men: to wit, this image exists in order to *heterosexualize* or straighten up homosocial relations that might otherwise be open to homophobic scrutiny. Take, for example, the large body of work of the actor Edward Everett Horton, who played feminized characters throughout the 1930s and '40s in Hollywood musicals such as *The Gay Divorcee* (1934), *Top Hat* (1935), *Shall We Dance* (1937), and *Brazil* (1944). In each of these musicals, Horton, who would normally be characterized as neither a singer nor a dancer, functions as a comical bungler who doesn't get the girl; this contrasts with the more skillfully suave performances of the lead male, usually Fred Astaire, but occasionally someone else, like Tito Guízar. In each of these performances, Horton's hilarious comic abilities work to refigure femininity and masculinity, so that the audience is asked to look at the singing, dancing male lead as masculine and the ineffectual, inelegant sidekick as feminine. Horton's comedic skill in this regard is especially evident in Ernst Lubitsch's *Design for Living* (1933) – nominally based on Noel Coward's play – which stars Miriam Hopkins, Fredric March, and Gary Cooper as a threesome who love one another dearly and who seem to work better as a throuple than each does separately. It's a delightfully queer pre-Code comedy that manages to avoid the implication that the two central male characters might be homosexually inclined through the casting of Edward Everett Horton as a boring (straight) nerd who eventually marries Miriam Hopkins' character but who is nevertheless consistently coded as a sissy. In other words, although the March and Cooper characters live together, are physically affectionate with one another, finish each other's sentences, and have trouble functioning when they're apart, it is Horton's *heterosexual* character who is framed as effeminate, a move that masculinizes the two leads and effectively disavows the much more obvious queerness of their relationship.

The Closet and the 1960s Musical

The 1960s world of *Promises, Promises* puts the history of this stock figure into stark relief. What is so intriguing about the accusation that Sean Hayes's performance in the show is closeted or "has something to hide" is that the entire premise of the musical is about sneaking around and hiding sexual activity. To put it another way, *Promises, Promises* is a show for which the closet is the single most important plot element – except that *Promises*' closet *is inhabited exclusively by heterosexual men who are cheating on their wives.*[27] Neil Simon's libretto, which is based on the I.A.L. Diamond–Billy Wilder film *The Apartment* (1960), follows a mild-mannered office worker named C.C. Baxter (he's called Bud or Buddy-boy in the movie and Chuck in the musical) whom nobody ever notices.[28] Chuck is in love with his coworker Fran Kubelik, who can't seem to remember his name and (like everyone else) takes no notice of him. In order to ingratiate himself with his bosses, Chuck begins lending out his apartment to the company's many vice presidents for their extra-marital flings. Through a series of farcical situations – undercut by the much more serious portrayal of Fran's suicide attempt – Chuck and Fran become good friends, and the show ends with the possibility of romance between the two.

As might be expected, in Wilder's film, the eponymous apartment is the key location for meaning making. Thematically, as scholar Steven Cohan argues, "on film the bachelor pad functions as a symptom of the playboy's immaturity, since he fashions a lifestyle out of his refusal to settle down as husband and breadwinner. [Billy Wilder's] comedies therefore view his modern, urban apartment as a sexual playpen, which inevitably has to be replaced by another type of dwelling in the suburbs," when the bachelor finally settles down.[29] This doesn't quite work as it should for C.C. Baxter, since he barely gets to spend any time alone in the apartment, but it still functions as a site of privacy and solitude. Baxter's apartment is visually contrasted with the much more open – that is, open to observation – sites of the insurance office where he works, the Chinese restaurant where Mr. Sheldrake takes women on dates, the bar on the corner, and Central Park. The work of film scholar Pamela Robertson Wojcik, in her books *The Apartment Plot* and *The Apartment Complex*, draws attention to apartments as a driving force in post-World War II narratives. Her analysis of Wilder's film emphasizes the way that the apartment figures Baxter as a playboy bachelor, but also produces cycles of secrecy and disclosure. Baxter himself is a regular Joe, unmarried but unable to maintain the playboy lifestyle, and unremarkable at the office. However, through the activities of the married men who host numerous women at the apartment, he appears to his neighbors to be a ladies' man, partying hard and sleeping little.[30]

The apartment, in this way, becomes a space for both hiding and revealing – it is a location that hides extra-marital trysts from some people (the men's wives) and reveals them to others (Baxter's neighbors).

Baxter's apartment and the movie that is named after it, then, make extensive use of a central metaphor that looks a great deal like a closet. As film historian Ian Brookes has argued, *The Apartment* also dramatizes a "culture of surveillance," in which jilted secretaries expose married men's dalliances, nosy neighbors make unfounded assumptions about sex, and office boys run apartment keys up and down the elevators of the Consolidated Life building.[31] Everyone is watching everyone else in *The Apartment*, and Brookes argues that this is reflective not only of postwar Fordism and the panoptic corporation but also of Cold War politics in the United States:

> This was a culture in which virtually everyone was under the constant threat of investigation by the power of the state, predominantly through the House Un-American Activities Committee (HUAC) and the Federal Bureau of Investigation (FBI). The committee exploited information provided by anonymous informers together with unsubstantiated allegations and other testimony, frequently perjured, from colleagues, neighbors, and acquaintances.[32]

HUAC's campaign against men suspected of homosexuality is well documented, but *The Apartment* does not directly address homosexuality or LGBTQ politics *per se*.[33] Still, it is notable that the subject matter from which *Promises* was adapted was already fundamentally about sexual secrecy, surveillance, and the constant threat of exposure.

Simon's stage adaptation of *The Apartment* makes fewer alterations to Diamond and Wilder's screenplay than might be expected. In *Promises*, the Marge MacDougall scene at the bar is greatly expanded, but some scenes – such as Chuck and Mr. Sheldrake's first meeting and most of the comedy with Dr. Dreyfuss – retain almost all of the film's dialogue. Simon makes a few other intriguing changes. Mr. Sheldrake, for example, gives Chuck Baxter tickets to a Knicks game in *Promises*, prompting the song "She Likes Basketball," whereas in *The Apartment*, the tickets are to an evening performance of *The Music Man* at the Majestic on 44th Street. Most important dramaturgically, however, is that Simon introduces a pattern of direct address in *Promises* that is mostly absent from the movie. Bud in *The Apartment* speaks in voiceover at the beginning of the film, but he does this only to set up the plot. In *Promises*, Chuck opens the show speaking to the audience and keeps this up throughout the musical's two acts, repeatedly addressing us in asides – even in the middle of conversations with other characters – in order to tell us his feelings and to give us information of which the other characters onstage are ignorant.

I noted in this book's introduction that musical numbers have the effect of doubling characterization, giving us another version of the character we have come to know.[34] During a song, characters often communicate thoughts and feelings to the audience that they are attempting to keep hidden from other characters. This is one of the reasons why Bradley Rogers suggests that "we might understand the musical as a genre of the closet, a genre whose pleasures lurk at once in plain sight and completely underground, awkwardly obscured by the rhetorical fig leaf of 'integration.'"[35] But Neil Simon's transformation of C.C. Baxter so that he addresses the audience directly, even during scenes in which he's *not* singing, adds an additional level to Chuck's character. This dramaturgical choice compounds the amount of disinformation and subterfuge at work in *Promises*. Or, rather, Simon's libretto *stages for the audience* the character's desire to hide his feelings. Take, for example, this exchange from Chuck's first meeting with Mr. Sheldrake:

CHUCK. Mr. Kirkeby thinks I'm bright?
SHELDRAKE. Yes, they're all keen on you. Vanderhof, Kirkeby, Dobitch . . . even Mr. Eichelberger.
CHUCK. *(To the audience)* I think they overdid it. He's going to want to know what makes me so popular.
SHELDRAKE. Tell me, Baxter, what makes you so popular?
CHUCK. Well, I imagine it's . . . Well, they probably . . . I don't know.
. . .
SHELDRAKE. I know everything that goes on in this building. In every department, on every floor.
CHUCK. *(To the audience)* All right, don't get nervous. Because if you get nervous, I'll get nervous. *(To* SHELDRAKE*)* On every floor?[36]

Certainly, this sequence illustrates the culture of surveillance in the postwar United States described by Cohan (Sheldrake knows everything that goes on in the building); it also hints queerly at Chuck's relationships with his male superiors (they're all keen on him). Even more importantly, this sequence stages Chuck's attempts to hide his feelings from a character onstage while directly communicating those same feelings to us. In fact, we watch Chuck lie repeatedly in *Promises*, though he seems always to tell *us* the truth. Recall that in Ramin Setoodeh's reading of Hayes's performance, it's "as if he's trying to hide something, which of course he is." Such duplicity is embedded already in the musical's dramaturgy – and made more explicit in Simon's 1968 adaptation than it was in the 1960 film. Indeed, at the end of this scene, Chuck and Mr. Sheldrake move into the duet "Our Little Secret," a song nominally devoid of homoerotics but one in which they emphasize their commitment to one another: "'Cause it's no one else's business / But our own anyhow, / Our little secret, oh yes, it's yours and mine."[37]

To return briefly to the feminizing/masculinizing function of the sissy in these narratives, one of the other important changes Simon's libretto makes is to expand the roles of four of *The Apartment*'s philandering executives – Vanderhof, Kirkeby, Dobitch, and Eichelberger. In *Promises*, the four men act as more of a unit than they do in the movie. They function as a secondary antagonist to Chuck, and they usually appear onstage together. Bacharach and David give them their own song in act 1 – "Where Can You Take a Girl?" – which, in the 2010 revival, was reprised near the end of act 2. The song's lyrics describe a longing for bachelorhood. The men wonder where to take a young woman to drink and party "Like other guys who live alone can do."[38]

The four married men articulate their jealousy of guys who live alone, who have the freedom to take a girl "home for a little fun" or "put on some records and then go berserk" or "dance her around so fast she starts to shout."[39] They describe what they want to do with the women they're dating, but they constantly compare their own situations with those of unmarried men (the very men the narrative codes as potentially queer): "Most married men play cards / Most single men play house / We'd like to play house too," they sing. In the 2010 revival, the men tried on a series of different dance styles as they sang about their desperation, eventually breaking off into pairs and dancing with one another. Two of the men then *dipped* the others as they sang, "Most married men just waltz / Most single men make out / We'd like to make out too." As Ashford choreographed it, the men turned their faces toward one another as they sang this last line, and there was just a hint that the men *might* actually "make out." They didn't, moving instead into the song's next verse. As with the two men in the throuple in *Design for Living*, the four executives in *Promises* tease the audience with the homoerotic potential of their relationships, but the possibility of their own homosexual activity comes to seem absurd when there's a young man nearby who can be made to look like an ineffectual loser.[40]

In *Promises*, it is the married, heterosexual men who are duplicitous: they sneak around, deceive both their wives and their girlfriends, discuss having sex in Central Park, and use bribery and blackmail to keep other people quiet.[41] Chuck is the upstanding guy in this situation; he lies to protect other people's secrets, most especially Fran's. Nevertheless, Simon's libretto insists on Chuck's deviance from traditional masculinity: in the play's first scene when Mr. Dobitch asks if he can speak to Chuck "man to man," Chuck replies "Gee, Mr. Dobitch, I never thought you considered me that way,"[42] and much later, at the beginning of act 2, Marge apologizes to Chuck, rather half-heartedly: "I didn't mean to imply that you're *not* masculine. In your own off-beat way, I suppose you are."[43] Chuck even begins the show by referring to himself as "*puny*," and his opening number is titled "Half as Big as Life," in which he sings that he feels small and doesn't like what he sees when he looks at himself seriously.[44]

Chuck's position in the show, then, is consciously and purposely effeminized by the musical's creators; his is a failed attempt at being a man that the libretto and lyrics contrast with the traditional version of masculinity – the one defined by making a lot of money, eating in executive dining rooms, treating underlings disrespectfully, and having sex with secretaries. Chuck sees himself as puny because he accepts these attributes as characterizing successful manliness. And the show, for the most part, agrees with this assessment or at least doesn't argue with it. Indeed, dramaturgically, the function of the sissy in *Promises, Promises* is – as in *Design for Living* – to masculinize the other men and affirm their manliness as untainted. But this isn't a project designed by the sissy himself; rather, *it is the project of traditional masculinity to feminize men who do not behave the way they do.*

Promises originally arrived on Broadway in December 1968, a significant moment in musical theatre history that marks it as one of the last shows before the Stonewall uprising in June 1969, an event that D.A. Miller pinpoints as the time after which musicals could no longer plausibly deny their gayness. Miller describes pre-1969 musicals such as *Promises* as formally operating using the technology of the closet:

> By contrast to the opera, or Bette Davis movies, or any other general cultural phenomenon that enjoys, as we say, a gay *following* – in other words, that gay subjectivity comes to invest only after a creation at which it wasn't presumably present – the Broadway musical, with "disproportionate numbers" of gay men among its major architects, is determined from the inside out by an Open Secret whose fierce cultural keeping not all the irony on a show queen's face can ever quite measure, nor all his flamboyance of carriage undo.[45]

The closet, then, is essential not just to *Promises* or other 1960s musicals but to the form in general. John Clum, for example, finds "something closeted about [Cole] Porter's insistent vagueness, the repetition of the idea that what is most desirable cannot be spoken, much less defined."[46] In Clum's detailed reading of the lyrics of Porter, Lorenz Hart, and Noel Coward, he argues that these pre-Stonewall lyricists "represent more than ghosts of closets past. . . . To some of us, they also represent a lost style that is in great part a gay style."[47]

Basic to both *Place for Us* and *Something for the Boys* is a kind of longing for the old days when musicals were closeted, when many gay male audience members expected to identify very differently with the performers and characters in a musical; neither Miller nor Clum has a very high opinion of the post-Stonewall musical. One hears, perhaps, a similar nostalgia for a well-constructed closet in Setoodeh's (and others') complaints about Hayes being too gay to play the role of C.C. Baxter in *Promises*. Forty years after Stonewall and the musical's original production, the revival of *Promises* staged all of the old deceptions, surveillances, and failed masculinities in the original script, but audience members, like Setoodeh and others, saw way too many closets for their liking on stage at the Broadway Theatre in 2010.

I've noted the closetedness of the musical as a form and the masculinizing function of the effeminate sissy in order to put Sean Hayes's performance in the revival of *Promises* within the larger context of Hollywood and Broadway musicals, but I want to close this section with yet another contextualization. As I read Clum's longing for "a lost style," I can't help but consider that style's overwhelming whiteness and the way the "gay style" to which he refers is bounded within a particular cultural milieu populated only by *some* gay men. I draw attention to this because *Promises, Promises*, both in its original production and in its revival, was an overwhelmingly white musical. Given the frequency of casting practices that aimed for more racial diversity onstage in 2010, the whiteness of *Promises'* cast was surprising. In the context of this kerfuffle about the closet, *Promises'* overwhelming whiteness is also worth noting because so much of the discourse about the closet at the turn of the twenty-first century was explicitly racialized using the racist language of *the down low*.

Analysis of the down-low figure helps us to see some of the other operations at work in the Straight Jacket affair. As queer theorist Riley Snorton argues in *Nobody Is Supposed to Know*,

> If we are ever to truly understand the full weight of the closet in its contemporary operation, we must consider the example of the down-low figure not as an instance of a closeted gay man but as a mass-mediatized form that exists in a particular moment in HIV/AIDS history.[48]

The closeted figure in this analysis is not a *person* who is in the closet, then, but an image created by journalists, bloggers, commentators, and others in order to justify mass-media scrutiny – particularly as it pertains to sexual desires and sexual freedom. For Snorton, "The fact that the down low persists in popular culture requires examinations of the complex relationships among identifications, sexual expression, and new technology in a rapidly increasing culture of surveillance."[49] I have described how *Promises* and *The Apartment* staged the post-World War II culture of surveillance, but Snorton argues that we see a new version of this culture of surveillance in the twenty-first century as websites report on the personal activities of Black celebrities and attempt to uncloset or out those who are "suspect."[50]

One of the key insights of *Nobody Is Supposed to Know* is Snorton's argument that "the closet is a site structured by queer oppression, yet the rhetoric of the closet cannot fully capture what queer oppression looks like or the way the closet acts as both shelter from and a manifestation of domination."[51] The discourse of the closet frames a person as *trapped within it*; this rhetoric insists that all one has to do is gather the courage to step out or open the door. The idea of the closet as a key structure of queer sexualities and queer identities behaves as though homophobic oppression and transphobic oppression are internal to the "closeted" person rather than part of the constant rhetoric of a homophobic and transphobic society. Snorton notes that "the closet [can also be] a shelter from oppression; it functions rhetorically as an indication of the specific forms of legal and cultural persecutions that queer people face."[52] It would also benefit us to let go of:

> the presumption that the "outside" of the closet is a less regulated – if not utopian – space for the unrepressed, unencumbered, and unregulated queer

subject. Comparative interpretations of the closet rely on a set of logics that place darkness and enlightenment and concealment and freedom in opposition to one another. These logics are put in crisis in the case of blackness, where darkness does not reflect a place from which to escape but a condition of existence. In other words, there can be no elsewhere when darkness is everywhere. In the context of blackness, the closet is not a space of concealment but a site for observation and display.[53]

Snorton's argument is that Black sexuality is always figured as queer or deviant and that this manufactured deviance then functions as a justification or rationale for the heightened surveillance, discipline, and incarceration of Black bodies. Blackness demonstrates that the discourse of the closet makes a set of value judgments that privilege the "outside," although – and this is especially true in the case of LGBTQ celebrities – to "come out" is often to open oneself up to still more surveillance, regulation, ridicule, and judgment. This is precisely what happened to Sean Hayes.

Playing Gay and Playing Straight

Although it was written a decade before the Straight Jacket affair, one might be surprised to find the second edition of John Clum's *Acting Gay* (2000) prefaced by a prescient discussion of Hayes, his sexuality, and his first film, *Billy's Hollywood Screen Kiss* (1998). Clum describes Hayes as "the sort of actor one would hire to play a stereotypical gay character. He's slender, cute, sweet, with a very expressive face and a high tenor voice."[54] Clum finds Hayes and his film charming but is impatient with the coy way Hayes avoids discussing his sexuality: "Hayes plays his own games about being and acting gay. On the *Billy's Hollywood Screen Kiss* website, both Hayes and [costar Brad] Rowe claim to be heterosexuals. They may well be," Clum remarks drily, "but we all know the official Hollywood mythology: There are no gay actors, only gay roles."[55] Clum's frustration with Hayes's claims to be straight in 1998 and his later statement – repeated during the original run of *Will & Grace* – that he wanted "to keep his sexuality a mystery" was shared by many in the gay media.[56]

As out and proud as Jack McFarland was, Hayes himself officially came out a mere month before appearing in *Promises*. His revelation was the *Advocate* cover story for April 2010, the same month *Promises* opened. The bright blue magazine advertised "The interview you've waited 12 years to read." Inside, Hayes says that "He's not happy about sitting down with the magazine" and tells his interviewer that he was not in the closet but trying to keep his options open as an actor: "Faced with the very real prospect of jeopardizing his chance at landing straight roles down the road, he started reciting stock answers."[57] But "I am who I am," Hayes says. "I was never in, as they say. Never." As Steven Schelling notes in the gay magazine *Xtra!*, however, long before 2010, Hayes "drew speculation as to his sexual orientation. (Okay, straights speculated – the gays knew.) But despite urging and prodding from gay advocates and gay media, he refused to speak on the record about his sexuality" until he started doing press for *Promises*.[58] The *Advocate* interview was clearly aimed at promoting the Broadway revival to gay readers: the article is upfront about that promotion, and the piece includes a synopsis of the show and quotations from both Chenoweth and *Promises* producer Craig Zadan.

Schelling's claim that "the gays knew," however, directs us toward questions central to the politics of the closet: To whom is one *out*? And what might it even mean to be *in the closet* if "the gays" already know? Indeed, we would do well to ask what it is that "the gays" believe themselves to *know* about Hayes's or anyone else's sexualities. As I noted in the introduction, queer people differ from one another in numerous ways, including gender, class, race, preferred sexual practices, religion, and political affiliations – a fact often occluded by those who wish to look at us as a political group or market niche. Queer theorist Eve Sedgwick reminds us – as the first axiom of *Epistemology of the Closet* – that "People are different from each other," and even *homosexuality* as a blanket term describes a wide variety of practices, desires, and subjectivities.[59]

If "the gays knew," then, we truly didn't know much. As queer theorist David Halperin puts it in *How to Be Gay*, "gay male desire actually comprises a kaleidoscopic range of queer longings – of wishes and sensations and pleasures and emotions – that exceed the bounds of any singular identity and extend beyond the specifics of gay male existence."[60] Coming out, on the other hand, is a practice that publicly defines a sexuality, linguistically encompassing and making sense of a collection of desires that in fact make little sense. Once declared, this sexuality brings with it a set of meanings that allows others to believe they better understand the person so defined. For Wayne Koestenbaum, "Coming out is a way of telling a coherent story about one's sexuality, and it has worked political wonders. . . . But coming out is only one version of the vocalization underlying sexuality itself."[61] For the sake of LGBTQ politics, activists or fans might wish for celebrities to define their sexualities, but as Sedgwick notes,

> there are remarkably few of even the most openly gay people who are not deliberately in the closet with someone personally or economically or institutionally important to them. Furthermore, the deadly elasticity of heterosexist presumption means that . . . every encounter with a new classful of students, to say nothing of a new boss, social worker, loan officer, landlord, doctor, erects new closets.[62]

It is hardly unreasonable to argue that Hayes and other actors – performers in the business of embodying the desires of their audiences – might want to keep their own desires private, even secret, in order to maintain a public image as a desirable sexual object. (In the theatre, this tradition dates back to the first celebrity actors.) But even setting aside the argument that secrecy about a performer's private desires is good for business, we would do well to heed Halperin's and Sedgwick's reminders that terms such as *gay* and *lesbian* are never comprehensive and always remain inadequate descriptions of the capaciousness of desire. Indeed, although it can distance a speaker from the heterosexist presumption Sedgwick describes, "coming out of the closet" actually tells us precious little about a person's desires, longings, gender identities, fantasies, and styles. Coming out appears to explain something personal, to "tell a coherent story" about the self, but it opens up a universe of new questions because sexuality is simply not as coherent as a label might make it appear.

The critics and media commentators of the Straight Jacket affair, however, discussed "heterosexuality" and "homosexuality" as both essential and self-explanatory attributes, expressed either badly or well, rather than describing desire as multiplicitous, complex, or confusing. Chenoweth, Black, and Setoodeh treat homosexuality as though it were an essential component of a person rather than a dynamic, mutable relationship between bodies or a journey of discovery on which one might embark. Hayes, on the other hand, with his careful silence and the coy periphrasis he employed to discuss his sexuality, long resisted committing to such a coherent story about sexual desire.[63] "I don't see sexuality," the actor said in 2016, and the reasons he gave for resisting a public categorization of his sexual life were neither meritless nor ill-advised.[64] In this way, the Straight Jacket affair calls attention not only to the politics of the closet but also to the politics of outing – that is, publicly condemning someone for hiding their homosexuality.

As the April 2010 *Advocate* cover notes, Hayes had been famous for 12 years before coming out, but the *Advocate* had itself already outed him. In 2006, in an antagonistic piece entitled "Sean Hayes: The Interview He Never Gave," the *Advocate* reminded readers that the actor had "played two very well-known gay characters," had never publicly dated a woman, and had refused to be interviewed by the magazine for eight years.[65] That Hayes was reluctant to do an interview with this same magazine in 2010, then, should have come as no surprise. The *Advocate*, of course, claims a largely gay readership; *Newsweek*'s audience is more mainstream, and it seems likely that Setoodeh's April 2010 piece outed Hayes to a broader audience. As Richard Ouzounian noted in the *Toronto Star*, "There might still have been millions of people who hadn't known before that Hayes or [Jonathan] Groff or Cynthia Nixon or Neil Patrick Harris or Portia de Rossi were gay. . . . But everyone now sure knows."[66] Further, Setoodeh's article *accuses* Hayes of homosexuality – "the big pink elephant in the room" – and censures other critics for lying about it. *Newsweek*, in other words, resurrected the old trope linking homosexuality to insincerity and deviousness, outing Hayes with language approximate to the hostile outings of homophobic politicians in the 1990s.

To complicate matters further, Setoodeh's opponents employed precisely this same politics of outing in their counterattacks. Chenoweth's open letter notes that she'd been "told on good authority that Mr. Setoodeh is a gay man himself,"[67] and GLAAD's Barrios and Black refer to "openly gay Setoodeh's own issues with sexuality and femininity." An overwhelming majority of the articles written during the Straight Jacket affair go out of their way to speak, as the *Atlantic* does, about "Setoodeh, who is openly gay,"[68] or to lament with Ryan Murphy that "Mr. Setoodeh is himself gay."[69] Thus, these articles, while praising out actors and ostensibly celebrating gay identity, take pains to out Setoodeh – to tell readers that the man calling an actor too gay for his job is also a gay man. In either case, the writers doing the outing use the sexuality of others as a weapon. Both writers frame the sexualities of their targets as coherent and essential, and while Setoodeh clearly accuses Hayes of attempting to hide his sexuality, the responding articles obliquely accuse the critic of precisely the same thing. The actor's sexuality, in this case, was expressly used against him by the critic; the critic's sexuality was, in turn, used against him by others. If, to paraphrase Foucault, sodomy used to be something one was charged with doing, *homosexuality remains something one is accused of being*.[70]

It's important to note, as well, that those commentators who announced to readers that Ramin Setoodeh is a gay man did so in order to register a kind of betrayal of mainstream gay culture or to point out his divergence from accepted LGBTQ values. *This man is gay too, and so his opinions should not be what they are*. These comments reveal a profound puzzlement about the lack of *identity* among LGBTQ-identified folks. He is gay, and so he is expected to toe the line in terms of how we all talk about other LGBTQ people and what we all are supposed to say about LGBTQ politics. Setoodeh's viewing practices and ideas did not accord with those of the mainstream LGBTQ news media, and they took pains to out him in order to push both his sexuality and his politics to accord better with something more popularly coherent.

Femininity on Display

Musical theatre has long been recognized as a rich, complex site for the various operations of gay and lesbian desire. These queer desiring relationships have been noted by Miller, Wolf, Clum, Halperin, and David Savran, among others.[71] A teenaged Wayne Koestenbaum even "worried, listening to records of *Darling Lili, Oklahoma!, The Music Man, Company*, and *No, No, Nanette*, that [he] would end up gay: . . . I had a clear impression," he says in *The Queen's Throat*, "that gays liked musical comedy."[72] Indeed, as Miller quips in *Place for Us*, "In the admittedly monstrous case that he isn't gay, the aficionado of the Broadway musical must resign himself to being thought so, or work as hard as Frank Rich to establish his improbable but true sexual orientation."[73] Miller argues that "though not all gay men – nor even most – are in love with Broadway, those who aren't are hardly quit of the stereotype that insists they are."[74] Audiences seem to agree with this overwhelming critical consensus: a year after the Straight Jacket affair, 2011 Tony Awards host Neil Patrick Harris would joke in his opening number that "Broadway has never been broader; it's not just for gays anymore!"[75]

One of the fundamental arguments in *Place for Us* is that queer desire's relationship to the Broadway musical shifted profoundly after Stonewall. Miller argues that before 1969, musical comedy could function as a kind of expression or vehicle of identificatory possibility for a widespread, unlocalized homosexual desire for an entire range of men, that it was a form designed "to indulge men in the thrills of a femininity *become their own*."[76] After Stonewall, however, with the ascendance of gay identity, U.S. American culture "could no longer help sensing that the Broadway musical was 'a gay thing,'" irremediably associated with homosexuality.[77] Miller is no doubt correct, but if the musical initiates queer operations of desire, these operations are not uniform. Rather, the audience's desire for the musical performer works in several modes at once, relating simultaneously to identification, eroticism, and virtuosity. An audience member can desire a character in multiple ways – to be the character, to sing like the character, to be loved *by* the character, to be loved *like* the character.[78] The audience member might also desire simply to sing, dance, act, perform.

The critic, in the guise of a dispassionate observer, catalogs and evaluates, frequently pretending that this description and assessment are unrelated to and uninflected by the complexities of desire. The distance necessary for criticism, however, has not often stopped critics from using the language of desire to discuss performances and performers. Indeed, the history of theatre criticism is filled with critics speaking more or less openly about the desirability of the performers they are watching. In his original review of *Wicked*, for example, Ben Brantley described Elphaba, or rather Idina Menzel, as "the slinky babe with green skin on the broom."[79] One of the reasons I find the Straight Jacket affair so intriguing is that the critic is honest and upfront about how he perceives the sexuality of the actor onstage and the character in the show. He tells us, in no uncertain terms, what he was hoping to see and how the show failed to deliver on the promises it seemed to offer.

Setoodeh describes his viewing experiences in an almost uncomfortably candid way: after saying Jonathan Groff's performance on *Glee* reminds him of "your average theater queen," he says, "It doesn't help that he tried to bed his girlfriend while singing (and writhing to) Madonna's 'Like a Virgin.' He is so distracting I'm starting to wonder if Groff's character on the show is supposed to be secretly gay."[80] This is a harsh remark and not only because Setoodeh is saying that Groff is not believable in the show. He's also saying that Groff possesses a femininity that he should be hiding better if he's going to portray a straight guy on screen, especially one who covers iconic Madonna songs.

But why? Setoodeh's assumptions here about what the terms *gay* and *straight* are supposed to describe are simply unsupportable. Are not men who desire sex with women just as susceptible as anyone else to the charms of 1980s pop music?[81] Don't men who desire sex with women also possess differing levels of femininity? Don't plenty of women find such varying levels of femininity sexually desirable in their male partners? Setoodeh appears to be objecting to performances of homosexuality, but his objections circulate around femininity. The critic's remarks in "Straight Jacket" accept the same conventions about maleness, heterosexuality, and masculinity that Neil Simon and the four philandering executives insist upon in *Promises*. As I argued earlier in this chapter, traditional masculinity shores itself up, it insists upon its own veracity, by feminizing men who do not behave according to traditionally masculine rules. But men behave in all sorts of ways; we perform our genders in an array of styles, and predicting sexuality based on a perceived gender performance – or a predilection for Madonna classics – leaves plenty of room for error.

Hayes may claim not to "see sexuality," but critics of *Promises, Promises* certainly did – and Ramin Setoodeh was not alone. Other critics mentioned sexuality, as well; they just weren't as open about the subject matter at hand. In the *New York Times*, Brantley reported that Hayes's "relationship with Ms. Chenoweth's Fran feels more like that of a younger brother than a would-be lover and protector."[82] In a subsequent piece for the *Times*, Brantley described *Promises* as mostly lacking in "sexual energy," commenting that throughout the play's first act "[Hayes] – despite being cast opposite the appealing Kristin Chenoweth – has given the impression of someone still waiting for a playmate to bring out the devil inside him."[83] Similarly, in the *Toronto Star*, Richard Ouzounian wrote that "Hayes has a winning personality as Baxter, but he's too sweet. You . . . don't really believe he's in love with Kubelik. A puppy-dog crush, maybe, but little more."[84]

Perhaps even more telling is a remark made by the *New York Post*'s Michael Riedel when the show's casting was announced – a full two years before *Promises* opened. "Hayes," worried Riedel, "doesn't seem quite virile enough to play a role originated by Jerry Orbach, one of Broadway's greatest leading men."[85] The comparison to Orbach contrasts the masculinity of one actor with another, but let's be clear that *virility* is a quality not even remotely associated with *Promises'* Chuck Baxter, the lonely bachelor who lets his superiors at work use his apartment for sex. Chuck is, to the contrary, a character whom critics consistently describe as a nebbish and who, in his opening monolog, refers to himself as "the kind of person that people don't notice."[86] In *The Apartment*, Mr. Kirkeby derisively refers to Baxter as "Little Lord Fauntleroy," and in both the movie and the musical, Baxter carries his own thermometer and nasal spray with him. As I've argued, the show's characterization of Chuck, in fact, is precisely the opposite of masculine. Chuck *knows* he lacks masculinity: it is a lack essential to his character. Riedel's comparison to Orbach, then, had nothing to do with whether or not Hayes was right for the role; I see it, rather, as simply a coded way of publicly wondering if Hayes was "too gay" for the part. In other words, although Setoodeh bore the brunt of the criticism during the Straight Jacket affair, numerous male critics (of differing sexualities) apparently felt entitled to comment on Hayes's perceived lack of masculinity *as long as they pretended they were talking about something else.*

Those angry about Setoodeh's article, then, might well accuse the critic of having "issues with sexuality and femininity," but *so do most of us*, straight and gay alike. Indeed, in *How to Be Gay*, David Halperin charts the rise in mid-century gay literature of "the straight-acting and -appearing gay man."[87] In the 1950s, this image or type became the romantic ideal for many gay men, and this ideal "was built on systematic contrasts with other, earlier, queerer types [like Vito Russo's sissies]; in fact, it thrived on explicit put-downs of effeminate or gender-deviant men, from whom the hero or the author recoiled in horror."[88] The sissy is ridiculed for his femininity on all sides, including by many gay men. One need only look briefly on gay male social media to see such shaming at work and note the enormous number of men whose profiles include the phrase "masc 4 masc." But this eroticization of masculinity among gay men and its attendant ridicule of femininity contradict the out-and-proud story we've all agreed to tell straight people about gay culture. For Setoodeh to say, in a mainstream publication like *Newsweek*, that Hayes's perceived femininity interrupted the pleasures of the critic's evening of musical theatre – desires that are normally disavowed by critics – was a kind of uncloseting all its own. The Straight Jacket affair, in many ways, outed the mainstream gay community's own biases against men who aren't quite "masc" enough.

All of this returns us to the operations of desire at work between the critic and the Broadway performer. Setoodeh's article details, however clumsily, a failed experience at the theatre. The audience is supposed to want to *be* Chuck Baxter, to be loved by him, to be loved the way he is loved, to sing like him, simply to *sing*, or some complex combination of these desires. This desiring operation did not work for Setoodeh, and in the case of *Promises, Promises*, we might do better to blame heterosexist masculinity instead of queer sexuality and the closet itself rather than the person in (or out of) it. But what the Straight Jacket affair makes most apparent is that the critic – like any other audience member – is a desiring sexual subject, whose judgments about an actor's performance are affected by what we find attractive, and that the actor is the object of that erotic investment, a figure of fantasy on which each of us projects our desires.

Straight Jacket Revisited

I want to close this chapter by jumping ahead roughly a decade to a much smaller media kerfuffle but one that revisited the issues raised by the Straight Jacket affair in several key ways. Ryan Murphy's film version of *The Prom* (2020) adapted a Broadway musical from the 2018–19 season with music by Matthew Sklar, lyrics by Chad Beguelin, and a libretto by Beguelin and Bob Martin. At the Longacre Theatre on West 48th Street, *The Prom* starred Beth Leavel and Brooks Ashmanskas. The movie version (as with nearly all movie musicals in the last 20 years) starred half a dozen very big movie and television stars: *The Prom* boasted the talents of Meryl Streep, James Corden, Nicole Kidman, Keegan-Michael Key, Kerry Washington, and Andrew Rannells, all of whom appeared on *The Prom*'s poster. The two high school girls at the film's center were played by Ariana DeBose – would win an Oscar in 2022 for Steven Spielberg's *West Side Story* remake – and Jo Ellen Pellman; *The Prom* was the first significant film credit for both. Few critics loved Murphy's adaptation, but the conversation about *The Prom* that emerged upon the film's release centered primarily on Corden's performance as Barry Glickman, a gay musical theatre actor who, as one of the plot's narratives, processes his pain about the homophobia he experienced in his family as a teenager.

Corden's work in *The Prom* (like his performance as Bustopher Jones in Tom Hooper's 2019 adaptation of *Cats*) was mostly panned. Gay male critics, especially, took issue with Corden's performance: Samuel Spencer titled his review for *Newsweek* "James Corden Offensively Miscast in Messy Netflix Musical"; the *Telegraph*'s Tim Robey called his "James Corden Tries to Solve Homophobia with a Musical – and Fails"; and, as I noted at the beginning of this chapter, the headline for Richard

Lawson's *Vanity Fair* review was "James Corden Should Have Been Banned from *The Prom*."[89] I say gay male critics, especially, because Manohla Dargis took no issue with Corden's performance in her *New York Times* review, and *Variety*'s Owen Gleiberman liked him a lot, saying that "Corden may be criticized in some quarters for portraying Barry as a gay stereotype, but like Christopher Guest in 'Waiting for Guffman' he burrows so deeply into the character's quibbling insouciance that he gives him a three-dimensional essence."[90] The "some quarters" to which Gleiberman refers were, overwhelmingly, critics who identify as gay men.

As a mass-mediated conversation about casting and sexuality, much of the same ground was covered in December 2020 that was covered by the Straight Jacket affair in April and May of 2010. In fact, many critics seemed to think the conversation had been exhausted by the end of the decade, with Zach Sharf of IndieWire referring to "the age-old debate about whether or not straight actors can play gay characters," and the *Guardian*'s Benjamin Lee saying that "Whenever the debate over whether straight actors should be allowed to play gay characters has reared its head (and with time, that's gone from every year to every week), I've found myself largely dismissive."[91] There are, however, a few key differences between the situations surrounding *Promises, Promises* and *The Prom* that are worth discussing. I also want to highlight some of their surprising similarities as a way, first, to take stock of the currently accepted twenty-first-century wisdom related to casting and identity and, second, to note some of the assumptions about sexuality, performance, and the closet that have endured over the course of the decade.

If the Straight Jacket affair was about a gay actor (allegedly) being too feminine to play a straight character, the Corden–Glickman drama was about a straight actor (allegedly) playing a gay character as too feminine or in a way that read as falsely feminine. The sissy, in other words, appears to have made a comeback. This time, however, the character of Barry Glickman is himself a satirical figure. He's ridiculously shallow, but he's also a gay man who has experienced homophobia; in short, he might be what Ramin Setoodeh would call "your average theater queen" if he weren't also a big Broadway star. This sissy's function in the narrative of *The Prom* is *not*, as it is in *The Apartment* or *Promises, Promises*, to deflect attention away from the homoerotic possibilities in the other male characters' relationships. Masculinity doesn't need shoring up in *The Prom* the way it does in *Promises*, and the movie doesn't make an effort to do that because the important homoerotic relationship in *The Prom* is between two high school girls. Still, the sissy retains his power, managing to induce shame – or anger, or at least aversion – in so many of his gay male viewers.

Although in both of these situations the issue under discussion appears to be casting, who gets to play whom, and what an authentic portrayal might look like, the problematic figure in each case – and across a decade of musical theatre performance – continues to be the too-feminine man. In their critiques of *The Prom*, one gay male critic says, "It's painful to watch James Corden lean into effeminate gay stereotypes and play up sassy gay flourishes"; another refers to Corden's "cliched queening"; still another describes him as "flitting and lisping around in the most uninspired of caricatures, miss[ing] all potential for nuance, and thus never find[ing] even a hint of truth in the role."[92] For gay male critics, Corden's Barry Glickman is a stereotype of "a bustling Queer Eye nightmare."[93] I draw attention to these critiques neither to excuse Corden nor to invalidate these responses; I want, rather, to note the continuing power of the effeminate man to draw the ire of the gay men in the audience, who vehemently disavow his presence on stage or onscreen. Benjamin Lee gets it right in his summation of the Corden–Glickman drama when he says that "Corden mindlessly crashing his way through the film, mincing and often lisping for gruesome effect recalls exactly the kind of caricature we'd hoped was locked and buried in the past."[94] These gay male audience members do not see themselves in Corden's portrayal – they disavow his performance as inauthentic, caricatured, and stereotyped – but the figure offends because we know that the sissy *continues to be a way of talking about us* out here in the audience. Corden's performance is offensive because although the sissy is not necessary to shore up masculinity within the narrative structure of *The Prom*, the figure is still constantly used to shore up masculinity in the real world where gay men live.

Another fascinating aspect about all of these reviews of *The Prom* is that the critics, in order to discuss the sexualities of these fictional characters, have to figure out ways to disclose their own identifications and attempt, in addition, to refer to the various identifications of performers, directors, and screenwriters. For the critic this isn't so difficult: he can use the only somewhat inelegant phrase "as a gay viewer" or (as one critic does) refer to himself as "batting for the same team" as Barry Glickman. But there's no smooth way to do this when talking about the film's artistic contributors. Critics find themselves using phrases like "Corden, a straight actor yet to truly prove his worth in film," "Corden, a straight, married dad, may not have direct experience of what Barry faced," or "Corden, who is straight, is so bad in *The Prom*."[95] The term *straight* seems, on the surface, to be straightforward enough, and perhaps it is. But things get more complicated for the film's other artists, whom critics describe using phrases such as, "[Ryan] Murphy, an openly gay writer-director-producer," or "[Jo Ellen] Pellman, as a queer woman herself, connected with Emma's optimism," and made friends with "[Ariana] DeBose, a fellow queer woman."[96] In its references to people who are "openly gay" or "openly queer," such language often refers insistently back to the closet, marking distance from it.[97] These journalistic pieces also invariably perform the same function as the language of outing I discussed earlier: not that Murphy, Pellman, or DeBose do not or did not wish to be referred to as gay or queer, but that describing them as such – and describing Corden as straight – is a method of linguistically fixing their sexualities, of attempting to tell a coherent story about these artists' desires, sexual practices, and erotic orientations.

This variant language of *openly queer/openly gay/openly* LGBTQ draws attention, yet again, to the differences *between* queer-identified people, even if many in the news media behave as if all queer people possess identity. The language around being "open" should remind us that there are lesbians, gay people, bisexuals, trans folks, nonbinary individuals, and other queer people who cannot be described "openly," who don't have easy language with which to describe their identifications, or who prefer to keep their identifications to themselves. This quite simple fact, though often overlooked, makes the idea of "authentic" portrayals more of a conundrum than many of us might like, especially for *characters* who are not open or whose identifications change over the course of a film or play's narrative. Almost everyone who commented on the Corden–Glickman drama agreed that they wouldn't restrict "gay" roles only to "gay" actors. (This question is, apparently, something that the Straight Jacket affair *did* settle for a majority of commentators.) Most writers making this argument cite acclaimed portrayals of queer characters by actors who identify as straight such as Trevante Rhodes, Timothée Chalamet, and Darren Criss. But their logic also makes sense in light of the arguments I am making: queer people are different from one another, our experiences of queerness differ widely, and our desires are not easily contained within the restrictive labels of sexuality available to us at any given time. To cite an example from the Corden–Glickman drama, one thing that appears in Jo Ellen Pellman's interviews about *The Prom* is a discussion of how different she is from Emma, the teenage character she plays. Pellman describes growing up in an accepting household with a gay single mother and never being bullied. She says she hasn't had to face the homophobia experienced by the character. Pellman is also fairly careful about referring to herself as "queer," explicitly identifying herself with a different term for her sexuality than the one which Emma in *The Prom* uses – "lesbian."

Still, there's something about openness and being "out" that's important to those commenting on the Corden–Glickman drama that we have not yet discussed. In a May 2022 piece in the *Gay & Lesbian Review*, Adam Odsess-Rubin makes the case for "casting queer actors in queer roles" so that we can "tell our own stories on our own terms."[98] Odsess-Rubin describes being moved to come out as gay in 2008 after seeing Sean Penn in the film *Milk*, but he quickly pivots to argue that because Penn is an actor who identifies as straight, "I lost out on a role model and a vision for my future as a successful gay actor." What I see in Odsess-Rubin's challenge to actors (and directors and producers) is less a call for "authenticity" than it is a statement of a desire for identification with the actor as well as the character. What appears initially to be a call for better representation ought more accurately to be reframed as a desire for actors to be open about their (varying) queer sexualities.[99] One of my arguments in this chapter is that many actors who *do not* "openly" describe themselves as gay (or bi or queer or trans or nonbinary) might have private lived experiences that make their performances very authentic indeed. I'm also arguing that it's very difficult to pinpoint what "authenticity" actually looks like when we're all so different from one another – even among those who in some way identify underneath the umbrella of LGBTQ. But my arguments do not solve the problem presented by Odsess-Rubin, who is calling for more "out and proud role models on stage and screen.... When queer people grow up with proud gay role models, we become proud adults." It is true that coming out tells a coherent story about a sexuality that is anything but; it is also true that LGBTQ identity can never fully describe the capaciousness of queer desire and the multiplicity of queer longings. But Odsess-Rubin remains correct that young people need a variety of queer role models with whom they can identify. On some level – one removed from the Corden–Glickman drama – this is precisely what *The Prom*'s message of acceptance and love had failingly attempted to do.

Notes

1. Setoodeh, "Straight Jacket," 50. *Newsweek* 155.19 is dated May 10, 2010, but the article first appeared online on April 26, 2010 as "From Glee to Sean Hayes: Gay Actors Play Straight." Jensen and Chenoweth responded before the article appeared in print.
2. Setoodeh is the Co-Editor-in-Chief of *Variety* as of January 2022.
3. Setoodeh, "Straight Jacket," 50.
4. Setoodeh, "Straight Jacket," 51.
5. Jensen, "*Newsweek*'s Ramin Setoodeh Strikes Again."
6. Chenoweth quoted in Jensen, "Kristin Chenoweth 'Offended' by Ramin Setoodeh's Homophobic Article in *Newsweek*."
7. Barrios and Black, "*Milk* Scribe Joins GLAAD against *Newsweek*."
8. Wallenstein, "Why Newsweek need not apologize to GLAAD."
9. Sorkin, "Now That You Mention It, Rock Hudson Did Seem Gay."
10. Healy, "*Red* and *Memphis* Win Top Tony Awards," C1.
11. Setoodeh's second article has been removed by the *Daily Beast* and is now unsearchable on the Internet.
12. See McQuade, "Gay Actors and Ramin Setoodeh"; Jensen, "Ramin Gets it Wrong Again. Anyone Surprised?"
13. See, for example, Odsess-Rubin, "What We All Gain When We Cast Queer Actors in Queer Roles."
14. Lawson, "James Corden Should Have Been Banned From *The Prom*."
15. Wilder, *The Apartment*.
16. Bacharach, David, and Simon, *Promises, Promises*, 120.
17. Thompson, "Of Course Gay Actors Can Play Straight."
18. Setoodeh, "Straight Jacket," 50.
19. Dziemianowicz, "*Promises*: Say a Little Prayer," 24.
20. Scheck, review of *Promises, Promises*, 7.
21. See Piepenburg, "He's Playing God on Broadway," AR7.
22. Indeed, *Will & Grace*, which originally ran for eight seasons from 1998 to 2006, was revived in 2017, playing for three more seasons, with its final episode airing on April 23, 2020.
23. Hayes, "Offstage with Broadway Star Sean Hayes."
24. Schelling, "Can Gays Play Straight?" 19.
25. Bernardo, "Offstage with Sean & Kristin," 6.
26. Russo, *The Celluloid Closet*, 3–59.
27. Their heterosexual mistresses are there too, of course, although they are not in the closet. In *Promises*, the mistress almost always wishes she were a wife.
28. In the film, Bud tells us that C.C. is short for Calvin Clifford, neither of which is usually shortened to Chuck.
29. Cohan, "From Walter Neff to C.C. Baxter," 55.
30. Wojcik, *The Apartment Plot*, 122.
31. Brookes, "The Eye of Power."
32. Brookes, "The Eye of Power," 159.
33. See Johnson, *The Lavender Scare*.
34. McMillin, *The Musical as Drama*, 20–21.
35. Rogers, *The Song Is You*, 88.

36 Bacharach, David, and Simon, *Promises, Promises*, 26. This sequence is nearly identical in *The Apartment*, except that the libretto adds asides where none exists in the film.
37 Bacharach, David, and Simon, *Promises, Promises*, 34.
38 Bacharach, David, and Simon, *Promises, Promises*, 48.
39 Bacharach, David, and Simon, *Promises, Promises*, 48–49.
40 It seems worth noting that two of the four actors who played these straight characters in 2010 are gay.
41 The sex in Central Park seems particularly queer here. See Chauncey, *Gay New York*, 182–183.
42 Bacharach, David, and Simon, *Promises, Promises*, 6.
43 Bacharach, David, and Simon, *Promises, Promises*, 69. These are Neil Simon jokes; they don't appear in the Diamond–Wilder screenplay.
44 Bacharach, David, and Simon, *Promises, Promises*, 3–4. Emphasis in original.
45 Miller, *Place for Us*, 39.
46 Clum, *Something for the Boys*, 72.
47 Clum, *Something for the Boys*, 85.
48 Snorton, *Nobody Is Supposed to Know*, 5.
49 Snorton, *Nobody Is Supposed to Know*, 5.
50 Snorton, *Nobody Is Supposed to Know*, 122.
51 Snorton, *Nobody Is Supposed to Know*, 18.
52 Snorton, *Nobody Is Supposed to Know*, 17.
53 Snorton, *Nobody Is Supposed to Know*, 17–18.
54 Clum, *Still Acting Gay*, vii.
55 Clum, *Still Acting Gay*, viii.
56 Clum, *Still Acting Gay*, viii.
57 Karpel, "Sean Hayes: I Am Who I Am." In print, the article appeared in April 2010, pp. 32–37.
58 Schelling, "Can Gays Play Straight?" 19.
59 Sedgwick, *Epistemology of the Closet*, 22.
60 Halperin, *How to Be Gay*, 69–70.
61 Koestenbaum, *The Queen's Throat*, 174.
62 Sedgwick, *Epistemology of the Closet*, 67–68.
63 This changed in late 2016 when Hayes apologized for not coming out sooner and referred to himself as "a proud gay man." See Gardner, "Sean Hayes Says He's Sorry for Not Coming Out Sooner."
64 Piepenburg, "He's Playing God on Broadway," AR7.
65 Broverman, "Sean Hayes: The Interview He Never Gave."
66 Ouzounian, "Actors: What's Gay Got to Do with It?" E3.
67 Chenoweth quoted in Jensen, "Kristin Chenoweth 'Offended' by Ramin Setoodeh's Homophobic Article in *Newsweek*."
68 Thompson, "Of Course Gay Actors Can Play Straight."
69 Entertainment Weekly, "*Glee* Creator Ryan Murphy Pushes for *Newsweek* Boycott."
70 Foucault, *The History of Sexuality: Volume 1*, 43.
71 See Miller, *Place for Us*; Clum, *Something for the Boys*; Stacy Wolf, "'Defying Gravity'"; David Savran, "'You've Got That Thing.'"
72 Koestenbaum, *The Queen's Throat*, 11.
73 Miller, *Place for Us*, 16.
74 Miller, *Place for Us*, 16.
75 GilbeauxFan, "Neil Patrick Harris' 2011 Tony Awards Opening Number."
76 Miller, *Place for Us*, 90.
77 Miller, *Place for Us*, 134.
78 Again, see Wolf, *A Problem Like Maria*, 211.
79 Brantley, "There's Trouble in Emerald City," E1.
80 Setoodeh, "Straight Jacket," 51.
81 Cf. Mötley Crüe's 2019 cover of the same song.

82   Brantley, "Back in the '60s," C1. In case you didn't catch the unnecessary misogynist shade, Chenoweth is two years older than Hayes.
83   Brantley, "Promises, Promises Katie Finneran and Sean Hayes," AR15.
84   Ouzounian, "Promises Made, but Unfulfilled," E2.
85   Riedel, "Thick Web of Intrigue," 44.
86   Bacharach, David, and Simon, *Promises, Promises*, 3.
87   Halperin, *How to Be Gay*, 46.
88   Halperin, *How to Be Gay*, 46–7.
89   Spencer, "*The Prom* Review"; Robey, "The Prom, Review."
90   Dargis, "*The Prom* Review"; Gleiberman, "*The Prom* Review."
91   Sharf and Dry, "Why Are Critics Outraged over James Corden?"; Lee, "James Corden Proves Why Straight Actors Should Think Twice Before Playing Gay."
92   See Sharf in Sharf and Dry, "Why Are Critics Outraged over James Corden?"; McNulty, "Meryl Streep Is Queen of Netflix's *Prom*, an LGBTQ Message Musical Gone Hollywood"; and Lawson, "James Corden Should Have Been Banned from *The Prom*."
93   See Lee, "James Corden Proves Why Straight Actors Should Think Twice Before Playing Gay."
94   Lee, "James Corden Proves Why Straight Actors Should Think Twice Before Playing Gay."
95   Lee, "James Corden Proves Why Straight Actors Should Think Twice before Playing Gay"; McNulty "Meryl Streep Is Queen of Netflix's *Prom*, an LGBTQ Message Musical Gone Hollywood"; Lawson, "James Corden Should Have Been Banned From *The Prom*."
96   Lee, "James Corden Proves Why Straight Actors Should Think Twice Before Playing Gay"; Bahr, "New Star of *The Prom* Sees a Chance to Make L.G.B.T.Q. Characters Visible."
97   The terms "openly gay" and "out" appear frequently, for example, in Malkin, "*The Prom* Star Jo Ellen Pellman on Why Kate McKinnon Is Her Queer Role Model."
98   Odsess-Rubin, "What We All Gain When We Cast Queer Actors in Queer Roles."
99   Odsess-Rubin wonders, for example, "why a gay male actor has still never won an Academy Award for acting." This is not true. What is true is that an *out* gay male actor has still never won an Academy Award for acting.

References for Chapter 1

Bacharach, Burt, Hal David, and Neil Simon. *Promises, Promises*. New York: Random House, 1969.
Bahr, Sarah. "New Star of *The Prom* Sees a Chance to Make L.G.B.T.Q. Characters Visible." *New York Times*. 11 December 2020. www.nytimes.com/2020/12/11/movies/jo-ellen-pellman-prom-lgbtq.html. Accessed 21 May 2022.
Barrios, Jarrett, and Dustin Lance Black. "*Milk* Scribe Joins GLAAD Against *Newsweek*." *Hollywood Reporter*. 12 May 2010. www.hollywoodreporter.com/news/general-news/milk-scribe-joins-glaad-against-23554/. Accessed 15 May 2022.
Bernardo, Melissa Rose. "Offstage With Sean & Kristin." *Playbill* 28.9: 6–7, 2010.
Brantley, Ben. "Back in the '60s: Let's Tryst Again." *New York Times*. 26 April 2010. (C1).
Brantley, Ben. "*Promises, Promises* Katie Finneran and Sean Hayes." *New York Times*. 16 May 2010. (AR15).
Brantley, Ben. "There's Trouble in Emerald City." *New York Times*. 31 October 2003. (E1).
Brookes, Ian. "The Eye of Power: Postwar Fordism and the Panoptic Corporation in *The Apartment*." *Journal of Popular Film and Television* 37.4: 150–160, 2009.
Broverman, Neal. "Sean Hayes: the Interview He Never Gave." *Advocate*. 10 March 2006. www.advocate.com/arts-entertainment/television/2010/03/10/sean-hayes-interview-he-never-gave. Accessed 19 May 2022.

Chauncey, George. *Gay New York: Gender, Urban Culture, and the Making of the Gay Male World 1890–1940*. New York: Basic, 1994.

Clum, John M. *Something for the Boys: Musical Theater and Gay Culture*. New York: St. Martin's Press, 1999.

Clum, John M. *Still Acting Gay*. New York: St. Martin's Griffin, 2000.

Cohan, Steven. "From Walter Neff to C.C. Baxter: Billy Wilder's Apartment Plots." In *The Apartment Complex: Urban Living and Global Screen Cultures*. Edited by Pamela Robertson Wojcik. Durham: Duke University Press, 44–64, 2018.

Dargis, Manohla. "*The Prom* Review: Showbiz Sanctimony, and All That Zazz." *New York Times*. 10 December 2020. www.nytimes.com/2020/12/10/movies/the-prom-review.html. Accessed 20 May 2022.

Dziemianowicz, Joe. "*Promises*: Say a Little Prayer." *New York Daily News*. 26 April 2010. (24).

Entertainment Weekly. "*Glee* Creator Ryan Murphy Pushes for *Newsweek* Boycott." *EW*. 11 May 2010. ew.com/article/2010/05/11/ryan-murphy-newsweek-boycott/. Accessed 19 May 2022.

Foucault, Michel. *The History of Sexuality: Volume 1 – An Introduction*. Translated by Robert Hurley. New York: Vintage Books, 1990.

Gardner, Chris. "Sean Hayes Says He's Sorry for Not Coming Out Sooner." *Hollywood Reporter*. 24 October 2016. www.hollywoodreporter.com/news/general-news/sean-hayes-sorry-not-coming-940767/. Accessed 19 May 2022.

GilbeauxFan. "Neil Patrick Harris' 2011 Tony Awards Opening Number." *YouTube*. 13 June 2011. www.youtube.com/watch?v=-6S5caRGpK4. Accessed 8 August 2022.

Gleiberman, Owen. "*The Prom* Review: Ryan Murphy Turns a Message Musical about Tolerance into a Fizzy and Elating Showbiz High." *Variety*. 1 December 2010. variety.com/2020/film/reviews/the-prom-review-meryl-streep-james-corden-ryan-murphy-1234842681/. Accessed 21 May 2022.

Halperin, David M. *How to Be Gay*. Cambridge: Harvard University Press, 2012.

Hayes, Sean. "Offstage With Broadway Star Sean Hayes." *Fresh Air*. 11 June 2010. www.npr.org/transcripts/127556541. Accessed 19 May 2022.

Healy, Patrick. "*Red* and *Memphis* Win Top Tony Awards." *New York Times*. 14 June 2010. (C1).

Jensen, Michael. "Kristin Chenoweth 'Offended' by Ramin Setoodeh's Homophobic Article in *Newsweek*." *NewNowNext*. 7 May 2010. hwww.newnownext.com/kristin-chenoweth-offended-by-ramin-setoodehs-homophobic-article-in-newsweek/05/2010/. Accessed 15 May 2022.

Jensen, Michael. "*Newsweek*'s Ramin Setoodeh Strikes Again: Gay Actors Can't Play Straight." *NewNowNext*. 27 April 2010. www.newnownext.com/newsweeks-ramin-setoodeh-strikes-again-gay-actors-cant-play-straight/04/2010/. Accessed 15 May 2022.

Jensen, Michael. "Ramin Gets It Wrong Again. Anyone Surprised?" *NewNowNext*. 3 January 2011. www.newnownext.com/ramin-gets-it-wrong-again-anyone-surprised/01/2011/. Accessed 15 May 2022.

Johnson, David K. *The Lavender Scare: The Cold War Persecution of Gays and Lesbians in the Federal Government*. Chicago: University of Chicago Press, 2004.

Karpel, Ari. "Sean Hayes: I Am Who I Am." *Advocate*. 8 March 2010. www.advocate.com/arts-entertainment/people/2010/03/08/sean-hayes-i-am-who-i-am. Accessed 19 May 2022.

Koestenbaum, Wayne. *The Queen's Throat: Opera, Homosexuality, and the Mystery of Desire*. Boston: Da Capo Press, 2001.

Lawson, Richard. "James Corden Should Have Been Banned From *The Prom*." *Vanity Fair*. 1 December 2020. www.vanityfair.com/hollywood/2020/12/the-prom-movie-review-james-corden. Accessed 11 May 2022.

Lee, Benjamin. "James Corden Proves Why Straight Actors Should Think Twice Before Playing Gay." *Guardian*. 9 December 2020. www.theguardian.com/film/2020/dec/09/james-corden-the-prom-netflix-proves-straight-actors-playing-gay-should-think-twice. Accessed 20 May 2022.

Malkin, Marc. "*The Prom* Star Jo Ellen Pellman on Why Kate McKinnon Is Her Queer Role Model." *Variety*. 26 January 2021. variety.com/2021/music/podcasts/prom-jo-ellen-pellman-kate-mckinnon-1234892778/. Accessed 21 May 2022.

McMillin, Scott. *The Musical as Drama: A Study of the Principles and Conventions Behind Musical Shows from Kern to Sondheim*. Princeton: Princeton University Press, 2006.

McNulty, Charles. "Meryl Streep Is Queen of Netflix's *Prom*, an LGBTQ Message Musical Gone Hollywood." *Los Angeles Times*. 3 December 2020. www.latimes.com/entertainment-arts/story/2020-12-03/prom-netflix-review-ryan-murphy-meryl-streep-james-corden. Accessed 20 May 2022.

McQuade, Aaron. "Gay Actors and Ramin Setoodeh: Setting the Record 'Straight.'" GLAAD, 5 January 2011. www.glaad.org/2011/01/05/gay-actors-and-ramin-setoodeh-setting-the-record-straight. Accessed 15 May 2022.

Miller, D.A. *Place for Us: Essay on the Broadway Musical*. Cambridge: Harvard University Press, 1998.

Odsess-Rubin, Adam. "What We All Gain When We Cast Queer Actors in Queer Roles." *Gay & Lesbian Review Worldwide*. 10 May 2022. glreview.org/what-we-all-gain-when-we-cast-queer-actors-in-queer-roles/. Accessed 21 May 2022.

Ouzounian, Richard. "Actors: What's Gay Got to Do With It?" *Toronto Star*. 16 May 2010. (E3).

Ouzounian, Richard. "Promises Made, but Unfulfilled." *Toronto Star*. 26 April 2010. (E2).

Piepenburg, Erik. "He's Playing God on Broadway." *New York Times*. 22 May 2016. (AR7).

Riedel, Michael. "Thick Web of Intrigue." *New York Post*. 19 March 2008. (44).

Robey, Tim. "The Prom, Review: James Corden Tries to Solve Homophobia With a Musical – and Fails." *Telegraph*. 11 December 2020. www.telegraph.co.uk/films/0/prom-review-james-corden-tries-solve-homophobia-musical-fails/. Accessed 20 May 2022.

Rogers, Bradley. *The Song Is You: Musical Theatre and the Politics of Bursting Into Song and Dance*. Iowa City: University of Iowa Press, 2020.

Russo, Vito. *The Celluloid Closet: Homosexuality in the Movies* (Revised ed). New York: Harper & Row, 1987.

Savran, David. "'You've Got That Thing': Cole Porter, Stephen Sondheim, and the Erotics of the List Song." *Theatre Journal* 64.4: 533–548, 2012.

Scheck, Frank. "Review of *Promises, Promises*." *Hollywood Reporter*. 26 April 2010. (7).

Schelling, Steven. "Can Gays Play Straight?" *Xtra!* 17 June 2010. (19).

Sedgwick, Eve Kosofsky. *Epistemology of the Closet*. Berkeley: University of California Press, 1990.

Setoodeh, Ramin. "Straight Jacket." *Newsweek* 155.19: 50–1, 2010.

Sharf, Zach, and Jude Dry. "Why Are Critics Outraged Over James Corden? Debating Ryan Murphy's *Prom* Casting." *IndieWire*. 12 December 2020. www.indiewire.com/2020/12/james-corden-prom-offensive-gay-stereotype-1234603096/. Accessed 20 May 2022.

Snorton, C. Riley. *Nobody Is Supposed to Know: Black Sexuality on the Down Low*. Minneapolis: University of Minnesota Press, 2014.

Sorkin, Aaron. "Now That You Mention It, Rock Hudson Did Seem Gay." *Huffington Post*. 12 May 2010. www.huffpost.com/entry/now-that-you-mention-it-r_b_574210. Accessed 15 May 2022.

Spencer, Samuel. "*The Prom* Review: James Corden Offensively Miscast in Messy Netflix Musical." *Newsweek*. 1 December 2020. www.newsweek.com/prom-netflix-review-meryl-streep-james-corden-nicole-kidman-1551419. Accessed 20 May 2022.

Thompson, Derek. "Of Course Gay Actors Can Play Straight." *Atlantic*. 15 May 2010. www.theatlantic.com/entertainment/archive/2010/05/of-course-gay-actors-can-play-straight/56761/. Accessed 15 May 2022.

Wallenstein, Andrew. "Why Newsweek need not apologize to GLAAD." *Hollywood Reporter*. 12 May 2010. www.hollywoodreporter.com/news/general-news/why-newsweek-need-not-apologize-23553/. Accessed 15 May 2022.

Wilder, Billy, (director). *The Apartment*. Criterion Channel. 15 June 1960.

Wojcik, Pamela Robertson. *The Apartment Plot: Urban Living in American Film and Popular Culture, 1945–1975*. Durham: Duke University Press, 2010.

Wolf, Stacy. "'Defying Gravity': Queer Conventions in the Musical *Wicked*." *Theatre Journal* 60.1: 1–21, 2008.

2
IT GETS BETTER THAN BOYHOOD

As the story goes, the 1992 film *Newsies*, directed by Kenny Ortega and starring Christian Bale, was an attempt by Disney to revitalize the live-action movie-musical genre with a story based on real events from 1899. Impoverished orphan children selling newspapers in New York City went on strike when the price of the papers they were selling was raised by media moguls William Randolph Hearst and Joseph Pulitzer during the Spanish–American War. The boys sing, dance, and fight for organized labor, finally prevailing over the greed of their employers. *Newsies* was a resounding flop on the big screen – the *New York Times*' Janet Maslin called it "joyless," "pointless," and "bungled"[1] – but the picture gained enormous popularity on the expanding Disney channel, which needed content it could air, and then later on home video, becoming a kind of cult classic.[2] Twenty years later, the movie was crafted into a stage musical by book writer Harvey Fierstein, original composer Alan Menken, and original lyricist Jack Feldman. Directed by Jeff Calhoun, *Newsies* premiered at Paper Mill Playhouse in New Jersey in 2011. The production team claims that, fearing a repeat of the movie's flop, they were not planning for the show to go to Broadway. But to Broadway it went: *Newsies the Musical* had its first preview on March 15, 2012 and ran until August 2014, clocking over 1,000 performances at the Nederlander Theatre on West 41st Street. The show was nominated for eight Tony Awards and six Drama Desk Awards, winning at both ceremonies in the categories of Best Choreography and Best Score. After its Broadway run, *Newsies* toured nationally from 2014 to 2016.

Since then, *Newsies*-related media have proliferated, and if the show – like the characters in its plot – once appeared to have underdog status, it has since become a kind of cultural behemoth. In early 2017, Fathom Events released a filmed version of the *Newsies* tour starring some of the original Broadway cast: *Disney's Newsies: The Broadway Musical!* became Fathom's highest-grossing event to date. It screened in multiple movie theatres across the country on February 16, 2017, and it brought in a record $4.7 million for the company.³ *Disney's Newsies: The Broadway Musical!* was so wildly popular that Fathom screened it twice more in 2017 and again in 2018. The filmed theatre event was released digitally for purchase in May 2017, and it then appeared on the streaming service Netflix in September before moving over to competing streamer Disney+. Notwithstanding the popularity of *Newsies* as a digital musical theatre event starring many members of the original Broadway cast, *Newsies* has been even more popular as a licensed property, with hundreds of local productions annually since 2018, including at many high schools, colleges, and universities. In 2020, Music Theatre International released the licensing rights for *Disney's Newsies JR.*, part of their series of Broadway shows rewritten for kids and cut down to 60-minute running times. This, too, has been very popular with school groups and children's theatres. Audiences, in other words, don't want only to watch *Newsies*, they want to do the show too. Licensing was, after all, the reason the movie was adapted into a stage musical in the first place, and in order to discuss the impact of *Newsies* and its connections with LGBTQ politics, we must pay attention not only to the film version in 1992 and the show as it appeared on Broadway in 2012 but also to some of the ways it has been taken up by local performers putting on *Newsies* in Midland, Pennsylvania, or Roanoke, Virginia, or Sullivan, Illinois.

A family-oriented show (almost all reviews of *Newsies* remark on this), perhaps the most notable thing about the Broadway cast of *Newsies* is the number of men it contains. There are two significant female characters in the show, young reporter Katherine Plumber and wise chanteuse Medda Larkin. The cast also includes two other women, and women play nuns and other ensemble roles; the remainder of the cast is entirely male. But if its overwhelming maleness is what immediately strikes one about *Newsies*, what is most memorable about the show is its dancing. The young men in the show – most spectacularly in the number "Seize the Day" – outdo themselves, performing extraordinary feats of terpsichorean athleticism. In the first important review of *Newsies* at Paper Mill, the *New York Times*' David Rooney was delighted by the company's "spring-loaded backflips, airborne spins, rambunctious kicks and balletic pivots," noting the "irrepressible physicality" of "the athletic ensemble."⁴ Just before the show opened on Broadway, the *New York Post* reported that during previews, "there were three midshow standing ovations, triggered in each case by Christopher Gattelli's buoyant choreography."⁵ In the *Daily News*, Joe Dziemianowicz praised the fact that "Gattelli's awesome athletic choreography never quits. He keeps the young dancers flipping, tapping and twirling across the urban landscape."⁶ More descriptively, Wayman Wong described the "athletic and dynamic dances" as "pay[ing] homage to Ortega, Michael Kidd and Gene Kelly."⁷ The *Times*' Ben Brantley, who was decidedly less charmed by *Newsies*, compared the dancing young men to "toddlers on a sugar high at a birthday party," but his review still focused on the energy and athleticism of the dancers: "they keep coming at us in full-speed-ahead phalanxes, fortified by every step in a Broadway-by-the-numbers dance book. There are back flips, cartwheels, somersaults and kick lines galore, not to mention enough pirouettes to fill a whole season of *Swan Lake*."[8] There will be more to say later about the excess Brantley describes, but for now I want simply to note the way critics, almost without exception, describe Gattelli's choreography as energetic, athletic, and most importantly possessing a kind of stamina or relentlessness.

Gattelli won both the Tony Award and the Drama Desk award for his choreography, and since then, the "Seize the Day" dance number has become *Newsies*' calling card: the chorus of dancing newsies made rousing appearances on television, demonstrating Gattelli's athletic choreography not only on the broadcast of the Tony Awards but also on the daytime talk show *The View* and the primetime variety program *Dancing with the Stars*. Further, Disney's education and outreach team taught the "Seize the Day" choreography to visiting groups of adolescents. These visits from schools proved extraordinarily popular: as the program's director Lisa Mitchell noted, "We taught twice as many kids *Newsies* in half a year as we did for *Mary Poppins* and *The Lion King* combined for all of 2012."[9] As part of a fitness program called "*Newsies* Get up and Go!" Gattelli and dancers Michael Fatica and Jacob Guzman even appeared in an instructional video on YouTube, teaching a version of the "Seize the Day" choreo intended to "encourage active lifestyles through dance." This video was released as part of First Lady Michelle Obama's "Let's Move" campaign, an initiative designed to combat childhood obesity and promote children's health. The choreography for the show's hit song was modified specifically for children between 12 and 18.[10]

It makes sense that the *Newsies* publicity team would lead with dance. Many of the artistic contributors to the show refer to dance as the reason they connected with the original 1992 film. Lyricist Jack Feldman has said:

> nothing was as moving to me as the conversations I had with a number of the young actors who told me that it was the movie of *Newsies* that gave them the courage to go to dance class – a socially risky and possibly dangerous decision for a boy even today – and dare to dream of a career in the arts.[11]

Casting director Justin Huff adds that:

> the movie challenged my belief that musicals weren't cool. Finall[y] there was something that allowed me to believe that cool guys do musicals. Christian Bale's rough-and-tumble Jack Kelly . . . gave permission for boys like me to follow their dreams of performing.[12]

Associate director Ricky Hinds notes that even though he had already decided upon a career in musical theatre at age 11, "it wasn't until [he] saw those newsboys dancing their hearts out that [he] realized it was okay to be a boy in the performing arts."[13] Gattelli's own story mirrors these: "I remember sitting in the movie theater and being blown away seeing that many guys my age dancing like that. . . . I just remember sitting there and being so inspired. I saw that it was possible to be a guy and be able to dance like that."[14] The dancing male body, in other words, was a figure with whom many of *Newsies*' contributing artists identified when they were young. The athletic, rebellious newsboy who fought for his rights, joined a union, and stood up to capitalist greed while also singing and dancing was a figure not merely of inspiration but of identity, reassurance, and desire. The men describe seeing the film, recognizing themselves as identical in many ways to the dancing young men, and subsequently feeling more comfortable, more confident about their own desires to sing and dance.

Disney's *Newsies* is intriguing for many reasons, but I focus here on the way that the musical aims for this identification with its audience, especially young people. This chapter argues that the *Newsies* version of maleness is a reinvented one, a maleness that expands in order to include the chorus boy teased by his schoolmates for preferring the athleticism of dance to the fancy footwork and fluidity of football and basketball, a maleness that welcomes the musical theatre kid into its fold. This chapter will examine a new gender performance offered by the men who created *Newsies*. It is my argument that the show realigns maleness in relation to three other figures from the turn of the twentieth century when *Newsies* is set: the child, the woman, and the fairy. First, however, this chapter places *Newsies the Musical* in the context of some of the most important concerns of LGBTQ politics in 2012, anti-bullying campaigns and chosen family. In order to do this, we will examine the chief differences between the 1992 film and the 2012 Broadway show. Next, we will consider how the musical understands mentorship and growing up, including how the musical rethinks *Newsies*' role models – for the boys onstage and the young people in the audience. This chapter will close with one version of that future by moving past the Broadway show and into the local theatres, high schools, and middle schools that are producing *Newsies* not only *for* young people but also starring them.

The Family and the Future

When we compare Kenny Ortega's 1992 film *Newsies* with its twenty-first-century stage version, we are able to see the important shifts Harvey Fierstein made, not only to the structure of the narrative but also to its themes. The show's plot remains one of labor-solidarity and generational struggle, but Fierstein and his collaborators stress very different issues in 2012 than the original screenwriters, Bob Tzudiker and Noni White, did in 1992. These shifts are even more notable because *Newsies* is not a musical about queer people – neither on film nor onstage. It has no characters who identify as lesbian, gay, bisexual, or trans, and it makes no obvious references to queerness. My analysis here, however, is not a "queering" of *Newsies*. To the contrary, I take for granted that the creative team behind *Newsies* in 2012 comprised primarily gay men – Fierstein, Feldman, Calhoun, Gattelli, and producer Tom Schumacher – so that despite an absence of queer characters onstage, I already assume that *Newsies* has an investment in queer youth.[15] What I want to do here is illuminate how the shifts in focus that Fierstein makes in the libretto illustrate some of the most important topics in LGBTQ politics at the beginning of the decade and how this musical addresses those issues.

Tzudiker and White's original *Newsies* screenplay takes part in the long tradition of films released through Walt Disney Pictures about childhood and coming of age. Particular to the mid-1980s and early-1990s, however, was an examination of childhood through the lens of the historical past. *Newsies* was one of several Disney movies from this period that examined the subject of childhood by placing its young heroes and heroines in the past, with films set (especially) during the Great Depression or the nineteenth century. These movies include *The Journey of Natty Gann* (1985), *Return to Oz* (1985), *White Fang* (1991), *Shipwrecked* (1991), and *Wild Hearts Can't Be Broken* (1991). As coming-of-age narratives, each of these films also includes a challenge to traditional gender roles: Tomboy Natty learns to rough it as she finds her way across the country, Jack Conroy in *White Fang* struggles with masculinity as he tries to fulfill his father's dream, and *Wild Hearts* is about the diving-horse rider Sonora Webster. All of these narratives also involve growing up without parents – learning to deal with being abandoned by a loving father or a hostile aunt or becoming the sole support of a family because of the injury of a parent.

Newsies emphasizes its orphanhood/parenthood theme from the very beginning. The film opens by panning up a statue of Horace Greeley, the man who said "Go West, young man, and grow up with the country." At Greeley's feet are a pair of sleeping orphans, and another child lies cradled, asleep in the statue's lap. It's an image that immediately recalls the photographs of orphaned children in turn-of-the-century New York by reformer Lewis Hine, but it recalls these images with a twist. Added to Hines' usual images of abandoned kids is now a material symbol of the absent father. There, where the children's father should be, is an unresponsive bronze effigy. The importance of this opening image is underlined by repetition – in the film's first act, after Jack and Davey have become friends and Jack has gone home to dinner with the Jacobs family, the camera catches Jack looking back inside from the fire escape as Davey's mother cradles little Les in her lap and sings quietly. It is this image that prompts the first bars of "Santa Fe," which, in the film's version, begins:

> So that's what they call a family
> Mother, daughter, father, son
> Guess that everything you heard about is true.
> So you ain't got any family,
> Well, who said you needed one?
> Ain't you glad nobody's waitin' up for you?[16]

In the movie, "Santa Fe" functions as a plaintive but dynamic "I want" song – with a dance break and a horse – in which Jack sings about finding somewhere outside of New York City where he might have a home, where he might find the kind of traditional family Davey and Les have. The concept of Santa Fe figures as the father or mother for whom Jack searches, and he sings to the Southwestern city as an anthropomorphized entity: "Santa Fe, are you there? / Do you swear you won't forget me? / If I found you would you let me come and stay?" Jack has told Davey that his family is out west in Santa Fe, and so he sings, here, to an imagined parent.

On film, *Newsies* repeatedly figures the family along traditional lines. Davey's mother and father are a loving couple who scold the kids good-naturedly and call Davey in to go to bed when it gets too late. When Jack goes to dinner at their house, he arrives the night before Mr. Jacobs' birthday, and his wife Esther has been hiding a cake in the cupboard for the occasion. The images are of domestic contentment, troubled only by the father's lack of a union to fight for him when his bosses discard him after his arm injury. Jack's exclusion from this family unit is immediately clear, but Jack underlines it explicitly in a scene in act three:

JACK. You see, I ain't got nobody tucking me in at night like you. It's just me. I gotta look out for myself, all right?
DAVE. You had the newsies.
JACK. Oh, what did being a newsie ever give me but a dime a day and a few black eyes? You know, I can't afford to be a kid no more, Dave.

Again the film makes clear what is missing in Jack's life, even if he says otherwise: here is a young man who actually *does* need someone tucking him in at night. It's a problem that is solved in the film's final moments, which emphasize Jack's adoption into the Jacobs family unit: Jack walks arm-in-arm with Davey, Sarah, and Les, framed on either side by Denton and Crutchy.[17]

In Ortega's film, the proper functioning of the family is contrasted, on the one hand, by the figure of the orphan and, on the other, by the mistreated child laborer. By act three, *Newsies* fundamentally becomes a film about child labor as such. This is a kind of narrative surprise in the movie, a trump card discovered and then played by the newsboys when their strike feels at its lowest point. Denton, the reporter for the *New York Sun*, writes an article that reveals – to the characters and to the film's audience – that the reason no one is willing to talk about the newsies strike is that 1890s New York runs on child labor. Jack, Davey, and company print the article, and the newsies distribute it – not to the public at large but to the working children of the city – and the film gives us numerous images of underage laborers, working as smiths, housekeepers, delivery boys, and many other jobs. As the newsies deliver the paper, they repeatedly ask the children "Can you read?" reminding the audience that we ought not to assume that they can. This repeated question emphasizes a much more widespread lack of care experienced by the children of the city – they are unloved, uneducated, and destitute.

The problems of the injustices of turn-of-the-century New York City are not solved in any satisfactory way in *Newsies*. Crutchy is released from The Refuge, the juvenile prison, and the evil Snyder, who runs it, is locked up by Governor Roosevelt instead. Pulitzer, too, has been bested by Jack and the newsies, but it is unclear what the outcome of the strike is. Jack says they won and that the strike is over, but this has no real bearing on the hundreds of child laborers who've marched in support of the newsies' strike. These other young people, at last, are not really very important. The film operates on the assumption that the issue of child labor so central to the film's third act is not really a political issue in 1992. As I noted earlier, *Newsies* is just one of a series of movies from the late 1980s and early 1990s that involve escapes into versions of childhoods from the past; these films contrast their stories with the U.S. American childhood of the '80s and '90s, an imagined childhood of suburban safety, positive feelings, good education, and plenty of food to eat. In many ways, then, Ortega's *Newsies* is firmly focused on the children of the past; it doesn't ask its viewers to consider their own political situations or issues affecting young people in the 1990s. Or, to put it a different way, the solutions to the problems of the young people in Ortega's *Newsies* are the usual ones you might expect from the different political factions of the Reagan–Bush era: on one hand, the traditional family and, on the other, the organized labor movement.

Harvey Fierstein's libretto for *Newsies the Musical* places its emphases in different places altogether. Fierstein abandons the film's orphanhood/parenthood theme. Rather than aligning with their parents, the young people in the stage production who have parents actively oppose them. This is most clearly literalized when we find out right before "Once and for All" that Katherine, the daughter of Joseph Pulitzer, has recruited Darcy and Bill, the sons of two other newspaper publishers, to defy the will of their fathers by publishing "The Children's Crusade." We can see it in other subtle ways, as well. The retooled lyrics for "Seize the Day" no longer include the bridge "Neighbor to neighbor / Father to son / One for all / And all for one," a phrase that gets repeated in the film. In 2012, Feldman gave us, instead, "Houston to Harlem / Look what's begun!" replacing the references to neighbors, fathers, and sons.[18] And Mr. and Mrs. Jacobs, whom we meet in the movie's long sequence in which Jack is invited to stay for dinner, have been cut for the stage show. They're mentioned but remain offstage.

The contrast between Davey and Les's happy family and Jack's lack of the same is a central theme and struggle in Ortega's *Newsies*, resolved by the film's final section. The concept of family is still a central concern in the *Newsies* libretto, but in Fierstein's adaptation, family looks very different than it does in the film, and he's completely discarded the orphan/adoption theme. The first song Jack sings in *Newsies the Musical* is "Santa Fe." It's a surprisingly downbeat number with which to open a rousing musical. Fierstein describes his attempts to sell the idea to Alan Menken in his 2022 memoir:

> "You want to open with what?" Menken was perplexed to say the least.
> "'Santa Fe,' sung as a lullaby to Crutchie. Yes! It's his promise to make life better for them":
> *Don't you know that we's a family?*
> *Would I let you down? No way!*
> *Just hold on, kid, till that train makes Santa Fe!*[19]

In the film, Jack sings about "Santa Fe" as a substitute for the "Mother, daughter, father, son" relationships he doesn't have. Fierstein and Feldman have replaced the absent family in the movie with a different family onstage. The lyrics Fierstein quotes here appear at the end of the song, but even earlier in this retooled "Santa

Fe," Jack sings, "Soon your friends are more like fam'ly / And they's begging you to stay," and in the middle of the song, Jack and Crutchie have this (spoken) exchange:

CRUTCHIE. You got folks there?
JACK. Got no folks nowhere. You?
CRUTCHIE. I don't need folks. I got friends.[20]

These three references to friends as family all occur in the prologue to *Newsies*, setting up the show's central relationships, and this theme recurs throughout the show.

Crutchie and Jack's relationship is transformed for the musical so that they become best friends – this is totally absent from the film, in which Jack's friendships with Racetrack, Mush, Spot Conlon, and Boots are all more important than his relationship with Crutchy. The closeness of their relationship onstage is especially evident in "Letter from The Refuge," in which Crutchie signs the letter "Your friend . . . / Your *best* friend . . . / Your brother."[21] The musical, thus, insistently alters the definition of family so that it emphasizes chosen family over biology. In an earlier moment in his "Letter from The Refuge," for example, Crutchie sings "On the rooftop you said that a fam'ly looks out for each other / So you tell all the fellas for me to protect one another," teaching us that the boys are, in fact, each other's family. The message becomes especially clear when comparing the movie with the stage musical. The film's final line, in which Jack decides to stay in New York because, as he says, "I've got family here," emphasizes his incorporation into the Jacobs family unit, his relationships with Sarah, Davey, and Les. This is altered for the stage musical's libretto so that it is Crutchie, instead, who tells Jack, "New York's got us. And we're family."[22] Crutchie's phrase is not the same as the fraternal language used in organized labor – although that too makes an appearance in "Seize the Day" ("You're still our brothers / And we will fight for you.") – *Newsies* onstage gives us the language of chosen family.[23]

The alternative of chosen family was a central tenet of LGBTQ politics in the early part of the decade. Certainly, the issue of marriage equality dominated political discussions related to gay and lesbian people during this period, but the idea of a chosen family also formed one of the core messages of the It Gets Better campaign, which focused on preventing the suicides of LGBTQ-identified teenagers and young people. Appearing in September of 2010, the phrase *It gets better* became a rallying cry with the aim of reaching bullied young people and attempting to give them hope.

The first *It gets better* video was posted by Dan Savage and his husband Terry Miller as a response to the suicide of 15-year-old Billy Lucas, who killed himself after experiencing intense bullying and homophobia at his school in Indiana. Savage explained the impetus behind the videos this way:

> I wish I could have talked to this kid for five minutes. I wish I could have told Billy that *it gets better*. I wish I could have told him that, however bad things were, however isolated and alone he was, *it gets better*.

But gay adults aren't allowed to talk to these kids. Schools and churches don't bring us in to talk to teenagers who are being bullied. Many of these kids have homophobic parents who believe that they can prevent their gay children from growing up to be gay – or from ever coming out – by depriving them of information, resources, and positive role models.

Why are we waiting for permission to talk to these kids? We have the ability to talk directly to them right now. We don't have to wait for permission to let them know that *it gets better*. We can reach these kids.[24]

Savage called on other LGBTQ-identifying adults to make videos that communicated their own struggles as kids but that also, and more importantly, articulated what life can be like for queer kids in the future if they stick out the miseries of adolescence and decide against committing suicide.

The idea went viral very quickly, and just as quickly *It gets better* became a message that was being shared by *non*-LGBTQ-identified people, including some very famous ones. Less than a month after Savage's original video, and just days after U.S. Secretary of State Hillary Clinton released hers, U.S. President Barack Obama recorded an It Gets Better video, addressing queer young people with the messages "you are not alone" and "there is a whole world waiting for you filled with possibilities." Obama's message was addressed specifically to LGBT youth, but he folded the ideas of embracing our differences and things getting better for young queer people into a larger message of the nation itself getting better, noting that LGBT adults are more likely to fight discrimination in all its forms.

It Gets Better and related campaigns such as Love Is Louder were founded as anti-bullying, anti-suicide campaigns aimed directly at LGBTQ youth.[25] These campaigns were consciously linked almost immediately with musical theatre. In the first It Gets Better video, Savage told viewers, "I was picked on because, you know . . . I liked musicals, and I was obviously gay,"[26] and musical theatre performers were some of the first celebrities to make videos. Neil Patrick Harris's video – under the Love Is Louder banner – encouraged young people by saying: "You can act with strength, you can act with courage, you can act with class and stand tall, be proud of who you are. . . . This is a good time we live in, and we're being granted more and more rights, and it will continue in that direction, and, yeah, be proud."[27] Other connections between It Gets Better and musical theatre include the campaign's first public service announcement, which featured Nick Adams, Tony Sheldon, and Will Swenson from the cast of 2011's *Priscilla, Queen of the Desert*, and an ad for Google Chrome featuring Savage discussing It Gets Better, which aired during a May 2011 episode of *Glee*. Several theatre organizations, such as Center Theatre Group in Los Angeles, released It Gets Better videos, and a group of gay and straight Broadway stars released a video through Broadway Cares/Equity Fights AIDS. The BC/EFA video, which appeared in November 2010, featured 64 Broadway writers, directors, and actors, including Nathan Lane, Audra McDonald, Colman Domingo, Cherry Jones, Billy Porter, Robin de Jesús, and Lin-Manuel Miranda.

The usual structure of these videos was as follows: participants acknowledged the difficulties of being a gay, lesbian, or trans adolescent, they highlighted the benefits of getting older and becoming a queer adult, they told young people about the non-biological families that queer adults get to find and make, and they attempted to convince kids experiencing bullying to turn their attentions away from present difficulties and instead toward the possibilities ahead of them. The BC/EFA video, like many of these videos, took a further step – it switched over to address adults directly, encouraging them to help bullied youth and donate to the LGBTQ organizations Reach Out and the Trevor Project.[28]

Somewhat of a turning point for the movement came in late 2012 when the San Francisco 49ers became the first NFL team to release an It Gets Better video only later to have some of the players who appeared in the video distance themselves from supporting LGBTQ youth.[29] Two of the players denied making the video; they had apparently understood the It Gets Better campaign to be about bullying, but they had not agreed to encourage LGBTQ kids. I note this moment at the end of 2012 as a turning point because the players' confusion here signals that the philosophy of It Gets Better had become mainstream – not as a message specifically for queer young people but one standing in opposition to bullying and in support of bullied kids in general. Although organizations such as the New York City Fire Department, the Austin Police Department, and the Canadian Royal Mounties still made videos featuring gay and lesbian members of their organizations talking directly to LGBTQ kids, the figure of the teen who is bullied for reasons *other* than queerness had become more mainstream. On Broadway, this apparently straight bullied kid was soon to appear in *Dear Evan Hansen* (2016), *Be More Chill* (2019), and, of course, *Newsies*.

The period of 2010–2012 was peak It Gets Better popularity, with numerous new videos released each week, and these years overlapped precisely with *Newsies*' development: Fierstein began reworking the *Newsies* libretto in 2010, emphasizing chosen family over patriarchal structures.[30] Fierstein has not discussed It Gets Better's importance to *Newsies* as such, but in March of 2022, in an interview for *Time*, Alex Rees noted that the playwright had actually used this exact phrase in 1979 in the third part of *Torch Song Trilogy*: Mrs. Beckoff says "It gets better" to her son Arnold, attempting to help him with his grief about losing his partner – to a fatally violent act of homophobia no less.[31] Rees asked Fierstein to talk about the phrase and what it means to him, and his reply highlights the other fundamental change the playwright made to the libretto of *Newsies*:

> Whatever you survive becomes a triumph, right? And I think time, you know, does make things better. Does it bring somebody back to life? No. But [it] makes it easier to take that breath without that incredible pain underneath. Do things get better politically just because time passes? No. You actually have to do the work. One thing that people don't understand, and I don't understand why they don't understand, is that you can't go backwards. Nothing goes backwards! . . . [A]nd if you're not looking to the future you're not alive. You are saying, *I am no longer a force in the world. I am just a memory*. And that's no way to live.[32]

Unlike so many of Disney's films about childhood in the '80s and '90s, the libretto for *Newsies* onstage is focused – like the videos telling teens *it gets better* – on the future. Fierstein here has elaborated on the future-directed message of "The World Will Know," written for the 1992 film, but in the show this theme recurs repeatedly, beginning with Jack telling Crutchie "Just hold on, kid / Till that train makes Santa Fe" in the prologue, and continuing through Katherine's "Just look around / At the world we're inheriting / And think of the one we'll create" in "Watch What Happens" to Jack and Katherine's love song, in which they sing, "The world finds ways to sting you / And then one day decides to bring you / Something to believe in."[33]

I will have more to say later about this faith in the future that is central to *Newsies'* message, but I want to underline here how fundamentally the key tenets of the It Gets Better campaign have been incorporated into *Newsies*. There are no LGBTQ-identified adults in *Newsies* telling young people about how great their lives are now, but vital to the entire show is a commitment to making a better future for young people, a focus on chosen family, and constant encouragement that the world can be improved. At the show's climax, after the police attack the boys, Jack battles with his own grief, even using the language of suicidal ideation: "Just be real is all I'm askin'," he sings, "Not some paintin' in my head / 'Cause I'm dead if I can't count on you today."[34] Act 1 ends with Jack at his lowest point. He's brought out of these negative thoughts by a vision of the future articulated by Katherine and Davey, who tell him that the reason for the violence the newsies experienced was not because of anything the boys did wrong – it was because the men trying to keep them down were scared of *them*. These are the ideas that are central to Jack's first scene in act 2; his friends convince him not to give up, that what appears to be causing his grief is really his power, and that the people committing violence are the ones who are afraid. These are some of the same messages queer adults had been posting for queer adolescents on YouTube since 2010.

Something for the Boys Becoming Men

In *The Male Dancer*, Ramsay Burt's important foray into discussions of masculinity in dance, one finds a curious axis of comparison: although Burt describes an interest in the "male dancer," his text is "primarily concerned . . . with images of men in twentieth-century theatre dance."[35] The book finds itself describing men and masculinity in contrast, in the first place, to women and, later in the book, to gay men. What Burt most conspicuously leaves out of his discussion are male dancers who are *not* men. In fact, Burt consistently describes masculinity as though it is only legible when contrasted with femininity. He also invariably conflates male homosexuality with femininity; there is no concept of gay male masculinity in *The Male Dancer*.[36] Burt avoids altogether an entirely different yet common axis along which men describe their own maleness: boyhood. But as historian Michael Kimmel argues in his discussion of U.S. American masculinity in the eighteenth century, "Being a man meant also not being a boy. A man was independent, self-controlled, responsible; a boy was dependent, irresponsible, and lacked control."[37] Kimmel makes clear that definitions of masculinity and manhood would shift numerous times over the ensuing centuries, but being a man never only means not being a woman; it also means not being a boy – among other things. Masculinity need not only contrast with femininity; it is often described in contrast to juvenility.

The most significant feature of New York's newsboys in turn-of-the-century discussions of labor, poverty, and criminality was the fact of their minority. Jacob Riis's famous exposés *How the Other Half Lives* (1890) and *The Children of the Poor* (1892) describe abandoned, impoverished adolescents fending for themselves on the streets and often sleeping in alleyways, huddled together for warmth. He reports that "Three-fourths of the young men called on to plead to generally petty offences in the courts are under twenty years of age, poorly clad, and without means."[38] The street urchin, Riis says, "is as much an institution in New York as Newspaper Row, to which he gravitates naturally," and Riis feelingly describes the typical child:

> Crowded out of the tenements to shift for himself, and quite ready to do it, he meets [on Newspaper Row] the host of adventurous runaways from every State in the Union and from across the sea, whom New York attracts with a queer fascination, as it attracts the older emigrants from all parts of the world.[39]

Riis's photographs of these boys capture children as young as five clutching piles of newspapers and hawking them on the street. Some of the boys are older, a few are teenagers, but they are all quite obviously children, and there are thousands of them.

Jack Kelly, the main character in *Newsies*, is 17 years old ("Trapped where there ain't no future, / Even at seventeen," he sings in "Santa Fe"), and he is surrounded by boys of indeterminate age whom the musical asks us to assume are Jack's juniors.[40] He refers to the other newsboys as "kids" after the violent crackdown in Newsie Square; Katherine and Davey, too, both call the young men "kids," and Katherine titles her article about the strike "The Children's Crusade."[41] *Newsies* is insistent about its characters' youth. The Broadway show's educational packet, which was aimed at student groups visiting the show, features photographs by contemporary reformer Lewis Hine of children obviously under the age of ten, and under the heading "Child Labor!," the packet defines *newsie* as

> a term for a *child* who sold newspapers on the streets at the turn of the century. The newsies of New York City were popularly admired as "little merchants," for, unlike *children* working for a company in factories, the newsies were seen as being business people.[42]

Critics writing about *Newsies*, too, took the characters' minority for granted. Nearly all reviews of the musical compared the show to either *Annie* or *Oliver!* and, more often than not, to both of them.⁴³ *Oliver!* and *Annie* are both musicals about large numbers of scruffy, scrappy, orphaned children, but it is worth noting that these shows are also usually performed by child actors. *Newsies* on Broadway, however, was not performed by boys. There were child actors employed by the show, but these boys were alternates for the role of Les, Davey's 10-year-old brother; the other actors were 17 or older. Although Christian Bale, for example, was 17 when he played Jack Kelly in the 1992 film, Jeremy Jordan, who originated the role onstage and later became famous on the NBC series *Smash*, was nearly 27 when the show premiered in 2011. Ben Fankhauser, who played Davey (age 17 in the script), was a relatively young 21 during the Paper Mill run, but Andrew Keenan-Bolger, who played Crutchie (age 15), was 26. In its Paper Mill and Broadway runs, *Newsies* was almost entirely performed by adults in their 20s.⁴⁴

Popular criticism ignored this age discrepancy with near uniformity. In *Variety*, after the requisite mentions of *Oliver!* and *Annie*, Steven Suskin described the choreography as "16 boys jumping, bounding and comporting themselves like a gang of Jets on a West Side playground,"⁴⁵ and Elisabeth Vincentelli in the *New York Post* said that the newsies are "so adorable, you want to pinch their cheeks and give them whatever they want."⁴⁶ The term *newsboys* might seem natural enough when referring to the characters, of course, but pinching cheeks and boys on playgrounds? Calhoun's production of *Newsies* unabashedly treated these adult men as objects of desire. The newsies were even introduced in the bathroom at the top of "Carrying the Banner": two shirtless newsies entered first, and then another group came onstage in undershirts, arms exposed, biceps bulging. These were "boys" who apparently also found time to hit the gym.

If Disney Theatricals and popular news media were invested in referring to the adult male actors as kids or boys, they simultaneously laid no small stress on Jeremy Jordan's masculinity and power in the lead role of Jack Kelly. Chris Montan, Disney Theatricals' executive music producer, was glad "to have a guy like Jeremy, who could be masculine in the part and still sing a lot of numbers. It was like the old John Raitt days," he said, "where these really handsome guys enter and bang out these songs with self-confidence. Jeremy helped galvanize the whole cast around a strong, masculine Jack Kelly."⁴⁷ In the same review in which she reports wanting to pinch the actors' cheeks, Elisabeth Vincentelli calls Jordan a "hunk" and says he "hits a good balance of sexiness and humor."⁴⁸ Several other reviewers refer to Jordan's sex appeal and masculinity, and descriptions of this sort were also common among the show's main collaborators: the *Daily News*, for example, quotes Alan Menken as saying "Jeremy is a dream. In his looks and his acting, he's like a young Marlon Brando."⁴⁹ Menken's comment is both typical and intriguing: he refers to Jordan as both masculine and young. Brando, in fact, was three years *younger* than Jordan when he was on Broadway in *A Streetcar Named Desire* and 26 when he made the iconic film version, the same age as Jordan at the time of his debut in *Newsies*. To put it another way, Disney and the popular press described Jordan as a masculine *boy*, and in this way, they created an extraordinary slippage between the men onstage and the children they were portraying, not only as beings capable of achieving and demonstrating masculinity but also as objects of desire and identification for audience members.

Feminine Power

The most important structural change as *Newsies* moved onstage was Fierstein's decision to insert a love story. The love story in the film, between Jack and Davey's sister Sarah, is mostly an afterthought, not at all central to the plot. This is indicated, especially, by the music: Sarah is neither given a song of her own nor does she share a duet with Jack.[50] In Fierstein's libretto, love, while unquestionably taking a back seat to the chorus's dance moves, is much more important. The courageous reporter played by Bill Pullman in the movie has been transformed into a beautiful 18-year-old writer named Katherine (played by Kara Lindsay), unhappily stuck in the society pages. This gender switch necessitates the delightful lyric "Am-scray punk, / She's the king of New York!" and what it means for the plot is that the love story becomes a prominent feature of the show.[51]

Another result of this gender transformation is that the number of likable adult men in *Newsies* is significantly reduced. In the 1992 film, Davey and Les's father is a caring, thoughtful, and upbeat role model played by Jeffrey DeMunn. Even more importantly, the boys also have Bryan Denton, Bill Pullman's reporter character, as a role model: he pays the corrupt judge's fines to bail them out of jail, he picks up the check at the restaurant, and he contacts Theodore Roosevelt to get The Refuge shut down. There is also the caring Mr. Kloppman, who runs the boarding house where the newsboys live and loyally lies to the authorities about Jack's whereabouts. Fierstein's libretto dispenses with the roles of Mr. Jacobs, Denton, and Mr. Kloppman, and this means that with the exception of Theodore Roosevelt, there is, in fact, no adult male role model in the show. Joseph Pulitzer is the show's villain, and the other adult males in the show include Snyder, the evil proprietor of The Refuge, the cruel Wiesel, and a group of policemen who beat up the newsies when they try to go on strike.

Even the adult men who *don't* appear in the show function as poor models for the boys as they aim toward some kind of adult behavior. Jack's dad, we are told, was destroyed by New York City, and Davey and Les's dad is out of work, made disposable by his employers, and dependent on the boys so that the family can eat.[52] The rest of the men the newsies discuss are either referred to with derision ("Try any banker, bum or barber. / They almost all knows how to read"), fear ("Me father's gonna kill me anyway!"), or reflect a lack of care or even outright neglect ("Wait 'til my old man gets a load of dis. I won't be last in line for the tub tonight").[53] Indeed, as I noted earlier, when the newsies go to publish "The Children's Crusade," they find help from Darcy and Bill, the sons of the men who own the *Tribune* and the *Journal*. The boys in *Newsies* are actively opposed to the show's adult men.

Katherine does mention reformer and anti-racist liberal Horace Greeley – whose statue functions so prominently in the film – as a possible model in act 2, but Jack dismisses Greeley quickly as someone who was crushed by the city.[54] Not that the musical is completely without an adult male hero: Teddy Roosevelt charges in at the end of the show to save the day (a kind of *gubernator ex machina*), and he was indeed a voice for social reform, as well as a close friend of Jacob Riis. Michael Kimmel describes Roosevelt as "the perfect embodiment of American-as-adolescent boy-man. His definition of manhood was . . . a relentless test to be proved constantly and in every arena in which men find themselves."[55] But this is not *Newsies*' version of the governor. Roosevelt's interaction with the newsboys is limited to a handshake and a short word or two of advice. "Keep your eyes on the star[s] and your feet on the ground," he tells Jack. A bit later, and more significantly, Roosevelt asserts the important future-directed focus of the show itself: "Each generation must, at the height of its power, step aside and invite the young to share the day," he says to the group of assembled newsies. "You have laid claim to our world, and I believe the future, in your hands, will be bright and prosperous."[56] But rather than espousing a maleness that needs to prove itself around other men, this version of Roosevelt might more precisely be described as following the lead of the most important female voice in the show, Katherine, who, in act 1, sings the lyrics:

> Just look around
> At the world we're inheriting,
> And think of the one we'll create.
> Their mistake is they got old.
> That is not a mistake we'll be making,
> No, sir, we'll stay young forever!
>
> Give those kids and me
> The brand new century
> And watch what happens![57]

Following Katherine's lead becomes a thematic trend throughout the rest of the show.

After beginning the tap number "King of New York" and showing off their innovative dance skills using the props available to them – spoons, chairs, table – Race, Albert, Elmer, and the other young men invite Katherine to join the dance. They scoff at her first few moves, but the dance quickly becomes a call and response with Katherine leading and the other dancers following. This culminates in Katherine doing a leg extension, a dance movement typically performed by women. This movement, which extends the leg up to the dancer's head, also emphasizes the dancer's body as female, since it necessitates lifting her skirt. The femininity of this particular dance move is further underlined by the choreography: this time the other dancers don't copy Katherine's movement; instead, the characters scream with apparent pleasure and astonishment. Next, Katherine does a cross with the

80 It Gets Better Than Boyhood

same props the young men have used – the spoon, the chair, the broom – doing riffs on the boys' choreography. After this, they all dance together: now she's one of the boys.

What I am noting here is the way the choreography of the young men's movement physically incorporates the woman's moves. Narratively, the young men accept Katherine as one of their own, and this story is told through Gattelli's choreography. Whether the young men precisely mimic Katherine's feminine leg extension or not, then, this movement functions as a powerful and virtuosic flourish that works to incorporate traditionally feminine phrases into the range of choreographic possibilities available to the young men.

Jack, for his part, also follows Katherine's lead, taking very seriously her advice that "Being [the] boss doesn't mean you have all the answers. Just the brains to recognize the right one when you hear it."[58] Katherine's advice to Jack in this sequence is a calm, reasoned attack on traditional masculinity. Jack does not need to be a person who does everything on his own. Katherine reminds him: "The strike was your idea. The rally was Davey's. And now my plan will take us to the finish line. Deal with it."[59] She advocates teamwork over the posturing, solitary masculinity of the adult men in the show. Jack agrees and adopts this alternate masculinity for himself so much that he repeats Katherine's line in the play's penultimate scene. When Pulitzer declares with capitalist conviction that "Anyone who does not act in his own self-interest is a fool," Jack responds by telling Davey that "Guys like Joe don't talk with nothin's like us. But a very wise reporter told me a real boss don't need the answers. Just the smarts to snatch the right one when he hears it."[60] The young men, in other words, are not without role models; it's just that the primary role models in *Newsies* are women.

Theatricalized Gender

The most spectacular of the newsies' role models is, of course, the chanteuse and entrepreneur Medda Larkin. In Ortega's film, Medda is introduced as "the Swedish Meadowlark," a name that burlesques the "Swedish Nightingale," nineteenth-century soprano Jenny Lind, who toured the United States in the 1850s. This reference to Lind would have been obscure to viewers in the 1990s, but musical fans might now recognize Lind as the touring opera singer from 2017's *The Greatest Showman* who belted "Never Enough." In *Newsies*, the Swedish Meadowlark is played by Ann-Margret with a vague Swedish accent, and she has two songs – "My Lovey-Dovey Baby," which she sings early in the first act, and "High Times, Hard Times," which she and the boys sing together as entertainment at the newsies' rally. "High Times, Hard Times" was given the Razzie award in 1993 and named the worst original song of the year, but one wonders why they selected Medda's second song as worse than her first. "My Lovey-Dovey Baby" consists entirely of baby-talk lyrics designed to be both sexy and juvenile, including "I miss the coochie-woochie" and the phrase "I used to be your tootsie-wootsie / Then you said toodley-doo." Both of Medda's songs in the film are straightforward imitations of a certain type of teasing vaudeville number, but neither song is developed along the lines of the popular turn-of-the-century New York theatre scene. "My Lovey-Dovey Baby," the song that introduces Medda in the film, portrays her as an infantilized figure, speaking in baby-talk and begging for her man to come back to her.

In the Paper Mill production of *Newsies*, Medda was played by white actress Helen Anker. Capathia Jenkins took over the role on Broadway, and reviews began stating that the character was loosely based on the Black musical theatre star and "Queen of the Cakewalk" Aida Overton Walker.[61] In the lyrics to her song "That's Rich," however, Medda tells us that:

> Some guys give me ermine, chinchilla and mink,
> And [some] give me diamonds as big as a sink,
> But you wouldn't give me [so] much as a wink –
> Now baby, that's rich.

And if her reference to diamonds doesn't immediately recall the Mae West of *She Done Him Wrong* (1933), her double entendre in the same song – "Seems whatever I touch starts to rise" – ought surely to make us think of "is that a pistol in your pocket or are you just glad to see me?"[62] Fierstein and Feldman – clearly enjoying themselves with these references – drive home the comparison in *Newsies*' final scene, in which Medda exits on Teddy Roosevelt's arm saying "Come along, Governor[,] and show me the back seat I've been hearing so much about."[63]

Mae West flourishes like this abound in *Newsies*, and they drop hints (hairpins, if you will) to the audience about the existence of a different New York from the one on which this family-oriented show focuses, an adult world with which real newsies in 1899 would likely have been quite familiar. I refer, of course, to the vibrant gay world detailed by historian George Chauncey in the seminal book *Gay New York*. Chauncey describes a highly visible subculture of men prior to the invention of homosexuality, a subculture that was "participating in and expanding a street culture already developed by working-class youths seeking freedom from their families' supervision" in New York City's tenements.[64] One of the most colorful figures from 1890s New York was the *fairy*: the word described persons with recognizably male anatomy who adopted "effeminate mannerisms" as "a deliberate cultural strategy" that allowed them to "negotiate their relationship with other men."[65] There are, to be sure, no fairies onstage in *Newsies*, but in 1899 New York City, they were a fixture in places like Paresis Hall and other Bowery "resorts" in Manhattan's Lower East Side. The newsies' colorful handles in both history (Kid Blink, Crazy Arborn, Barney Peanuts, Scabutch) and the musical (Racetrack, Romeo, Specs, Buttons, Spot) certainly align them with the delightfully disreputable world of prostitutes, fairies, and queens, who have always given themselves *noms de guerre* (Violet, Blossom, Edna May, Big Tess, Loop-to-Loop).

Even the real-life performers on whom Medda Larkin (also an obvious pseudonym) is based were known for their gender-bending performances: Mae West was a great friend of drag queens in 1920s New York, and her persona was partially based on well-known turn-of-the-century female-impersonator Julian Eltinge; her 1927 play *The Drag* infamously included numerous drag performers, a plot about a gay murderer, and open discussion of contemporary sexological theories about homosexuality. Aida Overton Walker, too, became famous as a brilliant comedienne and dancer, performing with Bert Williams and George Walker in their pioneering Broadway musical *In Dahomey* (1903), but she was also an occasional male impersonator who sensationally stood in for a role her husband George usually played, and male drag numbers became one of Walker's specialties.[66] Male impersonation, of course, was a mainstay of burlesque performance in the late nineteenth century.[67]

In the period in New York City before "homosexuality" caught on as a way of classifying sexual desire, a fairy was a person who populated this turn-of-the-century world. Fairies were men who wanted to have sex with men and who, in order better to accomplish this, presented themselves as effeminate – as sharing identity with women. Chauncey says that because of this "the fairy, so long as he abided by the conventions of this cultural script, was tolerated in much of working-class society." Perhaps even more intriguingly, the fairy was so obviously a "third-sexer," a different species of human being, that his very effeminacy served to confirm rather than threaten the masculinity of other men, particularly since it often exaggerated the conventions of deference and gender difference between men and women.[68]

In other words, the existence of the fairy helps us see that turn-of-the-century maleness was shaped not only by men wishing to present as masculine but also by men wishing to present as feminine. In many ways, these queer men helped to shore up the borders of masculinity. They saw masculinity as a desirable feature in a sexual object but not a feature they wished to adopt in their own gender performance. The fairy, like the sissy discussed in Chapter 1, is a figure who verifies the masculinity of other men through difference. The sissy is a figure *created by* men who are policing their own codes of masculinity; the fairy, by contrast, *adopts* this feminine gender performance as a style in order to confirm the masculinity of other men.

As Menken, Feldman, Fierstein, Calhoun, and Gattelli have fashioned *Newsies*, maleness has been decoupled – as, indeed, it would have been in 1899 New York – from any ideas about so-called "sexual orientation." Ever so subtly, Feldman has even altered lyrics that make assumptions about the newsies' heterosexuality: in 1992, the newsboys dreamed of "a porcelain tub with boilin' water," and "a Saturday night with the mayor's daughter." In 2012, they sang, "Pastrami on rye with a sour pickle . . . / My personal puss on a wooden nickel."[69] At the same time as sexuality is de-emphasized, masculinity in *Newsies* has become attached to, even combined with, a figure against which it is traditionally placed in contrast – the boy. And if we see masculine power in the figures of these newsboys, working to make a living like little men in the city, *Newsies* asks us to see just as much power in the women who function as these young men's role models. The show finds strength in both femininity *and* masculinity, and it gives the newsies and those who identify with them access to both.

Gender Performance and the Neoliberal Future

Two more articles about masculinity and dance in musical theatre are worth noting. Musical theatre scholars George Rodosthenous and Judith Sebesta have both chosen to discuss masculinity in dance by analyzing musicals about boys rather than men, primarily *Billy Elliot* and *Spring Awakening*.[70] These scholars have turned their attention to boys attempting to perform a masculinity that they do not possess, as though one might better be able to visualize masculinity as such if it is removed from the bodies of men (this is an argument carefully outlined by queer theorist Jack Halberstam in *Female Masculinity*).[71] Both scholars refer to aggressive movements and athleticism in the boys' dances. They see masculinity as re-written in *Billy Elliot* and *Spring Awakening*, and Sebesta (following Rodosthenous) suggests the possibility that dance might "offe[r] the real potential for material change in our perception of, and constitution of, masculine identities."[72]

I also want to return to Ben Brantley's curmudgeonly but right-on-target *New York Times* review of the show. One of the things that bothered the critic about *Newsies* was that it didn't know "when to quit." Brantley found Gattelli's choreography excessive and insistent: "just when you think a number is over, it starts up again, and no sooner are you recovering from that one, then there's another one, with all the same darn back flips, pirouettes, etc."[73] Brantley is, no doubt, correct, but if the newsboys dance more than is necessary, working hard to demonstrate their agility, energy, athleticism, and stamina, in this way, they reflect a fundamental trait of masculinity itself as gratuitous performance, dependent on what queer theorist Robert McRuer has called "compulsory able-bodiedness."[74] Traditional masculinity is always excessive, a performance (simultaneously) of identity and individuality designed to stave off fears "that others will see [one] as weak, timid, frightened," but that also works to compete with and dominate others.[75] By emphasizing the extraordinary effort involved in executing the *Newsies* choreography, Gattelli, in fact, makes the theatrical element of masculinity abundantly clear. In this way, the show critiques masculinity, not by calling it bad, but by calling masculinity out as performance.

Newsies not only makes colorable the theatrical aspect of masculinity but also expands its own version of masculinity so that, for the newsies, desirable ways of moving in the world also include traditionally feminine movements. What is important about this is that *Newsies the Musical* is not aimed primarily at men and women but at children and adolescents. One could accurately describe a majority of the characters onstage as minor, and the key audience for whom they are performing is minor as well. But though the characters are boys, the actors who played them on Broadway were men. The feats of ability the dancers perform in "Seize the Day" demonstrate a virtuosity and skill that cannot be achieved by a majority of the show's intended audience . . . yet. *Newsies* actively courts identification between the newsies and the "fansies" as kids. Young people in the audience, particularly boys, are asked to identify with, and aspire to be, as athletic, powerful, graceful, and happy as the "boys" onstage. *Newsies*, in other words, does not attempt to remake or refashion masculinity for adults. What it does instead is attempt to expand the range of acceptable gender performance possibilities for the boys and girls identifying with these characters. And when they grow up – when, that is, they become adults of whatever gender, and it gets better – they might perhaps understand their own bodies as less constrained by masculinity than the generation previous.

As I noted earlier, *Newsies* actively hails this younger generation in the audience, underlining the generation gap between Pulitzer and the newsboys numerous times. The most anthemic musical phrase in the entire show (from the 11 o'clock number "Once and for All") is accompanied by the lyrics:

> There's change comin' once and for all.
> You're getting' too old,
> Too weak to keep holdin' on.
> A new world is gunnin' for you,
> And Joe, we is too,
> Till once and for all you're gone![76]

and this generational shift signals not only a new world (of labor equity, justice, teamwork, and family) but also a different type of gendered being-in-the-world, a new world with a new type of adult to inhabit it. *Newsies* uses choreography, lyrics, and music physically to enact the possibilities held by this new world gunning for its audience. For if the boys in the show have no male role models for their onstage version of masculinity, the men playing those boys serve as precisely that for a new generation of boys and girls who won't be afraid to dance – who will feel more comfortable moving, in other words, in ways that are traditionally considered feminine.

As we've been tracking the way *Newsies* works, and even though I've been arguing that the show embraces femininity in gender performance in a way the film did not, the *maleness* of this musical – its creative team, its narrative, and its performers – remains on full display. The men who created the show have primarily addressed themselves to queer youth who are also male, and indeed the teen suicides that prompted the work of the It Gets Better project were the deaths of young white males. But it is worth considering here what *Newsies the Musical*'s focus on maleness, the vulnerability of queer (white) boys, and a consistent future-directed orientation might be working to cover over. As queer theorist Jasbir Puar asks us to consider in a 2012 article for GLQ, "what is lost in the naming of a death as a 'gay youth suicide?'"[77] How might singling out suicide, especially the suicides of queer white boys, make invisible the way others are debilitated by capitalism and by the requirements of a neoliberal society? For Puar, "the queer neoliberalism embedded in the tendentious mythologizing that 'it gets better'" is almost so obvious that it isn't worth critiquing: "'It gets better' is a mandate to fold oneself into urban neoliberal gay enclaves: a call to upward mobility that discordantly echoes the now-discredited 'pull yourself up by the bootstraps' immigrant motto."[78] The movement's focus on the future asks young people to ignore the present, to suffer through it, and in this way, It Gets Better fails to deal with the very real problems that might cause a young person to want to commit suicide in the first place, instead shoring up urban gay life as an ideal existence (*New York's got us. And we're family*).

Puar places these teen suicides in the larger contexts of disability politics, labor, and the medical–industrial complex, asking instead why suicide is "considered the ultimate loss of life" and "connecting these suicides to the theorization of debility and capacity."[79] To attempt to move away from evaluating suicide as the ultimate loss of life is not to minimize the tragedy of these boys' deaths but rather to ask how a different concept of

> slow death might open us up to a range of connections. For instance, how do queer girls commit suicide? What of the slow deaths of teenage girls through anorexia, bulimia, and numerous sexual assaults they endure as punishment for the transgressing of proper femininity and alas, even for conforming to it?[80]

Puar's questions seem especially apt here because if *Newsies* is fundamentally indebted to the It Gets Better movement, it is also a musical about wage labor performed by young people, and, even more, one with a physically disabled teenager as a central character. It also mostly ignores the difficulties of being a girl, in favor of offering new ways to be a boy. Like much of the politics around It Gets Better, *Newsies* focuses on the future, attempting to reincorporate young people within a future-directed neoliberal politics. It is an attempt to reimagine queerness as on the side of reproductive futurism, refiguring queerness so that it might name the side of those "fighting for the children."[81]

Puar's reformulation asks us, on the other hand, to consider:

> Which debilitated bodies can be reinvigorated for neoliberalism, and which cannot? In this regard, Savage's project refigures queers, along with other bodies heretofore construed as excessive/erroneous, as being on the side of capacity, ensuring that queerness operates as a machine of regenerative productivity.[82]

All of which is to say that if *Newsies* is a musical deeply informed by a particular LGBTQ politics, these politics are doing very specific ideological work, reincorporating young people who are experiencing hopelessness, depression, and disability back into the labor force and the neoliberal order. *Newsies* asks them to focus not on their present difficulties or even on the day-to-day labor of selling papers but on the possibilities of an affluent life in a world they'll be fashioning and the connections they are going to make with a family they'll choose.

Just a Pretty Face

The arguments I've been making about the maleness of *Newsies*, the role models it provides, and the expanded possibilities for gender performance it offers for young audiences might work for the musical as it appeared on Broadway and on tour, as well as in the recorded performance of the show which played in cinemas and is available through streaming services. But these arguments about masculinity fail to account for the hundreds of different licensed performances of *Newsies* that happen annually around the country. In most of these performances, the newsies are *not* uniformly played by adult men. The cast of the national tour skewed younger, though the newsies remained all male, but casts of *Newsies* in various productions around the country have differed in all sorts of ways, with young women playing girl newsies, with young women playing newsies *as boys*, with girls playing little Les, and with young women playing Race or Crutchie.[83] Directors and producers of *Newsies* at high schools and universities have a great deal of leeway with how they can cast the show, and Music Theatre International, which licenses these productions, provides a handbook from Disney Theatrical Productions that specifically lists characters such as Crutchie, Spot Conlon, Snyder, and others as "gender-flexible."[84]

This is no afterthought; the DTP handbook contains the following message on its very first page:

> Disney Theatrical Productions is committed to making our titles accessible to, and inclusive of, everyone. Throughout this Production Handbook, you will find casting, costuming, and dramaturgical tips that offer nontraditional and gender-flexible approaches to *Newsies* and its characters. Similarly, . . . we have decided to embrace the singular "they" – for reasons of both inclusivity and efficiency – and we hope these efforts inspire you to approach this material, and the casting of your production, with an open mind and heart.

The fluid approach that DTP encourages here perfectly reflects its contemporary moment in LGBTQ politics, and it articulates a decided change from the representational practices of the 2012 Broadway production, although the show's perspective vis-à-vis these politics remains. The handbook's use of gender-neutral pronouns and its reconceptualization of the show as filled with characters who can be male, female, or nonbinary, depending on the actors and the needs of the production, doesn't rethink *Newsies*' messages of gender fluidity so much as it doubles down on them by addressing the show's ideas about expanded ranges of gender performance to young people assigned male at birth *and* young people assigned female at birth.

Newsies JR., the 60-minute adaptation of the musical designed to be licensed for elementary and middle schools, makes this even more explicit. In this version of the show, with an adapted libretto by David Simpatico, Katherine is given a "trustworthy photographer" named Darcy; the owner of the *Trib* has a daughter, Dorothy, instead of a son; and Medda's backup singers, the Bowery Brigade, now have lines and names – Ada, Ethel, and Olive.[85] The newsies, too, boast recognizably female names in their ranks, including Nancy, Muriel, Hazel, and Pigtails, and in *Newsies* JR., the girl newsies stand up for Katherine when Davey doesn't think she's "a real reporter" who is important enough to write about the strike:

HAZEL: Give her a chance, she's all right!
PIGTAILS: I'm with Hazel! If a girl can sell the pape, why can't she write it?
GIRL NEWSIES: *Yeah!*[86]

Further opening up casting options, Les is named as Davey's "younger sibling" in this adaptation, and Crutchie no longer refers to Jack as "brother" in "Letter from the Refuge," leaving Crutchie/Casey's gender identity open.[87]

I have argued in this chapter that the 2012 Broadway production hailed young audience members (especially boys) with the message that *It gets better*. I noted, too, that this particular political message, indebted to the LGBTQ politics of the early part of the decade, is not only an advertisement for the urban gay enclave but also "a call to upward mobility," as Puar has argued about the It Gets Better movement as a whole. We see this explicitly in *Newsies JR*.'s reworked 2020 libretto, which now addresses girls as well as boys with its message of hope for the future. Because *Newsies JR*. is adapted to be performed by young people, Medda Larkin can't sing her signature tune "That's Rich," with its double entendres and disavowal of monogamy – that would be decidedly beyond the pale of the particular LGBTQ politics promoted by DTP. The show's vaudevillian chanteuse is instead given a new song, "Just a Pretty Face," which reuses music from "That's Rich" but alters its message. In *Newsies JR*., Medda introduces her number by saying "Well hi-dee-ho everybody! Welcome to *my* theater. Yessiree, it's a brand new century with a brand new set of rules for women."[88] The new song is a defiant statement of modernity and gender equality, and Medda now sings:

> I'm more than just a pretty face.
> Don't try to keep me in my place.
> You think there's all these big things ladies can't do?
> Or is it that you're scared we'd do 'em better than you?[89]

The new tune goes further than simply giving girls famous female historical figures like Betsy Ross as role models; later in the song, Medda and the Bowery Brigade transform the tune into a rallying cry, singing, "Here come the women doctors and reporters and cops. / We won't have time for housework, but we'll lend you our mops," and Medda ends the song with the line "See you in Congress!"[90] *Newsies JR*., in other words, extends the cross-generational hailing of *Newsies the Musical* to the girls in the audience as well as the boys, promising them that it will get better for girls and women in the United States. In this way, *Newsies JR*. reflects the mainstreaming of the It Gets Better movement we saw in 2012 – as the anti-bullying message became more general and aimed less directly at kids identifying in some way as LGBTQ.

From one perspective, this is a welcome extension of the gender equality and gender fluidity suggested by DTP in its handbook for new productions of *Newsies*. That "Just a Pretty Face" includes police work and the U.S. Congress among the list of professions soon to be open to women, however, seems especially telling when we consider the queer disability studies critiques of the It Gets Better movement that Puar and others have made. From this perspective, the new song in *Newsies JR.* is not only a call to upward mobility but explicitly one that tells girls that they, too, can participate in the machinations of government power. That the cops, the judge, the news media, the wealthy elite, and the representatives of child social services were explicitly the *villains* in the original 1992 *Newsies* is mostly forgotten here in favor of both gender equality and a reincorporation into the neoliberal political order. The newsies (boys and girls) still strike, and they still publish their manifesto about child labor. Jack still wants Pulitzer to "know the next century belongs to us," and his words still, as Katherine says, "challenged our whole generation to help each other!"[91] The show hails its young audiences to band together, support one another, and fight the enemies of progress. But from 1992 to 2020, the villains whom the young people need to fight have been transformed into merely the show's representative adults – their problem is only their age.

Jack will become a political cartoonist, working for the news media and commenting on politics instead of driving them. Girls will grow up to be police and politicians, but the social order, with its cops, its government, its exploitative labor policies, and its "little merchants," will continue as before, with a younger generation simply taking the place of the old. *Newsies JR.* celebrates something in a fictional 1899 that women will long have achieved by 2020, and by doing so, this version of the show for young people returns us to the nostalgia of those 1980s and 1990s Disney films about young people in bygone eras, examining childhood and adolescence from the perspective of a complacent present. *Newsies'* reception over the last decade demonstrates an increasing awareness and approval of one strand of LGBTQ politics within mainstream culture. What we can also see here, however, is that as the politics of anti-bullying, chosen family, and expanded gender performance have become more widely accepted, they have been repurposed by the existing social order. In many ways, these LGBTQ politics have gone mainstream; at the same time, they have been reincorporated in service of precisely the enemies they had been organized to combat.

Notes

1 Maslin, "They Sing, They Dance, They Go on Strike," C17.
2 The film began rolling in April 1991. This oft-repeated story is ubiquitous in press about the show. See Cerniglia, *Newsies: Stories of the Unlikely Broadway Hit*.
3 McNary, "Box Office: Fathom Events Sees Soaring 2017 Performance."
4 Rooney, "Theater Review: *Newsies the Musical*," C5.
5 Riedel, "Good *Newsies* for Disney," 36.
6 Dziemianowicz, "*Newsies* a Doozie," 50.
7 Wong, "Making *Newsies*," 13.
8 Brantley, "Urchins With Punctuation," C1.
9 Mitchell quoted in Cerniglia, *Newsies: Stories of the Unlikely Broadway Hit*, 129.
10 Disney on Broadway, "NEWSIES – Seize the Day Dance Tutorial."
11 Feldman quoted in Cerniglia, *Newsies: Stories of the Unlikely Broadway Hit*, 45.
12 Huff quoted in Cerniglia, *Newsies: Stories of the Unlikely Broadway Hit*, 36.
13 Hinds quoted in Cerniglia, *Newsies: Stories of the Unlikely Broadway Hit*, 148.

14 Gattelli quoted in Cerniglia, *Newsies: Stories of the Unlikely Broadway Hit*, 34. Similar stories of how watching the film's dancing changed collaborators' lives abound in Miller, "Newsies – An Oral History."
15 As early as 1981, Fierstein wrote a play in which a major plot point was a gay man's adoption of a gay teenager.
16 Ortega, *Newsies*.
17 The boy's name is spelled Crutchy for the film and Crutchie for the show. In *Newsies JR.*, Crutchie's real name is Casey. This is a plot point developed for the shortened show that signals that neither the character nor the child-actor needs to identify as male. It also reflects Fierstein's frustration that the child is named for the specific physical challenges he faces. (Kid Blink – a newsboy with an eyepatch in the film who was based on a real person with the same name – disappeared as a character in the stage musical.) See Fierstein, *I Was Better Last Night*, 287–288.
18 Menken, Feldman, and Fierstein, *Newsies the Musical*, 61.
19 Fierstein, *I Was Better Last Night*, 287.
20 Menken, Feldman, and Fierstein, *Newsies the Musical*, 3.
21 Menken, Feldman, and Fierstein, *Newsies the Musical*, 72.
22 Menken, Feldman, and Fierstein, *Newsies the Musical*, 110.
23 Menken, Feldman, and Fierstein, *Newsies the Musical*, 58.
24 Savage, "Give 'Em Hope."
25 Love is Louder is a project now focused on mental health more generally. See jedfoundation.org/our-work/love-is-louder/. Accessed 28 May 2022.
26 It Gets Better Project, "It Gets Better: Dan and Terry."
27 Warner, "Neil Patrick Harris Encourages Gay Youth to 'Be Proud.'"
28 BroadwayItGetsBetter, "Broadway It Gets Better – BC/EFA, Broadway.com and Broadway Impact."
29 Manahan, "Niners' Brooks, Sopoaga Don't Recall Anti-Bullying Video."
30 Fierstein, *I Was Better Last Night*, 280–281.
31 See Fierstein, *I Was Better Last Night*, 122; see also Fierstein, *Torch Song Trilogy*, 148.
32 Fierstein quoted in Rees, "'Whatever You Survive Becomes a Triumph, Right?'"
33 Menken, Feldman, and Fierstein, *Newsies the Musical*, 4, 54, 94.
34 Menken, Feldman, and Fierstein, *Newsies the Musical*, 65.
35 Burt, *The Male Dancer*, 2.
36 See Burt, *The Male Dancer*, 104, 110, 127.
37 Kimmel, *Manhood in America*, 14.
38 Riis, *How the Other Half Lives*, 51.
39 Riis, *How the Other Half Lives*, 111.
40 Menken, Feldman, and Fierstein, *Newsies the Musical*, 64.
41 See Menken, Feldman, and Fierstein, *Newsies the Musical*, 74, 53, 72, 90.
42 Disney Theatrical Group Education Department, "*Newsies the Musical* Study Guide."
43 See Scheck, "Songs and Star Scoop *Newsies* Story," 36; Dziemianowicz, "It's Terrific 'News'!" 37; Sommers, "Good *Newsies*," 53.
44 The original audition notice for the Paper Mill run was for ages 18 and up. According to Gattelli, for the (union) tour the "singing/acting/dance ensemble is actually younger, on average, than we had in New York. We've got guys as young as 16, and an average age of 20–1." See Takiff, "Bristol Stomp."
45 Suskin, "Newsies: The Musical," 23. Suskin's mention of *West Side Story* here is notable primarily because of the absence of such references in other reviews. *West Side*, famously a show about "juvenile delinquency," was populated almost entirely with actors in their twenties. See Herrera, "Compiling *West Side Story's* Parahistories."
46 Vincentelli, "Striking Ensemble Is on Tap," 44.
47 Montan quoted in Cerniglia, *Newsies: Stories of the Unlikely Broadway Hit*, 86.
48 Vincentelli, "Striking Ensemble Is on Tap," 44
49 Menken quoted in Wong, "Read All About It," 4.

50 Cf. Raymond Knapp's suggestion that Sir Evelyn's lack of a song undermines the believability of the couplings at the end of *Anything Goes*. Knapp, *The American Musical and the Formation of National Identity*, 90.
51 Menken, Feldman, and Fierstein, *Newsies the Musical*, 69.
52 Menken, Feldman, and Fierstein, *Newsies the Musical*, 2, 24.
53 Menken, Feldman, and Fierstein, *Newsies the Musical*, 6, 61, 66.
54 Menken, Feldman, and Fierstein, *Newsies the Musical*, 73.
55 Kimmel, *Manhood in America*, 124.
56 Menken, Feldman, and Fierstein, *Newsies the Musical*, 104, 107.
57 Menken, Feldman, and Fierstein, *Newsies the Musical*, 53.
58 Menken, Feldman, and Fierstein, *Newsies the Musical*, 90.
59 Menken, Feldman, and Fierstein, *Newsies the Musical*, 90.
60 Menken, Feldman, and Fierstein, *Newsies the Musical*, 101.
61 The other leads for the show remained white, but producers also added more people of color to the dancing chorus when the show moved to Broadway. The film, incidentally, includes several newsies played by actors of color.
62 Menken, Feldman, and Fierstein, *Newsies the Musical*, 28–29.
63 Menken, Feldman, and Fierstein, *Newsies the Musical*, 109.
64 Chauncey, *Gay New York*, 202.
65 Chauncey, *Gay New York*, 56.
66 Brooks, *Liner Notes for the Revolution*, 382.
67 See Knapp, *The American Musical and the Formation of National Identity*, 61.
68 Chauncey, *Gay New York*, 57.
69 Menken, Feldman, and Fierstein, *Newsies the Musical*, 68.
70 Rodosthenous, "*Billy Elliot the Musical*"; Sebesta, "Angry Dance."
71 Halberstam, *Female Masculinity*, 2.
72 Sebesta, "Angry Dance," 158.
73 Brantley, "Urchins With Punctuation," C1.
74 McRuer, *Crip Theory*, 2.
75 Kimmel, *Manhood in America*, 4.
76 Menken, Feldman, and Fierstein, *Newsies the Musical*, 99.
77 Puar, "The Cost of Getting Better," 149.
78 Puar, "The Cost of Getting Better," 149, 151.
79 Puar, "The Cost of Getting Better," 152.
80 Puar, "The Cost of Getting Better," 157.
81 See Edelman, *No Future*, 3.
82 Puar, "The Cost of Getting Better," 153.
83 Michelle LoRicco, who directed a 2022 production at Patrick Henry High School in Roanoke, for example, gave the young women in her *Newsies* the option of playing their characters, including Crutchie and Race, along whatever gender lines the actor chose.
84 Haverkate, *Newsies Production Handbook*, 24–25.
85 Simpatico, *Disney's Newsies JR.*, viii.
86 Simpatico, *Disney's Newsies JR.*, 43.
87 Simpatico, *Disney's Newsies JR.*, 65.
88 Simpatico, *Disney's Newsies JR.*, 28.
89 Simpatico, *Disney's Newsies JR.*, 29.
90 Simpatico, *Disney's Newsies JR.*, 31–32.
91 Simpatico, *Disney's Newsies JR.*, 87.

References for Chapter 2

Brantley, Ben. "Urchins With Punctuation." *New York Times*. 30 March 2012. (C1).
BroadwayItGetsBetter. "Broadway It Gets Better – BC/EFA, Broadway.com and Broadway Impact." *YouTube*. 2 November 2010. www.youtube.com/watch?v=YRwZfLpibh0. Accessed 29 May 2022.

Brooks, Daphne A. *Liner Notes for the Revolution: The Intellectual Life of Black Feminist Sound*. Cambridge: Harvard University Press, 2021.
Burt, Ramsay. *The Male Dancer: Bodies, Spectacle, Sexualities*. London: Routledge, 1995.
Cerniglia, Ken, (editor). *Newsies: Stories of the Unlikely Broadway Hit*. Glendale: Disney Editions, 2013.
Chauncey, George. *Gay New York: Gender, Urban Culture, and the Making of the Gay Male World 1890–1940*. New York: Basic, 1994.
Disney on Broadway. "NEWSIES – Seize the Day Dance Tutorial." *YouTube*. 15 July 2014. www.youtube.com/watch?v=LSEUR2gZUFc. Accessed 9 June 2022.
Disney Theatrical Group Education Department. "*Newsies the Musical* Study Guide." newsiesthemusical.com/pdf/NewsiesStudyGuide.pdf. Accessed 26 May 2022.
Dziemianowicz, Joe. "It's Terrific 'News'! Disney Musical Makes Headlines in New Jersey." *New York Daily News*. 28 September 2011. (37).
Dziemianowicz, Joe. "*Newsies* a Doozie." *New York Daily News*. 30 March 2012. (50).
Edelman, Lee. *No Future: Queer Theory and the Death Drive*. Durham: Duke University Press, 2004.
Fierstein, Harvey. *I Was Better Last Night: A Memoir*. New York: Alfred A. Knopf, 2022.
Fierstein, Harvey. *Torch Song Trilogy*. New York: Villar Books, 1979.
Halberstam, Jack. *Female Masculinity*. Durham: Duke University Press, 1998.
Haverkate, Julie, (editor). *Newsies Production Handbook* New York: Disney Theatrical Licensing. www.mtishows.com/newsies-0. Accessed 30 May 2022.
Herrera, Brian Eugenio. "Compiling *West Side Story*'s Parahistories, 1949–2009." *Theatre Journal* 64.2: 231–47, 2012.
It Gets Better Project. "It Gets Better: Dan and Terry." *YouTube*. 22 September 2010. www.youtube.com/watch?v=7IcVyvg2Qlo. Accessed 28 May 2022.
Kimmel, Michael. *Manhood in America: A Cultural History* (2nd ed). New York: Oxford University Press, 2006.
Knapp, Raymond. *The American Musical and the Formation of National Identity*. Princeton: Princeton University Press, 2005.
Manahan, Kevin. "Niners' Brooks, Sopoaga Don't Recall Anti-Bullying Video." *USA Today*. 31 January 2013. www.usatoday.com/story/sports/nfl/niners/2013/01/31/niners-ahmad-brooks-isaac-sopoaga-deny-antibullying-video/1880299/. Accessed 29 May 2022.
Maslin, Janet. "They Sing, They Dance, They Go on Strike." *New York Times*. 8 April 1992. (C17).
McNary, Dave. "Box Office: Fathom Events Sees Soaring 2017 Performance." *Variety*. 18 December 2017. variety.com/2017/film/news/box-office-fathom-events-2017-performance-1202643479/. Accessed 26 May 2022.
McRuer, Robert. *Crip Theory: Cultural Signs of Queerness and Disability*. New York: New York University Press, 2006.
Menken, Alan, Jack Feldman, and Harvey Fierstein. *Newsies the Musical* (Unpublished Broadway opening night script). Revised 29 March 2012.
Miller, Amanda Marie. "Newsies – An Oral History: How It All Happened." *Theatrely*. 25 March 2022. www.theatrely.com/post/newsies-an-oral-history-how-it-all-happened. Accessed 19 June 2022.
Ortega, Kenny, (director). *Newsies*. Disney+. 10 April 1992.
Puar, Jasbir K. "The Cost of Getting Better: Suicide, Sensation, Switchpoints." *GLQ: A Journal of Lesbian and Gay Studies* 18.1: 149–158, 2012.
Rees, Alex. "'Whatever You Survive Becomes a Triumph, Right?' Harvey Fierstein Looks Back – Even Though He Prefers Not To." *Time*. 9 March 2022. time.com/6154190/harvey-fierstein-interview/. Accessed 29 May 2022.

Riedel, Michael. "Good *Newsies* for Disney." *New York Post*. 28 March 2012. (36).
Riis, Jacob. *How the Other Half Lives* (Edited by Hasia R. Diner). New York: W.W. Norton, 2010.
Rodosthenous, George. "*Billy Elliot the Musical:* Visual Representations of Working-Class Masculinity and the All-Singing, All-Dancing Bo(d)y." *Studies in Musical Theatre* 1.3: 275–92, 2007.
Rooney, Dan. "Theater Review: *Newsies the Musical*." *New York Times*. 28 September 2011. (C5).
Savage, Dan. "Give 'Em Hope." *Stranger*. 23 September 2010. www.thestranger.com/seattle/SavageLove?oid=4940874. Accessed 28 May 2022.
Scheck, Frank. "Songs and Star Scoop *Newsies* Story." *New York Post*. 27 September 2011. (36).
Sebesta, Judith. "Angry Dance: Postmodern Innovation, Masculinities, and Gender Subversion." In *Gestures of Music Theater: The Performativity of Song and Dance*. Edited by Dominic Symonds, and Millie Taylor. New York: Oxford University Press, 146–58, 2013.
Simpatico, David. *Disney's Newsies JR*. New York: Disney Theatrical Licensing, 2020.
Sommers, Michael. "Good *Newsies*: Disney's Crowd-Pleaser Delivers." *Variety*. 3 October 2011. (53).
Suskin, Steven. "Newsies: The Musical." *Variety*. 30 March 2012. (23).
Takiff, Jonathan. "Bristol Stomp: *Newsies* Winning Choreographer Hails From Bucks." *Philadelphia Daily News* [*Philadelphia Inquirer*]. 29 October 2014. www.inquirer.com/philly/entertainment/movies/20141024_Bristol_stomp___Newsies__winning_choreographer_hails_from_Bucks.html. Accessed 24 October 2020.
Vincentelli, Elisabeth. "Striking Ensemble Is on Tap." *New York Post*. 30 March 2012. (44).
Warner, Kara. "Neil Patrick Harris Encourages Gay Youth to 'Be Proud.'" MTV News. 1 October 2010. www.mtv.com/news/1649200/neil-patrick-harris-encourages-gay-youth-to-be-proud/. Accessed 28 May 2022.
Wong, Wayman. "Making *Newsies*: How a Disney Flop Became a Stage Hit." *New York Daily News*. 2 October 2011. (13).
Wong, Wayman. "Read All About It: Meet Jeremy Jordan, Broadway Star of Disney's *Newsies*." *New York Daily News*. 25 March 2012. (4).

3
A GENDER OF ONE, A SEXUALITY OF MANY

In hindsight, it is not at all coincidental that the journal TSQ: *Transgender Studies Quarterly* announced its first issue and call for papers in July 2012 at the same time as negotiations were underway to mount a Broadway revival of the musical *Hedwig and the Angry Inch* and just 11 months before Neil Patrick Harris was finally announced as the show's star in June 2013. In their introduction to the first volume of TSQ, Paisley Currah and Susan Stryker describe (in quotation marks) the "'transgender turn' in recent affairs" and articulate their hopes that the journal will be able to analyze that turn in depth in its future volumes.[1] Directed by Michael Mayer, *Hedwig and the Angry Inch* began previews at the Belasco Theatre on March 29, 2014, and ran for more than 500 performances until September 13, 2015. *Hedwig* then went on a national tour from October 2016 to July 2017. The visibility of trans issues in the United States skyrocketed during the period of time between June 2013 and September 2015 when *Hedwig* was in the news: Chelsea Manning came out as transgender in August 2013; U.S. Secretary of Defense Ashton Carter made a statement in February 2015 that led to the Obama administration's inclusion of trans people in the military; Caitlyn Jenner's *Vanity Fair* cover story "Call Me Caitlyn" appeared in the magazine in June 2015; the Kilroys, a group dedicated to promoting plays by women, trans, and nonbinary playwrights, was founded in 2013 and produced their first annual list in June 2014, vowing to incorporate more trans and nonbinary plays for their 2015 list. At the same time, the question of transgender bathroom use became highly politicized, as states such as Arizona, Kentucky, Florida, and Maryland debated transphobic so-called "bathroom bills" during the election cycle in 2015.[2] But 2015 also saw the largest survey ever of transgender people in the United States. The *2015 U.S. Transgender Survey* gathered data on trans issues pertaining to employment, harassment, family life, communities of faith, health, income, military service, violence, housing and homelessness, policing, and more.[3] This was a watershed document in the history of trans people in the U.S.

DOI: 10.4324/9781003317470-4

2015 was also the most fatal year on record for trans people in the United States. According to a Human Rights Campaign report released in November 2015, "more transgender people were killed in the first six months of this year than in all of 2014."[4] Since 2015, fatal violence affecting trans people of color, primarily Black trans women, has remained at extremely alarming rates.[5] Meanwhile, actress Laverne Cox became the first trans person to appear on the cover of *Time* magazine in June 2014 – with the headline "The Transgender Tipping Point" – and in July of that year, she became the first transgender actor to be nominated for an Emmy award.[6] The comedy *Transparent* also debuted on Amazon Prime in 2014, and many commentators saw this as television's "trans tipping point"; by 2019, critic Joy Press would hyperbolically quip in *Vanity Fair* that "some days it seems like every lead character in TV has a trans sidekick."[7]

One of the problems with the concept of the "tipping point" is that it celebrates a triumph, assuming that we are somehow in a time that is post anti-trans prejudice, violence, policing, and surveillance. I've placed the widespread use of the phrase "trans tipping point" during this period next to the murders of trans women and the rise in anti-trans politics and anti-trans legislation as one way of demonstrating the interconnectedness of these phenomena. In other words, *representations* of trans people had become much more mainstream in the middle part of the decade, and these achievements in representation were attended by a rise in attacks on the safety and bodily autonomy of trans kids and trans adults.

It is perhaps worth noting alongside these significant moments in trans history a steep rise in the popularity of the gender-reveal party, a ceremony that explicitly celebrates and commemorates the gender binary.[8] In Queens, New York, the Gender Reveal Cakery, devoted *only* to making gender-reveal cakes, was founded in 2013. With new stories and new visibility for trans and nonbinary people on television and other entertainment media, one might look at the gender-reveal cake, with its insistence on *either* blue *or* pink, as evidence of renewed anxieties about gender identity, stability, and traditions, but we might also see the gender-reveal party and its accompanying pastry as demonstrating an interest in the fungibility of genders. If the blue or pink arrive with a measure of finality as the climax of the party, the gender-reveal party itself is a celebration of gender possibility, and we can see in its popularity, at the very least, a renewed interest in gender as a concept, its opportunities, and its plasticity.[9]

I map the details of this "transgender turn" because these news items related to trans visibility, anti-trans violence, and trans and anti-trans politics overlap with *Hedwig and the Angry Inch*'s visibility in mainstream media. If *Hedwig*'s first appearance at the Jane Street Theatre in 1998 was shocking, punk, and "unapologetically genderqueer," *Hedwig*'s appearance at the Belasco *coincided* with an astounding rise in trans visibility – for *some* trans people – as well as with the apparent ubiquity of trans issues and trans politics in LGBTQ media and other media aimed at queer consumers.[10] This ostensible coincidence is, of course, no coincidence at all, and this chapter finds that *Hedwig* is an excellent lens through which to examine trans issues and LGBTQ politics in the years 2013–2016. This is not because *Hedwig* is "good" trans representation — in fact, many trans writers have objected to *Hedwig*'s central character — but rather because *Hedwig* exposes some of the tensions between what audiences seem to want from trans performances and the ways that trans people describe themselves and their experiences. In 2014, *Hedwig and the Angry Inch* went mainstream, and that popularity is an intriguing marker not of how far we've come along a path of progressive politics but of *which* paths those politics have taken.

This chapter approaches three topics that *Hedwig* on Broadway illuminates. First, we will explore the central question of Hedwig's gender and her failure as trans representation. What I'm interested in here is how critics and audiences have spoken about what John Cameron Mitchell has called Hedwig's "gender of one."[11] How we speak about this fictional character is central to questions of identity and identification, and so this section will explore how people described Hedwig — in 1998, in 2001, and then in 2014 — as one way of examining how audiences have identified *with* her. Second, this will lead us to the question of casting, where we can look, especially, at the way the actors who played Hedwig on Broadway understood themselves in relationship to her (that is, their identity with her and differences from her). Third, we will see how *Hedwig*'s moment on Broadway charts a larger shift in transgender and LGBTQ politics in the United States. Running through all of these discussions of *Hedwig* — and taking us all the way back to *Hedwig*'s citation of Plato's *Symposium* — is a continual slippage between talking about gender and talking about sexuality. *Hedwig*, as we will see, tends toward fluidity precisely where many would like it to be more fixed.

A Gender of One

Almost from its humble beginnings in the mid-1990s, *Hedwig* has been decidedly popular with academics — a particularly niche audience. They've loved *Hedwig* much more than the other musicals addressed in *Love Is Love Is Love*, and there is rather a large amount of academic writing on the Jane Street Theatre production in 1998, the 2001 film adaptation of *Hedwig and the Angry Inch*, and the Tony-award-winning 2014 Broadway revival, as well as other productions.[12] In fact, the first academic article on the musical described a production on the campus of California State University Monterey Bay in 2003, and Hyewon Kim has written about the immensely popular productions of the show in Seoul under the titles *Hedwig* and *Hedwig: New Makeup*.[13] Kim doesn't describe herself as a *Hed*-head, but she does say she's seen the show at least a dozen times.[14] Most scholarly interest in the show has focused on *Hedwig*'s ideas about gender, but scholars have also written extensively about the musical's engagement with Plato's *Symposium*.[15] In addition, Chris Eng has pointed out the way that the 2014 production, especially, treated the violent destruction caused by the U.S. military in Iraq as a joke and disavowed Asian labor even while Asian American actors were onstage performing as Hedwig and Yitzhak, and Erik Hollis has used critical responses to Taye Diggs's performance in *Hedwig* to understand "the ruptured relation blackness has with performance itself and, in particular, its incapacity for performing gendered 'realness,' be it normative or otherwise."[16]

These critical examinations of *Hedwig* display a powerful amount of affection for this musical. Susan Stryker's *Transgender History* mentions *Hedwig* approvingly, and Cameron Awkward-Rich, in his award-winning article "Trans, Feminism: *or*, Reading like a Depressed Transsexual," asks us to hear a Hedwig song "in the background of my argument."[17] Caridad Svich opens her book on *Hedwig* with the charming sentence "I want to tell you a story of love."[18] Such love is palpable in most of the scholarship on *Hedwig*, though it is not usually declared quite so openly, and there are, of course, exceptions. But even an article such as Eng's, which argues convincingly that Hedwig's jokes about Asian people "induc[e] a sense of indifference within the audience members, redirecting their gaze away from the materiality of racial labor and toward the campy glory of Hedwig's fabulosity," can't seem to help but conclude by talking about camp's "reparative ethos" and quoting Hedwig directly.[19]

Scholars have been struck by audiences' abilities to identify with the character of Hedwig; they have often described the diversity of *Hedwig*'s audiences and attempted to make sense of her identificatory power. As early as 1999, critics were wondering about the story's appeal to *non*-queer audiences (many had apparently assumed that *Hedwig* would only interest queer folks). In *Out* magazine, Mitchell explained that interest this way:

> It's totally queer, but it's very inclusive. Hedwig's central situation is something we can all relate to: trying to figure out what it means to fill up a hole after having had something ripped away – and what do you do with the inch you've been given? A lot of unexpected people really respond to it, especially middle-aged women.[20]

Audiences have identified with "Hedwig's central situation," but critics have charted this identificatory process in many different ways over the last 25 years of the *Hedwig* phenomenon.

In reviews of the original Jane Street production in 1998, critics referred to the show's eponymous character as a *transvestite*, a *transsexual manqué*, a *drag queen*, *transgender*, and *gender-bending*; reviews also frequently described Hedwig as a *wannabe* or possessing *uncertain sexual identity*, but the word most frequently used for Hedwig in the late 1990s was *transsexual*. Reviews of the 2001 film had a more diverse vocabulary, using *transsexual*, *transgender*, *drag queen*, and *gender-bent* and adding the words *ambisexual*, *bisexual*, and *cross-dressing* to this list. By contrast, almost every review and description of the Broadway run of *Hedwig* referred to the character as *transgender*, although occasionally a critic would use the terms *transsexual* or *genderqueer*. This near uniformity in description and widespread use of *transgender* are developments of the late 2000s and early 2010s, readily apparent in comparison to descriptions of productions in the 1990s and the 2001 movie.

The distance between 1998 and 2014 is very important here, and *Hedwig* helps us see the way these terms were consolidated in a relatively short amount of time. From the very wide range of gender identities used to describe Hedwig in the previous decade to the time of the revival, the word *transgender* had emerged as *the* accurate descriptor for *Hedwig*'s central character, without, we should note, any help from the character herself, who doesn't tell us anything about how she identifies. As ethnographer David Valentine details in *Imagining Transgender*, "the conventional definition" of *transgender* is that it is an "'umbrella' term that includes all people who are in some ways gender-variant," but Valentine also reminds us that the borders of transgender – who, that is, comes to be included *under* the umbrella – are constantly shifting and frequently contradictory.[21] Critics' consistent use of the term *transgender* when discussing Hedwig in 2014 and 2015 is related to the ease with which the term can describe a specific person in a non-specific way:

> The very flexibility of transgender, its strength as a tool of political organizing, makes it possible to use without specifying who is being invoked in particular instances. . . . The capacity to stand in for an unspecified group of people is, indeed, one of the seductive things about "transgender" in trying to describe a wide range of people, both historical and contemporary, Western and non-Western.[22]

In this way, *transgender* solves the journalistic confusion that attended earlier reviews of *Hedwig*, which is to say that although many critics referred to *the character* as confused or ambiguous, we should more accurately consider the *reviewers* as those who were confused about Hedwig's gender identity. The term *transgender* resolves that identificatory conundrum, appearing to explain a gender that hasn't been explained at all. Valentine argues that the term can describe a person using a vague concept of gender variance (and in some cases gender performance), but that is not all. *Transgender* can also – and he makes a strong case for this in *Imagining Transgender* – offer an imagined identity that can be mobilized to unite a wide range of folks as a political coalition.

Journalistic description of Hedwig as *transgender* also used the umbrella term to side-step the criticism of *Hedwig* made by some trans activists who have taken issue with the show's apparent portrayal of a transsexual woman. Critic Jordy Tackitt-Jones summarizes the identity portion of this critique as follows:

> The character of Hedwig is not actually a transsexual woman, nor is John Cameron Mitchell, the man who created the character Hedwig, and who has played her on stage and screen. Hedwig is, rather, an overt citation of a transsexual woman, and Mitchell, as Hedwig, is a non-transsexual gay man *in drag as his fantasy of a transsexual woman*. Through the figure of transsexuality, Mitchell explores his own relation to male femininity through an identity other than his own.[23]

I don't want to argue at all with Tackitt-Jones' well-known conclusions about *Hedwig* – in any case, his argument is quite a narrow one: Hedwig is not a transsexual woman. His argument, however, is dependent on a series of assumptions about the show, and about sexuality and gender, that can help us understand both *Hedwig*'s complex politics and what the show might newly be able to accomplish in this (ongoing) period of the transgender turn.

Hedwig, when we meet her in the revival, is an "internationally ignored song stylist" performing for us on the stage of the Belasco Theatre.[24] She was born in East Berlin as Hansel Schmidt, she tells us, and Hedwig's mother consistently refers to little Hansel as her "son."[25] When Hedwig's future husband Luther meets Hansel, he also assumes Hedwig's gender to be male, saying, "Damn, Hansel, I can't believe you're not a girl, you're so fine."[26] When *we* first meet her, however, Hedwig refers to herself, even as a child, using a genderqueer term, describing the kid she was as a "slip of a girlyboy."[27] Gender ambiguity suffuses Hedwig's other descriptions of her childhood, as she talks about her identification with "the American Masters" – Toni Tennille, Debby Boone, and Anne Murray – and "the crypto-homo rockers," Lou Reed, Iggy Pop, and David Bowie.[28] If her mother and Luther understand that Hansel is a boy, or at least "not a girl," it is clear that Hedwig's childhood understanding of herself exceeds the terms of binary gender.

This child's conception of gender as more fluid and nonbinary can apparently be traced to a story Hedwig's mother told her when she was small, one that adapts Aristophanes' description of love from Plato's *Symposium*. Hedwig sings this story to us as the show's second song, "Origin of Love," and in this way, the musical sets up its nonbinary idea of gender. In "Origin of Love," as in the Aristophanes section of the *Symposium*, there are three sexes.[29] Each of these sexes ("the children of the sun / and the moon / and the earth") has two heads, four arms, and four legs, but perhaps more importantly, each of these individual persons has two sets of genitals as well as two sets of secondary sex characteristics.[30] Plato's Aristophanes and little Hansel, then, both imagine an originary gender that is double, one that is *already* multiple.

To be more specific, as Aristophanes describes the children of the earth in the *Symposium*, he seems to describe a gender identity that is singular: "All women who are sliced off from woman hardly pay attention to men but are rather turned toward women, and lesbians arrive from this genus." However, once Aristophanes begins to describe the children of the sun, he twists things so that his explanation of the origin of love makes sense according to an *Athenian* understanding of male–male sexual practices:

> But all who are male slices pursue the males; and while they are boys . . . they are friendly with men and enjoy lying down together with and embracing men. . . . When they are fully grown men, they are pederasts and naturally pay no attention to marriage and procreation.[31]

Here Aristophanes doesn't describe two identical halves at all; the original children of the sun comprise two very different (male) sides or slices. In other words, Aristophanes describes three originary gender identities that are multiple – that contain numerous differences – and this is just as true for the apparently identical children of the earth and the sun as it is for the androgynous children of the moon.

We will return to Plato and "Origin of Love" at the end of this chapter, but I also want to note here that the description of these three sexes, in this mythological exploration, is simultaneously a description of sexuality *and* gender. One is used to explain the other. It is impossible to make sense of the genders in Aristophanes' story without understanding ancient sexuality. In this story, the gender of the sexual subject is defined by the sexual object. To put it another way, if we follow Aristophanes' story, we can only finally trace our original four-armed and four-legged genders when we know the object (the other half) of our desires. I can define myself as a child of the sun because I love a man – and so on. Our genders only make sense in this schema when we have another half.

"It is clear," Hedwig says as a child, "that I must find my other half. But is it a he or a she?"[32] Hedwig's other half, if she is using the phrase as it is colloquially intended, is a companion or lover, and much of the show's plot describes Hedwig's search for this person. Indeed, in the final sequence of *Hedwig and the Angry Inch*, Hedwig would appear to have found her other half – Hedwig's self-discovery, along with her freeing of her husband Yitzhak to perform as a drag queen, are the show's conclusion. The way this works in the musical, though, is not so simple. At the end of *Hedwig*, Hedwig transforms *into* Tommy Gnosis, her rocker ex-boyfriend. Hedwig (as Tommy) sings the song "Wicked Little Town," and when the song concludes, the stage directions say that Hedwig "is not sure where she is. Or even who she is. She sees her wig on the floor and picks it up. She wipes her forehead and finds [Tommy's] silver makeup on her hand. Pause. Finally, she looks to the guitarist who begins to play" the show's final song, "Midnight Radio."[33]

During this song, Hedwig does not replace her own wig on her head but gives the wig to Yitzhak, who leaves the stage and reappears "in stunning female drag."[34] Hedwig, in other words, performs her final number *as* Hedwig but dressed as Tommy. She sings the lyrics:

> Breathe feel love
> Give free
> Know in your soul
> Like your blood knows the way
> From your heart to your brain
> Know that you're whole[35]

The song and the show end simultaneously as Hedwig (still in drag as Tommy) walks upstage into bright light. The final stage direction tells us that "The broken eye from 'The Origin of Love' appears and, as the song ends . . . / . . . it merges and becomes whole."[36] This is a series of images that work together in the theatre. Hedwig seems to become both male and female; she has reconciled with who she was and embraces a "whole" future of freedom, breath, blood, heart, brain. She no longer needs Tommy to hate or Yitzhak to abuse. And the return of the image from "Origin of Love" signals that Hedwig has also found the other half of herself *as* herself.

Jordy Tackitt-Jones interprets this finale differently, arguing that at the end

> Hansel [is] reborn with the knowledge that Hedwig is the feminine within himself. Once he integrates this lost Other into his own person, he is able to turn away from the fantasy of transsexuality, and towards a normative male homosexuality.[37]

For Tackitt-Jones, Hedwig is a figure defined by her *sexuality* and not her gender. But this description assumes a fixed interpretation of the meaning of *Hedwig*'s final images where the show leaves things much more ambiguous. Neither Hedwig nor Yitzhak tells us how Hedwig now sees herself or what she plans to do next. Hedwig certainly does not say that she now wishes to be called Hansel. In fact, Hedwig doesn't tell us anything except that Yitzhak and we in the audience should "know that [we're] whole," that we're "doing all right," and that we should "hold on to each other."[38] If there is any clue at all as to how Hedwig understands herself vis-à-vis gender, we might look to the "strange rock-and-rollers" she toasts in this final song: Patti Smith, Tina Turner, Yoko Ono, Aretha Franklin, Nona Hendryx, and Nico. Far from abandoning her femaleness and incorporating femininity into a "normative male homosexuality" as Tackitt-Jones argues, Hedwig quite clearly salutes a diverse list of female rockers and then adds herself to this list of women.[39]

Tackitt-Jones sums up his discussion of the film version in the following way:

> *Hedwig* has been consistently referred to as a transgender film. This it well may be if the broadest definition of transgender is used, one in which drag, male femininity, cross-gender role-play, psychic bisexuality, et cetera are all included. Easily included within that definition would be *Hedwig* as a gay male rite of passage narrative, one that uses the figure of the transsexual to represent the path not taken – because it is the wrong path. It is important to note, however, that it is the wrong path specifically for Mitchell. There are many paths, and for others, transsexuality is definitely the right one. It is of utmost importance – socially, politically and spiritually – that the various paths remain open, unobstructed and viable so that each may pass in safety to his or her own proper destination.[40]

I am quoting Tackitt-Jones at length here because I take seriously the difficulties he has in identifying with Hedwig, and – as I argued in Chapter 1 – it can be richly productive to examine the responses of audience members for whom the show *doesn't* work and try to make sense of them.

I want, however, to offer that meaning in *Hedwig and the Angry Inch* is less fixed than Tackitt-Jones makes it out to be, and that far from foreclosing a series of paths, the show attempts to open them up. The musical's ambiguities – especially at the end – are what allow for the different identificatory possibilities so many audiences have experienced. Further, it is by no means clear that transgender will not be Hedwig's path when she leaves the theatre. Hedwig walks upstage into the light by herself while a gorgeous Yitzhak finishes the show with the Angry Inch. Hedwig communicates that she will not allow her other half to define her, but neither does she define herself for us. She simply *forges a new path*.

On the other hand, if Hedwig is not transsexual, she *does* seem to have answered trans theorist Sandy Stone's well-known call for the *posttranssexual*: Stone imagines the possibility that one might "forego passing, to be consciously 'read,' to read oneself aloud – and by this troubling and productive reading, to begin to *write oneself* into the discourses by which one has been written."[41] Stone's idea of the posttranssexual world is one in which a person might claim their gender position *as* trans without disappearing or "passing," a world in which, perhaps, a genderqueer rocker might sing the lyrics of "The Angry Inch" and talk to an audience about her surgery in detail, describing her pain and linguistically putting her anatomy on display.[42]

Hedwig's lyrics also seem to echo Susan Stryker in her famous essay from 1993, "My Words to Victor Frankenstein above the Village of Chamounix: Performing Transgender Rage," as she articulates a "transsexual embodiment": "As we rise up from the operating tables of our rebirth, we transsexuals are something more, and something other, than the creatures our makers intended us to be."[43] "I rose from off of the doctor's slab / Like Lazarus from the pit," Hedwig sings in "Tear Me Down," and Stephen Trask's lyrics for "Exquisite Corpse" speak of Hedwig's operation, her sex reassignment and its failed gender confirmation – "I'm all sewn up / A hardened razor cut / Scar map across my body" – but then move us above all toward an expression of Hedwig's rage, as she tells us she's "hollowed out."[44] How well these lyrics echo Stryker when she says

> we have done the hard work of constituting ourselves on our own terms, against the natural order. Though we forego the privilege of naturalness, we are not deterred, for we ally ourselves instead with the chaos and blackness from which Nature itself spills forth.

And how expertly Trask's lyrics seem to respond to the "monstrous benediction" with which Stryker concludes her famous essay: "May you discover the enlivening power of darkness within yourself. May it nourish your rage. May your rage inform your actions, and your actions transform you as you struggle to transform your world."[45] As the cast sings in "Exquisite Corpse," "The whole world starts unscrewing / As time collapses and space warps / You see decay and ruin."[46] It's a rage-filled song, bent on destruction and transformation.

If Hedwig is not a transsexual woman – and this makes sense; she never claims that identity – her performance and the stories she tells allow for possible points of identification for a multitude of people with differing gender identities. Recently, Mitchell has responded to the question of Hedwig being trans by declaring that *Hedwig* "is not a transgender story." As Mitchell understands Hedwig:

> He was a boy who was quite comfortable in his gender and was coerced into a mutilation, really, by a boyfriend, mother and really the patriarchy, if you

think about it. [Coerced by] the binarchy that says you have to be one or the other for certain things to happen, for you to get married and so on. . . . But it's not really a trans story. There's all kinds of gender fluidity and exploration. But to be trans you have to want to be. You choose to be.[47]

It's important to note that Mitchell doesn't define Hedwig's gender here. Even the boy who is "comfortable in his gender" isn't given a gender identity by the author, though he says that Hedwig isn't trans. I want to argue, however, that the "broadest definition" of *transgender* that Tackitt-Jones uses to make sense of the show (and to which he objects) is the better one for understanding what *Hedwig* can achieve as a piece of musical theatre. And it seems to me that the "gender fluidity and exploration" Mitchell describes is one of the reasons *Hedwig* has been so beloved since 1998 and was revived so successfully in 2014. There are, after all, many trans stories, journeys, and genders.

As Tackitt-Jones points out, the umbrella definition of transgender purports to represent a wide range of sartorial practices and gender identities, but the term also covers over that *there is no transgender identity as such*. Or rather, the great power of *transgender* is its ability to cover over the very real differences between trans stories, journeys, and genders – to offer an identity for the purpose of political coalition and personal belonging. As David Valentine and others have argued, the numerous different gender identities and gender practices that *transgender* works so well to describe are not the same as one another, and folks defined by the term are frequently at great pains to differentiate themselves from others whom social workers or government agencies might group together as part of a transgender identity.

I am arguing here that what Hedwig might be able to offer us – from her unique position – is the possibility of inclusion without identity, or of a *more capacious identity* defined only by gender difference or gender diversity. Stumbling out of the Jane Street Theatre in February 1998, Caridad Svich "wonder[ed] if the feeling of possibility and commonality I experienced in the strange, disconcerting, silly yet oddly profound musical I had just seen – a musical of all things! – could last."[48] *Hedwig* manages, through its peculiar alchemy and unique protagonist, to have this effect on people; audiences lift up their hands, they sing along, they perform in front of screens and host sing-alongs in movie theatres while showing the film, they dress up for the occasion. I refer to this as inclusion without identity, however, because although the musical has appealed to many, many different audiences from many different backgrounds and in many different venues, it is impossible to share a gender identity with Hedwig. She is unique, a gender of one, and so what she might offer us is a concept of togetherness or community – "possibility and commonality" as Svich puts it – without needing to be the same as one another.

Casting and Identification

The idea of inclusion without identity might best be examined by exploring the casting for the revival of *Hedwig*. As we consider identity and identification in theatre and film, casting is perhaps the identificatory gesture *par excellence*. The process of casting both asks audiences to identify a particular actor with a character – indeed often asks audiences to forget there is an actor at all – and also asks the actor herself to do the identificatory work of *becoming* the character. During the Broadway run and its national tour, Hedwig was played, over the course of hundreds of performances, by actors Neil Patrick Harris, Andrew Rannells, Darren Criss, Michael C. Hall, John Cameron Mitchell, Taye Diggs, Lena Hall, and Euan Morton. Lena Hall, who also won a Tony Award for her portrayal of Hedwig's husband Yitzhak, is the only woman of the eight. Diggs is the only Black Hedwig in this group, and Criss is the only other man of color. Mitchell has recently come out as nonbinary, but none of the eight performers has publicly identified as trans.[49]

This is hardly a uniform group of individuals, but these choices make it clear that Trask and Mitchell, at least, do not see *Hedwig* as a show about transsexual experience but instead have used transgender as a metaphor for something else – be that change, betweenness, acceptance, or difference. It also demonstrates that *Hedwig*'s Broadway casting mostly fails to ask audiences to consider the stories of Black trans folks and trans people of color, as both Erik Hollis and Chris Eng have argued. This is partially a consequence of the story's setting in the GDR, but this erasure is also a *de facto* result of the casting. *Hedwig* imagines gender fluidity as white, a fact which became all the more apparent when Taye Diggs replaced Mitchell near the end of the Broadway run. Diggs's first (rescripted) line in the show was "You're seeing straight: the bitch is black!"[50]

Hedwig is similarly silent when it comes to trans masculine experience. On Broadway, Hedwig's husband Yitzhak was played by Lena Hall and other non-transgender-identified women, including Rebecca Naomi Jones, Shannon Conley, and Hannah Corneau. *Hedwig* has always explicitly avoided defining Yitzhak's gender identification. The show's star consistently refers to Yitzhak using male pronouns, but until he married Hedwig, Yitzhak had been "the most famous drag queen in Zagreb," lip-syncing to songs from *Yentl* and calling herself Krystal Nacht.[51] In any case, although Yitzhak is a favorite of audiences as she stands up to Hedwig's bullying and hits some killer high notes, Trask and Mitchell's musical is not much interested in Yitzhak's personal journey, either as a trans masculine performer or as a drag queen. *Hedwig* is interested in Hedwig, and this has seemed true of both the show's audiences and the press reporting on it. Indeed, in *The Theater Will Rock*, musical theatre scholar Elizabeth Wollman documents composer Stephen Trask's frustration as *Hedwig* became popular and journalists began treating Mitchell as though he were the show's primary artist.[52] Hedwig draws focus at all times.

When Neil Patrick Harris was announced as the lead in *Hedwig and the Angry Inch*, *Hamilton*, with its diverse and unconventional cast, had not yet appeared on Broadway. The casting–identity scandal that plagued the closing of *Natasha, Pierre & the Great Comet of 1812* wouldn't happen until August of 2017, and Scarlett Johansson wouldn't withdraw from playing trans man Tex Gill in *Rub & Tug* until 2018.[53] *Hedwig* appeared on Broadway two years before Laverne Cox would be cast in *The Rocky Horror Picture Show: Let's Do the Time Warp Again* (2016) and four before Peppermint would appear as Pythio in *Head over Heels* (2018).[54] Back in

2014, Trask and producer David Binder were much more anxious to dispel accusations of stunt casting – that is, casting a celebrity in order to cash in on her fame or as a gimmick rather than for her talent *per se* – than they were to talk about issues of identity. As Suzy Evans wrote for the *Hollywood Reporter*,

> "It's not stunt casting!" the composer affirmed over and over about bringing the musical *Hedwig and the Angry Inch* to Broadway – with headliner Neil Patrick Harris. "There are plenty of people that if we just wanted to do stunt casting, we could have cast. Stunt casting is easy; we waited for the right guy."[55]

When John Cameron Mitchell took over the role in early 2015, he, too, told reporters that his decision to join the show was "not some stunt to sell tickets."[56] In fact, despite Tackitt-Jones' critique of *Hedwig* – which had been published in 2003 in the magazine *Other* and then republished in *The Transgender Studies Reader* in 2006 – during the Broadway run, none of the production team seemed concerned that they had not cast a transgender-identified actor to play the trans feminine rocker who headlined the show. Very few reporters pressed the point.[57]

As I have argued, however, casting *Hedwig* "correctly" could only ever be a failed enterprise, and what the casting of *Hedwig* might offer us instead is a different lens with which to see what *Hedwig* has been able to accomplish in popular media, especially in media aimed at LGBTQ audiences. I want to look now at how the eight actors who played Hedwig during this period spoke about their *own* identifications with the character and the work they did to cross the gulf between themselves and the character. The question of how to identify with someone with whom they do not have identity is central to the acting process for many actors, and although the interviews I'll cite in this section are obviously designed to promote the production, I'm assuming that these performers are also communicating some truths about how they worked to become Hedwig and what Hedwig allowed them newly to understand about their subjectivities.

In 2014, when the *New York Times*' Patrick Healy asked Neil Patrick Harris whether audiences would accept him as transgender, the actor dodged the question, saying that "the issue isn't sexuality [*sic*]; it's the score."[58] Harris emphasizes here that the central problem in his process of identification is whether he could hit the character's high notes. This bit of avoidance is typical for the actor's interviews about *Hedwig*. Harris tended to emphasize the physical labor rather than the emotional work he did in order to become Hedwig: "Once you get the bra on, once you get the fishnets on," he said in a different interview, "you're required to maintain a posture that is certainly much different from the posture that I generally carry."[59] His interviews often stressed the athleticism required of *Hedwig*: "this show is uniquely masochistic and somehow I'm spending most of my days just wincing about weird ailments, bruises and dislocations that I've incurred. My right hip is very sore today and I have no real idea why."[60] Harris and the press both seemed at pains to articulate his differences from Hedwig, emphasizing, for example, his weight loss and his height on *Good Morning America* and other places. The *New York Post* reported that "the 6-foot tall Harris said he lost 20 pounds. 'I used to buy him women's size 10 rehearsal clothes,' says Valerie Marcus Ramshur, the show's associate costume designer. 'Now he's down to a size 6.'" Later in the article, the *Post* reporter mused that one of Hedwig's brassieres "seemed as if it could fit Cinderella, not Harris' [*How I Met Your Mother*] character, Barney Stinson."[61] Harris already had numerous Broadway *bona fides*, but Hedwig was a far cry from the lothario he played on television, and it was this distance that he sold to audiences:

> while Harris expressed enthusiasm at the process, he admits that the femininity was the hardest part of the transformation for him to crack. "It's tough to strut around in high heels and not feel a fool, tough to manage a full wig of hair, to cock a wrist, to embrace a bra and not feel like you are somehow going to be exposed," says Harris, who also lost a lot of weight for the role. . . . "But in a role like this, you have to commit. You can't tip toe, you have to bulldoze. And the more I trusted, the further I went, the better it felt. Now her mannerisms seem second nature."[62]

Harris's *transformation into* Hedwig was the important thing in this advertising campaign, and his interviews tend, because of this, to stress the actor's masculinity, emphasizing the hard work it took for Harris to become feminine.

Andrew Rannells' interviews about *Hedwig* also tend to articulate his distance from the character. Instead of emphasizing his masculinity, however, Rannells' interviews tend to describe him as mild-mannered or stress his gentlemanly qualities. Headlines declared that "Nice Guy Andrew Rannells Channels His Inner Hedwig," and the Associated Press asked him how he felt about spitting on people:

> The Nebraska part of me is not comfortable with that. It's really not. I remember [performing as Hedwig] in Texas and being like, "I'm sorry!" I sort of decided I'm just going to go for it this time. Once you get that wig on and all that makeup, all of a sudden your politeness flies out the window.[63]

Interviews with Rannells also avoided the question of casting a non-transgender-identified actor: "People think it's just a punk rock musical about a trans performer," Rannells told Richard Ouzounian, "It's about something else. It's about feeling lost and looking for love and wanting to feel complete inside."[64]

As much as these promotional pieces note the actors' differences from the character, and as much as they both avoid the question of the actors not being transgender, these articles about *Hedwig* frequently – almost invariably – describe both Harris and Rannells as gay men, and some of them also describe the actors' (very different) processes of coming out.[65] The actors' sexualities (presumed to be identical), then, are understood to be part of the identification each has with Hedwig. It's notable that Harris and Rannells emphasized nearly opposite differences from the character – one is so much more masculine than Hedwig; one is so much more mild-mannered – but the actors are presumed to possess an identity (homosexuality) that helps them cross the distance between them and the character. I say *presumed* here because, as I argued in Chapter 1, gay male sexualities are not, in fact, identical to one another, and any detailed reading of Harris's and Rannells' interviews makes their different sexualities very clear, despite the identity-marker *gay*.

Michael C. Hall, the next actor to play *Hedwig* in the revival, told the *Daily Beast* in 2014, that *Hedwig* was allowing him to feel more free:

> Being called upon or invited to open yourself to, or welcome in your woman. I would recommend it for all men. And that it's not all softness – there's a certain kind of strength there. It's very liberating to dress up like a woman.[66]

A few years later, while starring off-Broadway in the play *Thom Pain (Based on Nothing)*, Hall came out as heterosexual but "not all the way heterosexual."[67] Some news media reported this as if it were a shocking revelation, but Hall was attempting to describe an idea that is really not very complicated – the concept of sexual fluidity in general. For him, acting helped him identify this fluidity in himself. "I think playing the emcee [in *Cabaret*] required me to fling a bunch of doors wide open because that character I imagined as pansexual," he told the *Daily Beast*. "I made out with Michael Stuhlbarg every night doing that show. I think I have always leaned into any fluidity in terms of my sexuality." The topic actually under discussion in this interview was the numerous gay roles Hall has played and whether or not "straight" actors should be playing LGBT characters. Hall had this question to ask about that issue: "How fundamental is one's sexual orientation or gender identity if both are in fact fluid, if there is some sort of spectrum and we [actors] are just moving the dial? Or is it more fundamental than that?" Hall's question is an intriguing provocation – and one I ask in this book's first chapter – but I want to note, here, how sexual orientation and gender identity move from being plural ("both") to being singular ("it") in Hall's sentence. When asked more directly if he's ever been sexually attracted to a man, Hall said yes: when he saw John Cameron Mitchell as Hedwig.

There are three more actors I want to mention briefly. In April 2015, Darren Criss started a two-and-a-half-month run as Hedwig. Like Hall, Criss has made a career playing gay characters but identifies as straight and in 2019 married his longtime girlfriend. In early 2018, when asked about his roles in *Glee*, *Hedwig*, and *The Assassination of Gianni Versace*, he said:

> I can definitely see how people in the LGBTQ community could be a little weirded out about the consistency of these roles. But it's not conscious. I'm not going, ooh, I'm going to go after all these queer roles. It's sort of no different than a gay actor only doing straight roles. I think in our political climate those things are important to talk about and important to notice.[68]

Later in that same year, Criss was quoted as saying that he wouldn't be playing gay characters anymore. He said he didn't want to be "another straight boy taking a gay man's role."[69]

When Taye Diggs took over for Criss as Hedwig in July 2015, James Hannaham wrote a beautifully in-depth piece about the actor for the *New York Times*, in which Diggs discusses femininity, Blackness, drag, and his own changing opinions about transgender acceptance and LGBT equality.[70] Talking to the tabloid TMZ before he took over the part, however, Diggs made headlines when he jokingly told a paparazzo, "I went through a stage where I was a drag queen in high school like tenth and eleventh grade; I experimented with homosexuality and ass play; . . . I worked the streets, male prostitution . . . I'm kidding," he said, flashing a big smile. Getting in his car – and away from the camera operator – he then said, "I have a flaming homosexual inside of me, so I'm raring to let that out."[71] This was a fascinating bit of trolling, and Diggs described many aspects of Hedwig's character – drag, homosexuality, sex work – but I'm especially interested in the way gender as such is left out of the actor's flippant comments. Rather, what's notable here is the way the flaming homosexual, ass play, and male prostitution *take the place* of transgender in Diggs's offhand remarks.

Finally, the following bit of dialogue is from an interview with Euan Morton, who played Hedwig on the National Tour in 2016 and 2017 before joining the cast of *Hamilton* as King George. Jerry Nunn of the *Windy City Times* asked Morton, "So you are a straight man who played gay in the past and, now, almost-trans?" Morton answered by saying,

> I wouldn't label myself any sexuality and I would prefer if you didn't. If I call myself straight then it turns into me being straight, or gay makes me gay, or transgender then transgender.
>
> I think what Hedwig does is transcend those labels.[72]

This is a confounding reply, but it is perhaps a reasonable thing to say for someone who had been playing Hedwig for a year. I want to note, in the first place, the way *transgender* becomes a "sexuality" in Morton's list. I am also interested in Morton's quite neat summation of J.L. Austin's concept of the performative here: *If I call myself straight then it turns into me being straight, or gay makes me gay*. Morton says that labels fix a person, foreclosing with performative force the fluidity that actually exists within sexual desire and gender identification. But the transcendence of which Morton speaks notwithstanding, he's explicitly saying that he *doesn't* identify as straight, gay, or trans, avoiding the possible political alliances those terms might designate and sidestepping the question of his appropriateness for the role.

I took us on this whirlwind tour of interviews these actors gave about playing Hedwig, playing gay, playing trans, and how Hedwig affected their senses of self because this group of actors was asked these questions publicly over a period of time at which the spotlight on transgender representation was getting much brighter. What I have been attempting to chart is a slippage between sexuality and gender – understood here as *homo*sexuality and *trans*gender – that obtained when actors, journalists, and audiences began to talk about *Hedwig and the Angry Inch*. This slippage became most apparent when the actors spoke about their identificatory experiences with Hedwig as a character. In this way, Neil Patrick

Harris's and Andrew Rannells' gay identities were understood as contributing to their ability to play Hedwig; Darren Criss grouped gay roles and Hedwig together under the same rubric; Michael C. Hall came out as sexually fluid, citing Hedwig as making him aware of himself in a new way. Taye Diggs has a "flaming homosexual inside."

I have quoted from numerous different news sources here, and it's worth reminding ourselves that these actors' ideas about gender and sexuality were prompted, in many ways, by the questions they were being fed by journalists and by the media team of *Hedwig* itself. There is necessarily, then, a flattening of nuance as these actors spoke about their subject positions and the work they did to identify with the character. One even hears an exhaustion with such questions, especially in Morton's and Diggs's answers. But these performers' public identifications with Hedwig and their identificatory practices in order to *play* Hedwig demonstrate a kind of snapshot of popular thought around trans embodiment and gay–trans identity. As I noted earlier, from the period of time when Harris began playing the role in 2014 to when Morton played the role in 2017, popular discourse around this topic had shifted dramatically. There was a significant change over the middle of this decade in the types of questions asked of the performers and the creative team. We moved from softball questions such as *Will audiences be able to accept you as transgender?* to sensitive ethical questions about non-transgender-identified actors portraying transgender characters. This was a palpable shift that we can track even in questions asked of actress Lena Hall in 2016, as she took over for Criss during longer residencies in San Francisco and Los Angeles.[73]

Alongside this, we should notice that for the most part, these actors got a lot smarter about replying to these questions and took more care with their answers. They began using more nuanced language near the end of and following *Hedwig*'s run: Diggs, Criss, Morton, and Lena Hall, as well as Mitchell and Trask, spoke carefully about transgender identity when talking to journalists – TMZ excepted – and Criss and Hall, in particular, carefully attempted to separate out homosexuality and transgender as two different though related phenomena. *Hedwig*'s revival, in other words, coincided with a very important sea-change in the ways in which performers and U.S. American news media spoke about transgender issues and transgender people – expressly distinguishing gender identity and sexuality from one another – even if *Hedwig* itself is intentionally much more fluid about the way that it discusses those same topics.

Identificatory Possibilities and Critical Queerness

As journalists and musical theatre performers were learning to separate sexuality and gender as different phenomena during this period of 2013–2017, another shift was happening in U.S. LGBTQ culture over this same time. In the middle of this decade, during the period in which *Hedwig* was on Broadway and on tour, transgender became newly joined *with* homosexuality as central to LGBTQ political struggles. The transgender turn in academic discourses coincided with – and indeed contributed to – a reinvigoration of trans politics within LGBTQ political circles. Following the nation-wide legalization of same-sex marriage by the U.S. Supreme Court in June 2015 and energized by a robust trans political movement, mainstream LGBTQ politics became much more invested in issues affecting trans folks in the United States. Despite the real work done by trans activists over the last two decades, the issue of same-sex marriage had dominated mainstream LGBTQ politics until 2015 at the expense of many other issues affecting queer communities, and this was especially notable because the politics surrounding marriage most obviously benefited white, middle-class men and women who wanted to marry their white, middle-class partners. Pro-marriage politics were the priority of the mainstream LGBTQ political organizations in a way that, for example, decriminalization of sex work or trans healthcare were not. This changed somewhat following the Supreme Court's decision, as these mainstream LGBTQ political organizations were able to claim victory in the fight for marriage equality, leaving room for new and different political battles.

This period of time marks a new and different level of inclusion of trans issues within mainstream LGBTQ organizations, and this is perhaps most obviously visible in the "progress pride flag," designed by nonbinary artist Daniel Quasar in 2018. Their design adds a chevron comprising the three colors of the transgender pride flag (light blue, pink, and white) and the colors black and brown (representing queer people of color) to the more common six-striped rainbow pride flag. Quasar's progress pride flag immediately went viral and is now widely used by LGBTQ organizations. Their flag is a visible demonstration of a new awareness among the LGBTQ community writ large that trans issues should be fundamental to LGBTQ politics.[74]

What I want to note here is that at the same time as many people, including journalists, began to disaggregate gender identification from sexuality as separate phenomena, there was a simultaneous movement *within* LGBTQ politics that emphasized the *identity* of queer sexuality and transgender, a movement that characterized trans politics as central to the coalitional LGBTQ political agenda. This should not be simply taken for granted. Histories of transgender folks in the United States have long charted the tenuousness of gay–trans political identity. Historians Aaron Devor and Nicholas Matte, for example, argue that, following the Stonewall uprising in 1969,

> while gay and lesbian rights organizing expanded rapidly, the distinctive gifts and needs of transgendered people were often marginalized by the leadership of early gay and lesbian organizations. Bull daggers and drag queens, transgendered and transsexual people, were largely treated as embarrassments in the "legitimate" fight for tolerance, acceptance, and equal rights.[75]

Devor and Matte chart painful histories of exclusion, accusation, and rampant transphobia among lesbian- and gay-identified groups. According to historian Joanne Meyerowitz,

> In the 1970s and 1980s gay men, lesbians, and feminists increasingly cast transsexuals variously as irrelevant, out of style, invasive, or conservative. The gay liberation movement moved away from its early embrace of gender transgression.[76]

This is a long, complicated, and ableist history that Meyerowitz, Abram Lewis, and others relate in detail, and if political coalition between gay-identified and trans-identified people now seems, from the perspective of the third decade of the twenty-first century, to be natural or obvious, this only demonstrates the power and speed of the change that happened following the legalization of same-sex marriage in 2015.[77] As Devor and Matte remind us, the Human Rights Campaign amended its mission to include transgender folks only as recently as March 2001![78]

In 2015, things were much different. For example, when a transphobic Change.org petition circulated in November of that year asking the *Advocate*, the Human Rights Campaign, GLAAD, and other organizations to "Drop the T" from LGBT, all of these mainstream LGBTQ political organizations rejected the campaign immediately and outright.[79] This petition's aim was to return these organizations to focusing on political issues mostly affecting white, middle-class gay men and lesbians and away from the political issues facing trans folks, especially trans people of color. The "Drop the T" petition was hardly an important moment in LGBTQ politics; it received fewer than 1,000 signatures and is now mostly forgotten.[80] But the existence of such a petition is evidence of the new power of trans politics within LGBTQ political organizations in 2015; this minority of transphobic gay- and lesbian-identified people discovered and articulated newfound feelings of marginalization within organizations they understood as belonging to them.

Transphobic white gays notwithstanding, historians of gender and sexuality in the United States have, to the contrary, carefully documented a great deal of overlap between people who identify as gay or lesbian and people who identify as trans. Meyerowitz notes that "In the early twentieth century homosexuality increasingly referred to same-sex object choice, as opposed to gender 'inversion.' . . . But with the new definitions, the 'inverts' who described themselves as men with female bodies or women with male bodies stood in taxonomy's limbo."[81] These categories were fundamentally confused in the early twentieth century. Indeed, historian Jules Gill-Peterson argues that as we look for trans histories in the archive, we will sometimes find those histories labeled as *homosexuality*:

> The fact that trans life could fall under the sign of "homosexuality" is actually an important clue for how to read the early twentieth-century medical archive, for the wider category of sexual inversion regularly mixed gay and trans connotations.[82]

This is not only true for the United States in the early twentieth century; anthropologists Evelyn Blackwood and Saskia Wieringa similarly "problematize the categories of 'homosexuality,' 'lesbian,' and 'woman'" in their edited volume – take note of the title – *Same-Sex Relations and Female Desires: Transgender Practices Across Cultures*.[83] The scholars in their book critically examine gender and sexuality without assuming that the categories are separate. Deborah Elliston, for example, finds in her studies in French Polynesia, that gender "is not contingent on or derived from sexual practices; rather, gender produces sexuality, or more accurately, Polynesians conceptualize gender difference as productive of sexuality."[84] All of which is to say that our current categories of sexuality and gender might very well be useful ways of making sense of the world in which we live, of describing how we feel, how we understand our bodies, our desires, our longings, our selves, but the *separation* between gender and sexuality is a historically contingent one.[85]

The period from 2014 to 2017 marks a particularly thorny moment for this separation, as many gender descriptors were consolidated under the term *transgender* and the term *nonbinary* emerged in full force (Google charts a rise in searches of the term beginning in 2014); meanwhile, mainstream LGBTQ organizations were emphasizing gay–trans identity as a political coalition. There has been, in other words, a significant slippage between gender and sexuality over time, and the second decade of the twenty-first century marked an important moment of both difference *and* identity. One can easily see this in the Darren Criss interviews I cited earlier: though he distinguishes carefully between transgender and homosexuality as concepts, he inevitably speaks about his roles in *Glee, Hedwig,* and *The Assassination of Gianni Versace* as "consistent" with one another. In other words, he "knows" that gender identity and sexual desire are not identical, but he aligns them with one another, as it were, "naturally." Compare Criss's casual slippage to Chris Eng's 2018 academic article on *Hedwig* in *Theatre Journal*, which purposely uses the phrase "queer/trans" more than 15 times in the course of his argument as well as in the article's subtitle.

What I want to posit is that this tendency to aggregate sexuality and gender, or to slide into confusion where there "ought" to be strict separation, is not only colloquially common among straight-identified people like Criss and queer scholars like Eng but also fundamental to the dramaturgy of *Hedwig and the Angry Inch* itself. Further, *Hedwig* might help us to see that our own taxonomies are more clearly delineated than they perhaps ought to be. Is, for example, Hedwig homosexual, heterosexual, bisexual, or something else? The answer to this question about sexuality necessarily depends on which of the genders you decide you believe Hedwig to be. And since she has not told us which gender(s) she identifies with (if any), Hedwig and her creators leave open the question *both* of her sexuality and her gender.

For Hedwig, and indeed for us, it would appear that gender and sexuality are dependent on each other for definition. But this is also true for the "gender" and "sexuality" of Yitzhak, Luther, and Tommy, Hedwig's sexual partners. Our understandings of their sexualities are dependent on her gender as much as on theirs. All of this is, perhaps, obvious and may also be getting annoyingly technical. Hedwig, Luther, Tommy, and Yitzhak are, after all, fictional characters, and their sexualities, such as they exist, have been crafted by Stephen Trask, John Cameron Mitchell, and the actors who've played the characters. Still, something always strikes me as odd when I read a scholar or critic referring to Tommy or Luther as "straight." It just isn't quite right. Or, rather, the definition is too fixed; *straight* is too solid of a description for a set of desires that are a great deal queerer.

I don't wish to conclude simply by saying that the show revels in gender confusion and sexual indeterminacy; anyone who has seen *Hedwig* doesn't need me to tell them that. I am much more interested in how *Hedwig* might respond to a question Judith Butler asked in *Bodies That Matter* back in 1993: "If we seek to privilege sexual practice as a way of transcending gender, we might ask at what cost the *analytic* separability of the two domains is taken to be a distinction in fact."[86] If, for the actors who have played Hedwig, for the audiences who have watched *Hedwig*, and for the critics who have talked about *Hedwig*, the distinction between queer sexuality and gender transcendence ceased to be imagined as a distinction at all – if these viewers had difficulty achieving the analytic separability Butler described – *Hedwig* has been doing more (and more interesting) work than we imagined. And doing it at the same time as many, many U.S. Americans started typing the word *nonbinary* into their search engines.

The structural instability of gender in *Hedwig* points up the implausibility of binary gender as such, and this articulates a specific strand of trans politics, as well. Trans activist Dean Spade has argued that medical surveillance technologies and the possibility of gender identity disorder (GID) diagnosis work to make gendered sense of *all* children:

> The diagnostic criteria for GID produc[e] a fiction of natural gender, in which normal, non-transsexual people grow up with minimal to no gender trouble or exploration, do not crossdress as children, do not play with the wrong-gendered kids, and do not like the wrong kinds of toys or characters.[87]

The very idea of a GID diagnosis assumes that *most* children are coloring within their correctly gendered lines. As Spade argues, this story is simply not credible, certainly for the slip of a girlyboy that Hedwig was as a child, but also for each of us in the audience. And if, as Jordy Tackitt-Jones argues, Hedwig is not a transsexual woman, *nevertheless Hedwig invites transgender identification rather than foreclosing it*, asking audiences to identify in ways we might not have identified before. She attempts to create identity – sameness – where we can see only difference, and she asks us to dwell *in* those differences while acknowledging new possibilities for identity now and in the future.

Finally, I want to return briefly to Aristophanes' speech in the *Symposium* and the "Origin of Love." In *One Hundred Years of Homosexuality*, classicist David Halperin reminds us that

> one consequence of the myth is to make the sexual desire of every human being *formally identical* to that of every other: we are all looking for the same

thing in a sexual partner, according to Plato's Aristophanes – namely, a symbolic substitute for an originary object once loved and subsequently lost in an archaic trauma.[88]

In other words, one of the ways *Hedwig* functions is that the musical asks audiences to consider *both* our genders and our sexualities as identical to everyone else's: "But I could swear by your expression / That the pain down in your soul / Was the same as the one down in mine."[89] It is true that the show does not adhere to today's particular way of parsing between (trans)gender and (homo)sexuality, but if *Hedwig* does not do our identity politics very well, it is committed instead to opening up identificatory *possibilities* for persons with a wide range of bodies, desires, and orientations.

Well, Almost. . .

No matter this musical's virtues, *Hedwig* has its limits, and the identificatory possibilities it offers are not infinite. I've been arguing in this chapter that *Hedwig* on Broadway captured a particular moment in the history of U.S. American understandings of gender, sexuality, and LGBTQ identity. That moment was characterized by the political victory of marriage equality and a subsequent shift in focus (at least apparently) within mainstream LGBTQ politics toward more issues affecting trans people and trans communities. It was long argued within LGBTQ political circles that the achievement of same-sex marriage most benefited middle-class white couples, but Robert McRuer has also argued that "intracommunity debates over gay marriage and other 'normalizing' issues are centrally about disability and disability oppression."[90] He points out, for example, that

> most of the complaints about lesbian and gay partners not being able to get health insurance through their spouse have not included an acknowledgement of how many people in general don't have adequate health insurance, let alone a broader critique of the corporate health insurance industry.[91]

I want to highlight this critique because it seems to me that scholars have not yet spent enough time considering *Hedwig* from the perspective of disability.

Earlier I noted Chris Eng's argument that the musical's jokes about Asian labor disavow that labor and create indifference in the audience for the "Bangladeshi children" who have made Hedwig's wigs as well the Korean women who played the mean rhythm section in the original iteration of the Angry Inch.[92] I also noted the way the show ignores both transmasculine experience and the experiences of trans people of color. But *Hedwig* is also strangely dependent on the citation of disability. Even before the show's second song, Hedwig tells the audience that she and Tommy were arrested for driving under the influence of cocaine and that they hit a bus filled with deaf schoolchildren. Indeed, this is a joke in the show with a further, ableist punchline: "one survived – now blind."[93] Just a few minutes later, Hedwig explains that when the Berlin wall went up, she "happened to be living on the East side and Mother was given a job teaching sculpture to limbless children."[94] Images of medical procedures, prostheses, injury, pain, debility, and scarring further suffuse *Hedwig and the Angry Inch*.

These images became especially potent during John Cameron Mitchell's return to the role – after developing the part in the 1990s and playing Hedwig in the 2001 film. Mitchell replaced Michael C. Hall as Hedwig at the Belasco in late January 2015, and in contrast to their focus on Neil Patrick Harris's masculinity or Andrew Rannells' politeness, journalists tended to emphasize Mitchell's age (51) and his physical vulnerability (an interview with Patrick Healy emphasized "a purplish bruise under his left eye" that he got during rehearsal when a microphone fell on his face).[95] Then, in mid-February, Mitchell was forced to leave the show when he sustained a knee injury. Hall returned to the role for a week before Mitchell took over the part again, this time with his knee in a brace. Hedwig returned to the stage sporting a crutch covered in glitter and propping her leg up on an apple crate.[96] Mitchell's own visible disability, however, did not stop Hedwig from making her usual jokes at the expense of other, different disabilities.

Hedwig, in other words, explicitly disavows disability; she distances herself from – and asks us to laugh at – the deaf children in the school bus who can't hear the musical's songs. At the same time, she describes in detail the pain, scarring, and trauma she experienced after her operation as well as the more existential pain of separation imagined as attendant to the "Origin of Love" myth. But while disavowing disabled *people*, Hedwig preaches one version of disability politics, telling the audience we should know that we're whole as we are, in whatever state we find ourselves, that we don't need anything else to complete us. Hedwig does this while simultaneously exhorting us to lift up our hands, a physical action not easy to accomplish if you're a limbless child studying sculpture in East Berlin – or, indeed, a 51-year-old internationally ignored song stylist barely standing before us and supporting herself using a be-glittered crutch.

Notes

1 Currah and Stryker, "Introduction," 3.
2 Steinmetz, "Everything You Need to Know About the Debate over Transgender People and Bathrooms."
3 James, Herman, Rankin, Keisling, Mottet, and Anafi, *The Report of the 2015 U.S. Transgender Survey*.
4 Human Rights Campaign, *Addressing Anti-Transgender Violence*.
5 Martinez and Law, "Two Recent Murders of Black Trans Women in Texas Reveal a Nationwide Crisis, Advocates Say."
6 Steinmetz, "The Transgender Tipping Point"; Gjorgievska and Rothman, "Laverne Cox Is the First Transgender Person Nominated for an Emmy."
7 Press, "*Pose*'s Rise, *Transparent*'s Bittersweet Finale, and the State of Transgender Representation on TV."
8 Severson, "It's a Girl! It's a Boy! and for the Gender-Reveal Cake, It May Be the End."
9 This idea is rather obviously indebted to queer theorist Elizabeth Freeman's *The Wedding Complex*. On plasticity, see Gill-Peterson, *Histories of the Transgender Child*.

10 Svich, *Mitchell and Trask's Hedwig and the Angry Inch*, 22.
11 Mitchell quoted in Ouzounian, "John Cameron Mitchell to Host Hedwig and the Angry Inch Sing-Along in Toronto."
12 Mitchell, *Hedwig and the Angry Inch*.
13 Salazar, "Hedwig and the Angry Inch."
14 Kim, "Domesticating Hedwig," 425.
15 See Sypniewski, "The Pursuit of Eros in Plato's *Symposium* and *Hedwig and the Angry Inch*"; Blood, "The Trouble With Icons"; Hsu, "Reading and Queering Plato in *Hedwig and the Angry Inch*"; and Pérez Bernal. "El Amor Como 'Aventura Solitaria' en Hedwig and the Angry Inch, de John Cameron Mitchell."
16 Hollis, "Figuring the *Angry Inch*," 26.
17 Awkward-Rich, "Trans, Feminism: *Or*, Reading like a Depressed Transsexual," 838.
18 Susan Stryker, *Transgender History*, 147; Svich, *Mitchell and Trask's Hedwig and the Angry Inch*, 1.
19 Eng, "'Give It Up, Kwang,'" 175.
20 Mitchell quoted in Hilferty, "John Cameron Mitchell: Rock and Role," 68.
21 Valentine, *Imagining Transgender*, 37.
22 Valentine, *Imagining Transgender*, 39.
23 Tackitt-Jones, "Gender Without Genitals," 450.
24 Trask and Mitchell, *Hedwig and the Angry Inch*, 21.
25 Trask and Mitchell, *Hedwig and the Angry Inch*, 24.
26 Trask and Mitchell, *Hedwig and the Angry Inch*, 38. Many scholars seem rather confused about this interaction, saying that Luther thinks Hansel is a girl when he first sees him. See, for example, Sypniewski, "The Pursuit of Eros in Plato's *Symposium* and *Hedwig and the Angry Inch*," 568; Kim, "Domesticating Hedwig," 424; Hsu, "Reading and Queering Plato in *Hedwig and the Angry Inch*," 109; Dean, "There Ain't Much of a Difference/Between a Bridge and a Wall," 112. Blood, "The Trouble with Icons," 205, discusses this moment in the musical more accurately.
27 Trask and Mitchell, *Hedwig and the Angry Inch*, 21.
28 Trask and Mitchell, *Hedwig and the Angry Inch*, 25.
29 Trask and Mitchell, *Hedwig and the Angry Inch*, 29.
30 Trask and Mitchell, *Hedwig and the Angry Inch*, 31.
31 Plato, *Symposium*, 21. As David Halperin puts it, "although his genetic explanation of the diversity of sexual object-choice among human beings would seem to require that there be some adult males who are sexually attracted to other adult males, Aristophanes appears to be wholly unaware of such a possibility, and in any case he has left no room for it in his taxonomic scheme." See Halperin, *One Hundred Years of Homosexuality and Other Essays on Greek Love*, 20–21.
32 Trask and Mitchell, *Hedwig and the Angry Inch*, 33.
33 Trask and Mitchell, *Hedwig and the Angry Inch*, 79.
34 Trask and Mitchell, *Hedwig and the Angry Inch*, 82.
35 Trask and Mitchell, *Hedwig and the Angry Inch*, 80.
36 Trask and Mitchell, *Hedwig and the Angry Inch*, 83.
37 Tackitt-Jones, "Gender without Genitals," 454. Tackitt-Jones is speaking about the *film* version, but the critique is mostly transferable. Tackitt-Jones' reading of the final image of the eye is that "the male and the female halves of the animated original androgyne reappear and merge, the halves made whole, the masculine and feminine integrated into the symbol of the fantasy of the remarked/unmarked body" (464).
38 Trask and Mitchell, *Hedwig and the Angry Inch*, 91.
39 Musicologist Judith A. Peraino also makes this point in *Listening to the Sirens*, 251.
40 Tackitt-Jones, "Gender Without Genitals," 465.
41 Stone, "The *Empire* Strikes Back," 232.
42 Trask and Mitchell, *Hedwig and the Angry Inch*, 47–49.
43 Stryker, "My Words to Victor Frankenstein Above the Village of Chamounix," 248.
44 Trask and Mitchell, *Hedwig and the Angry Inch*, 15, 75–76.

45 Stryker, "My Words to Victor Frankenstein Above the Village of Chamounix," 254.
46 Trask and Mitchell, *Hedwig and the Angry Inch*, 76.
47 Mitchell quoted in Abramovitch, "John Cameron Mitchell: *Hedwig* Is 'Not Really a Trans Story.'" *Pace* Mitchell, not everyone chooses to be trans; see, for example, Gill-Peterson's discussion of intersex children in *Histories of the Transgender Child*, 68–80.
48 Svich, *Mitchell and Trask's Hedwig and the Angry Inch*, 60–61.
49 Henderson, "Actor John Cameron Mitchell Comes Out as Nonbinary." Many nonbinary folks *do* identify as trans, of course, but Mitchell so far has not.
50 Lee, "Will *Hedwig* Return as a Star-Launching Show?"
51 Trask and Mitchell, *Hedwig and the Angry Inch*, 56
52 Wollman, *The Theater Will Rock*, 186–187.
53 Paulson, "Race, Money and Broadway"; Svachula, "Scarlett Johansson Withdraws From Transgender Role After Backlash."
54 See Crookston, "Can I Be Frank With You?"
55 Evans, "Tonys: How the *Hedwig* Team Turned Neil Patrick Harris Into a Bona Fide Rock Star."
56 Healy, "An Old Role, but New Tresses," AR1.
57 Anyone on the hunt can find scandals related to the casting of non-transgender-identified performers in transgender roles, but these scandals emerge in the period *after Hedwig*'s Broadway run. See, for example, the listicle "14 Cisgender Actors in Transgender Roles."
58 Healy, "A Week with Neil Patrick Harris, as He Heads as Far as Possible from His Sitcom," AR1. Note, here, that Healy asks about gender, but Harris answers by saying it's not about sexuality.
59 Schneier, "From Madonna to Hedwig, Dressing the Divas of Rock," E6.
60 Johnson, "Neil's Mo-ment in Time Is a Wild Ride," 81.
61 "Drag Deluxe," 39.
62 Evans, "Tonys: How the *Hedwig* Team Turned Neil Patrick Harris Into a Bona Fide Rock Star."
63 Kennedy, "Nice Guy Andrew Rannells Channels His Inner Hedwig."
64 Ouzounian, "Andrew Rannells talks Hedwig, Girls and Book of Mormon."
65 See, for example, Yuan, "Playing It Straight," 4ff; "Doing 'What Felt Right' Key to Actor's Success," E3.
66 Stern, "Michael C. Hall on Going Drag for *Hedwig and the Angry Inch* and Exorcising *Dexter*."
67 Teeman, "Michael C. Hall on His 'Fluid' Sexuality, *Dexter*, Death, and David Bowie."
68 Criss quoted in Fallon, "How Darren Criss Became Versace's Killer."
69 Carlin, "Here's Why Darren Criss Says He Won't Play Gay Characters Any Longer."
70 Hannaham, "Transformation," MM24.
71 "Taye Diggs: Channeling His Inner Homosexual . . . to Play Hedwig."
72 Nunn, "Euan Morton Takes the Lead in *Hedwig*."
73 Evans, "Lena Hall on Revisiting Yitzhak for *Hedwig and the Angry Inch* Tour & Finally Wearing Hedwig's Heels."
74 Taylor, "Trans, QPOC Inclusive Pride Flag Campaign Going Viral."
75 Devor and Matte, "ONE Inc. and Reed Erickson," 388.
76 Meyerowitz, *How Sex Changed*, 258; see also 180.
77 Lewis, " 'We Are Certain of Our Own Insanity.' "
78 Devor and Matte, "ONE Inc. and Reed Erickson," 389.
79 See Brydum, "LGBT Groups Respond to Petition Asking to 'Drop the T' "; and Strehlke, "Why More Than 1,000 People Have Signed a Petition to Drop the 'T' from LGBT."
80 There has been a resurgence of trans-exclusionary politics in some places, including the United Kingdom, where the advocacy group the LGB Alliance was founded in September 2019.
81 Meyerowitz, *How Sex Changed*, 170.
82 Gill-Peterson, *Histories of the Transgender Child*, 61.

83 Blackwood and Wieringa, *Same-Sex Relations and Female Desires*, ix.
84 Elliston, "Negotiating Transnational Sexual Economies," 238.
85 Kadji Amin, for example, uses the phrase "gender-sexuality (a term I prefer to 'gender and sexuality, since the two are, in reality, indissociable)." See Amin, "We Are All Nonbinary," 107.
86 Butler, *Bodies That Matter*, 238.
87 Spade, "Mutilating Gender," 321.
88 Halperin, *One Hundred Years of Homosexuality and Other Essays on Greek Love*, 20.
89 Trask and Mitchell, *Hedwig and the Angry Inch*, 32.
90 McRuer, *Crip Theory*, 80.
91 McRuer, *Crip Theory*, 82–83.
92 Trask and Mitchell, *Hedwig and the Angry Inch*, 34.
93 Trask and Mitchell, *Hedwig and the Angry Inch*, 22.
94 Trask and Mitchell, *Hedwig and the Angry Inch*, 24.
95 Healy, "Old Role, but New Tresses," AR1.
96 Patterson, "John Cameron Mitchell's Knee-Braced *Hedwig* Gets On-Stage Back Story."

References for Chapter 3

"14 Cisgender Actors in Transgender Roles." *Hollywood Reporter*. 5 May 2017. www.hollywoodreporter.com/lists/cisgender-actors-transgender-roles-elle-fanning-eddie-redmayne-more-998984/. Accessed 9 June 2022.

Abramovitch, Seth. "John Cameron Mitchell: *Hedwig* Is 'Not Really a Trans Story.'" *Hollywood Reporter*. 3 June 2019. www.hollywoodreporter.com/news/general-news/john-cameron-mitchell-hedwig-is-not-a-trans-story-1215285/. Accessed 12 June 2022.

Amin, Kadji. "We Are All Nonbinary: A Brief History of Accidents." *Representations* 158.1: 106–119, 2022.

Awkward-Rich, Cameron. "Trans, Feminism: Or, Reading like a Depressed Transsexual." *Signs: Journal of Women in Culture and Society* 42.4: 819–841, 2017.

Blackwood, Evelyn, and Saskia E. Wieringa, (editors). *Same-Sex Relations and Female Desires: Transgender Practices Across Cultures*. New York: Columbia University Press, 1999.

Blood, H. Christian. "The Trouble With Icons: Recent Ideological Appropriations of Plato's *Symposium*." *Helios* 35.2: 197–222, 2008.

Brydum, Sunnivie. "LGBT Groups Respond to Petition Asking to 'Drop the T.'" *Advocate*. 6 November 2015. www.advocate.com/transgender/2015/11/06/lgbt-groups-respond-petition-asking-drop-t. Accessed 16 June 2022

Butler, Judith. *Bodies That Matter: On the Discursive Limits of "Sex."* New York: Routledge, 1993.

Carlin, Shannon. "Here's Why Darren Criss Says He Won't Play Gay Characters Any Longer." *Bustle*. 18 December 2018. www.bustle.com/p/darren-criss-wont-play-gay-characters-any-longer-for-a-truly-great-reason-15525677. Accessed 15 June 2022.

Crookston, Cameron. "Can I Be Frank With You? Laverne Cox and the Historiographic Dramaturgy of *The Rocky Horror Picture Show*." *GLQ: A Journal of Lesbian and Gay Studies* 27.2: 233–252, 2021.

Currah, Paisley, and Susan Stryker. "Introduction," *TSQ: Transgender Studies Quarterly* 1.1–2: 1–18, 2014.

Dean, Sharon G. "There Ain't Much of a Difference/Between a Bridge and a Wall." *Journal of Bisexuality* 5.4: 107–116, 2006.

Devor, Aaron H., and Nicholas Matte, "ONE Inc. and Reed Erickson: The Uneasy Collaboration of Gay and Trans Activism, 1964–2003." In *The Transgender Studies Reader*. Edited by Susan Stryker, and Stephen Whittle. London: Routledge, 387–406, 2006.

"Doing 'What Felt Right' Key to Actor's Success." *Toronto Star*. 28 June 2014. (E3).

"Drag Deluxe." *New York Post.* 27 April 2014. (39).

Elliston, Deborah A. "Negotiating Transnational Sexual Economies: Female *Māhū* and Same-Sex Sexuality in 'Tahiti and Her Islands.'" In *Same-Sex Relations and Female Desires: Transgender Practices Across Cultures.* Edited by Evelyn Blackwood, and Saskia E. Wieringa. New York: Columbia University Press, 232–252, 1999.

Eng, Chris A. "'Give It Up, Kwang': Disavowing Asian Labor and Queer/Trans of Color Critique in *Hedwig and the Angry Inch.*" *Theatre Journal* 70.2: 173–193, 2018.

Evans, Suzy. "Lena Hall on Revisiting Yitzhak for *Hedwig and the Angry Inch* Tour & Finally Wearing Hedwig's Heels." *Billboard.* 4 November 2016. www.billboard.com/articles/news/7565529/lena-hall-on-revisiting-yitzhak-for-hedwig-and-the-angry-inch-tour-finally. Accessed 15 June 2022.

Evans, Suzy. "Tonys: How the *Hedwig* Team Turned Neil Patrick Harris Into a Bona Fide Rock Star." *Hollywood Reporter.* 6 June 2014. www.hollywoodreporter.com/news/tonys-how-hedwig-team-turned-709922. Accessed 9 June 2022.

Fallon, Kevin. "How Darren Criss Became Versace's Killer (and Why He Keeps Playing Gay)." *Daily Beast.* 17 January 2018. www.thedailybeast.com/how-darren-criss-became-versaces-killer-and-why-he-keeps-playing-gay. Accessed 15 June 2022.

Freeman, Elizabeth. *The Wedding Complex: Forms of Belonging in Modern American Culture.* Durham: Duke University Press, 2002.

Gill-Peterson, Jules. *Histories of the Transgender Child.* Minneapolis: University of Minnesota Press, 2018.

Gjorgievska, Aleksandra, and Lily Rothman. "Laverne Cox Is the First Transgender Person Nominated for an Emmy – She Explains Why That Matters." *Time.* 10 July 2014. time.com/2973497/laverne-cox-emmy/. Accessed 9 June 2022.

Halperin, David M. *One Hundred Years of Homosexuality and Other Essays on Greek Love.* New York: Routledge, 1990.

Hannaham, James. "Transformation." *New York Times.* 26 July 2015. (MM24).

Healy, Patrick. "A Week With Neil Patrick Harris, as He Heads as Far as Possible From His Sitcom." *New York Times.* 23 February 2014. (AR1).

Healy, Patrick. "An Old Role, but New Tresses." *New York Times.* 18 January 2015. (AR1).

Henderson, Taylor. "Actor John Cameron Mitchell Comes Out as Nonbinary." *Pride.* 4 March 2022. www.pride.com/comingout/2022/3/04/actor-john-cameron-mitchell-comes-out-nonbinary. Accessed 12 June 2022.

Hilferty, Robert. "John Cameron Mitchell: Rock and Role." *Out* 7.7: 68, 1999.

Hollis, Erik. "Figuring the Angry Inch: Transnormativity, the Black Femme and the Fraudulent Phallus: *Or* Fleshly Remainders of the 'Ungendered' and the 'Unthought.'" *Feminist Theory* 19.1: 23–40, 2018.

Hsu, Wendy. "Reading and Queering Plato in *Hedwig and the Angry Inch.*" In *Queer Popular Culture: Literature, Media, Film, and Television.* Edited by Thomas Peele. London: Palgrave Macmillan, 103–117, 2011.

Human Rights Campaign. *Addressing Anti-Transgender Violence: Exploring Realities, Challenges and Solutions for Policymakers and Community Advocates.* 2019. assets2.hrc.org/files/assets/resources/HRC-AntiTransgenderViolence-0519.pdf. Accessed 16 June 2022.

James, Sandy E., Jody L. Herman, Susan Rankin, Mara Keisling, Lisa Mottet, and Ma'ayan Anafi. *The Report of the 2015 U.S. Transgender Survey.* Washington, DC: National Center for Transgender Equality, 2016.

Johnson, Neala. "Neil's Mo-ment in Time Is a Wild Ride." *Advertiser.* 1 June 2014. (81).

Kennedy, Mark. "Nice Guy Andrew Rannells Channels His Inner Hedwig." *Associated Press Online.* 20 August 2014. https://apnews.com/article/neil-patrick-harris-nebraska-archive-andrew-rannells-nancy-meyers-9971bda71f614837a5c6a61e96ec8e45. Accessed 15 November 2022.

Kim, Hyewon. "Domesticating Hedwig: Neoliberal Global Capitalism and Compression in South Korean Musical Theatre." *Journal of Popular Culture* 51.2: 421–445, 2018.

Lee, Ashley. "Will *Hedwig* Return as a Star-Launching Show? Taye Diggs, Composer Reflect on 'Spiritual' Broadway Run (Q&A)." *Hollywood Reporter*. 7 September 2015. www.hollywoodreporter.com/news/hedwig-angry-inch-taye-diggs-820810. Accessed 9 June 2022.

Lewis, Abram J. "'We Are Certain of Our Own Insanity': Antipsychiatry and the Gay Liberation Movement, 1968–1980." *Journal of the History of Sexuality* 25.1: 83–113, 2016.

Martinez, Gina, and Tara Law. "Two Recent Murders of Black Trans Women in Texas Reveal a Nationwide Crisis, Advocates Say." *Time*. 12 June 2019. time.com/5601227/two-black-trans-women-murders-in-dallas-anti-trans-violence/. Accessed 9 June 2022.

McRuer, Robert. *Crip Theory: Cultural Signs of Queerness and Disability*. New York: New York University Press, 2006.

Meyerowitz, Joanne. *How Sex Changed: A History of Transsexuality in the United States*. Cambridge: Harvard University Press, 2002.

Mitchell, John Cameron (director). *Hedwig and the Angry Inch*. Criterion Channel. 20 July 2001.

Nunn, Jerry. "Euan Morton Takes the Lead in *Hedwig*." *Windy City Times*. 8 March 2017. www.windycitymediagroup.com/lgbt/nunn-on-one-theater-euan-morton-takes-the-lead-in-hedwig/58366.html. Accessed 15 June 2022.

Ouzounian, Richard. "Andrew Rannells Talks Hedwig, Girls and Book of Mormon." *Toronto Star*. 27 June 2014. www.thestar.com/entertainment/2014/06/27/andrew_rannells_talks_hedwig_girls_and_book_of_mormon.html. Accessed 15 June 2022.

Ouzounian, Richard. "John Cameron Mitchell to Host Hedwig and the Angry Inch Sing-Along in Toronto." *Toronto Star*. 18 June 2014. www.thestar.com/entertainment/stage/2014/06/18/singalong_hedwig_and_the_angry_inch_comes_to_lgbt_film_fest.html. Accessed 14 June 2022.

Patterson, Richard. "John Cameron Mitchell's Knee-Braced Hedwig Gets On-Stage Back Story." *Playbill*. 5 March 2015. www.playbill.com/article/john-cameron-mitchells-knee-braced-hedwig-gets-on-stage-back-story-com-343425. Accessed 17 June 2022.

Paulson, Michael. "Race, Money and Broadway: How *Great Comet* Burned Out." *New York Times*. 29 August 2017. www.nytimes.com/2017/08/29/theater/great-comet-broadway-race.html. Accessed 9 June 2022.

Peraino, Judith A. *Listening to the Sirens: Musical Technologies of Queer Identity From Homer to Hedwig*. Berkeley: University of California Press, 2006.

Pérez Bernal, Ángeles Maria del Rosario. "El Amor Como 'Aventura Solitaria' en Hedwig and the Angry Inch, de John Cameron Mitchell." *Escritos* 30.64: 136–148, 2022.

Plato. *Symposium*. Translated by Seth Benardete. Chicago: University of Chicago Press, 2001.

Press, Joy. "*Pose*'s Rise, *Transparent*'s Bittersweet Finale, and the State of Transgender Representation on TV." *Vanity Fair*. 13 August 2019. www.vanityfair.com/hollywood/2019/08/the-state-of-transgender-representation-on-tv. Accessed 9 June 2022.

Salazar, Rosa. "Hedwig and the Angry Inch: A Radical Affront to Conventional Renditions of Gender." *Culture, Society & Praxis* 3.1: 69–78, 2004.

Schneier, Matthew. "From Madonna to Hedwig, Dressing the Divas of Rock." *New York Times*. 17 April 2014. (E6).

Severson, Kim. "It's a Girl! It's a Boy! and for the Gender-Reveal Cake, It May Be the End." *New York Times*. 17 June 2019. www.nytimes.com/2019/06/17/dining/gender-reveal-cake.html. Accessed 9 June 2022.

Spade, Dean. "Mutilating Gender." In *The Transgender Studies Reader*. Edited by Susan Stryker, and Stephen Whittle. London: Routledge, 315–332, 2006.

Steinmetz, Katy. "Everything You Need to Know About the Debate over Transgender People and Bathrooms." *Time*. 28 July 2015. time.com/3974186/transgender-bathroom-debate/. Accessed July 2022.

Steinmetz, Katy. "The Transgender Tipping Point." *Time*. 29 May 2014. time.com/135480/transgender-tipping-point/. Accessed 10 June 2022.

Stern, Marlow. "Michael C. Hall on Going Drag for *Hedwig and the Angry Inch* and Exorcising *Dexter*." *Daily Beast*. 4 December 2014. www.thedailybeast.com/michael-c-hall-on-going-drag-for-hedwig-and-the-angry-inch-and-exorcising-dexter. Accessed 15 June 2022.

Stone, Sandy. "The *Empire* Strikes Back: A Posttranssexual Manifesto." In *The Transgender Studies Reader*. Edited by Susan Stryker, and Stephen Whittle. London: Routledge, 221–235, 2006.

Strehlke, Sade. "Why More Than 1,000 People Have Signed a Petition to Drop the 'T' From LGBT." *Teen Vogue*. 9 November 2015. www.teenvogue.com/story/drop-the-t-petition-backlash. Accessed 16 June 2022.

Stryker, Susan. "My Words to Victor Frankenstein Above the Village of Chamounix: Performing Transgender Rage." In *The Transgender Studies Reader*. Edited by Susan Stryker, and Stephen Whittle. London: Routledge, 244–256, 2006.

Stryker, Susan. *Transgender History*. Berkeley: Seal Press, 2008.

Svachula, Amanda. "Scarlett Johansson Withdraws From Transgender Role After Backlash." *New York Times*. 13 July 2018. www.nytimes.com/2018/07/13/movies/scarlett-johansson-rub-and-tug-transgender.html. Accessed 9 June 2022.

Svich, Caridad. *Mitchell and Trask's Hedwig and the Angry Inch*. London: Routledge, 2019.

Sypniewski, Holly. "The Pursuit of Eros in Plato's *Symposium* and *Hedwig and the Angry Inch*." *International Journal of the Classical Tradition* 15.4: 558–586, 2008.

Tackitt-Jones, Jordy. "Gender Without Genitals: Hedwig's Six Inches." In *The Transgender Studies Reader*. Edited by Susan Stryker, and Stephen Whittle. London: Routledge, 449–467, 2006.

"Taye Diggs: Channeling His Inner Homosexual . . . to Play Hedwig." TMZ. 21 May 2015. www.tmz.com/2015/05/21/taye-diggs-hedwig-broadway-video/. Accessed 15 June 2022.

Taylor, Jeff. "Trans, QPOC Inclusive Pride Flag Campaign Going Viral." *NewNowNext*. 8 June 2018. www.newnownext.com/trans-qpoc-inclusive-pride-flag-campaign-going-viral/06/2018/. Accessed 16 June 2022.

Teeman, Tim. "Michael C. Hall on His 'Fluid' Sexuality, *Dexter*, Death, and David Bowie." *Daily Beast*. 9 November 2018. www.thedailybeast.com/michael-c-hall-sexuality-dexter-death-bowie-and-me. Accessed 15 June 2022.

Trask, Stephen, and John Cameron Mitchell. *Hedwig and the Angry Inch: Complete Text & Lyrics to the Smash Rock Musical – Broadway Edition*. New York: Overlook Duckworth, 2014.

Valentine, David. *Imagining Transgender: An Ethnography of a Category*. Durham: Duke University Press, 2007.

Wollman, Elizabeth L. *The Theater Will Rock: A History of the Rock Musical, From Hair to Hedwig*. Ann Arbor: University of Michigan Press, 2006.

Yuan, Jada. "Playing It Straight." *Sunday Telegraph*. 18 May 2014. (4ff).

4
ALL MY LIFE I HAD TO FIGHT

At the 2016 Tony Awards ceremony, Oprah Winfrey introduced the performance by the (newly reworked) cast of the (newly revised) musical *The Color Purple* this way:

> This story has been a part of my life for over thirty years – as a novel, first, then a film, and, of course, the stage musical. And yet, as it does for *everybody* who experiences it, this new production succeeds in stunning, in surprising, and in catapulting us to our feet as if it were completely new.

Winfrey's introduction told viewers at home that although it's likely that they'd heard the story of Celie, Nettie, Shug, Albert, Sofia, and Harpo before, the 2015 revival was doing something different.

The Color Purple first appeared in 1982 as an epistolary novel written by Alice Walker. The book was partially based on members of Walker's own family, especially her beloved grandmother and grandfather. Set in the early twentieth century, *The Color Purple* follows sisters Celie and Nettie as they write letters first to God, and then to one another, over the course of four decades. In 1983, *The Color Purple* received the Pulitzer Prize and the National Book Award, and Walker became the first Black woman to win the Pulitzer Prize for fiction.[1]

In February 1984, Walker granted the film rights to Steven Spielberg and Quincy Jones, and she began working on a *Color Purple* screenplay, which she finished that June. Walker worked as a consultant and collaborator on the film, but Spielberg did not use her screenplay, choosing a very different one by the Dutch writer Menno Meyjes instead. In December 1985, the sumptuous film version of *The Color Purple* was released, directed by Spielberg and starring Whoopi Goldberg, Danny Glover, Margaret Avery, Oprah Winfrey, and Adolph Caesar. The film was nominated for 11 Academy Awards in early 1986, though Spielberg was famously snubbed in the Best Director category, and the movie did not take home any statues at the March ceremony.[2] Walker's relationship with the film version proved to be complicated and painful, (more on this later), and so the author was understandably hesitant when the producer Scott Sanders asked Walker to allow him to develop *The Color Purple* into a piece of musical theatre. Walker eventually gave Sanders her blessing, but it was Spielberg's film company that actually owned the rights; Sanders got those too.

The Color Purple musical adaptation was developed over many years, with the composer–lyricist team of Brenda Russell, Allee Willis, and Stephen Bray writing the songs and Marsha Norman writing the libretto.[3] The show was directed by Gary Griffin, first appearing at the Alliance Theatre in Atlanta in September 2005 and then giving its first preview at the Broadway Theatre on West 53rd Street on November 1. *The Color Purple* received 11 Tony Award nominations, and LaChanze, in the team's only win, took home the award for Best Actress in a Musical. Though it received mixed reviews, *Purple* was an unqualified hit, clocking 910 performances and running until the end of February 2008. Indeed, in 2007, while the show was still playing on Broadway, a second Gary Griffin-directed production of *Purple* opened in Chicago, starring former members of the Broadway cast Jeannette Bayardelle and Felicia P. Fields, as well as Michelle Williams of Destiny's Child; the show toured until the end of February 2010. *The Color Purple* then went on a *second* (non-equity) North American tour from March 2010 to June 2011. Amateur and stock licensing rights were made available in February 2012.

The original production was barely out of the public consciousness when John Doyle, in his signature directing style, stripped *The Color Purple* down for the first London production in the Summer of 2013 at the Menier Chocolate Factory. This new, spare *Purple* received raves, and in Fall 2015, Scott Sanders brought Doyle's production – and its breakout star Cynthia Erivo – to Broadway just ten years after the original production had opened. The new revival was deemed a triumph. "Give thanks this morning, children of Broadway, and throw in a hearty hallelujah," crowed Ben Brantley at the *New York Times*, inflecting his review with religious terminology. "'The Color Purple' has been born again, and its conversion is a glory to behold":

> The heart-clutching, gospel-flavored musical that opened at the Bernard B. Jacobs Theater on Thursday night – in a production led by an incandescent new star named Cynthia Erivo and, in her Broadway debut, an enchanting Jennifer Hudson – share a title, the same characters, the same source of inspiration . . . and most of the same songs with "The Color Purple" seen on Broadway a decade ago. But, oh, what a difference there is between them.[4]

Cynthia Erivo's incandescence drove the success of the new *Color Purple*, and Doyle's production won two Tony Awards in 2016 – one for Erivo and one for Best Revival. It ran for 450 performances.

In all of its iterations, *The Color Purple* is a queer text. This is true even of Spielberg's film, which settles for a chaste kiss shared by Celie and Shug while the camera pans away. The novel's central themes, which include the (re)definition of "God," the power of family, sisterhood, the slow and steady development of the protagonist's voice, African and African American identity, misogynist violence, and anti-Black racism, are all inflected by the queerness of the main character.[5] Celie's perspectives on the themes explored in the novel are deeply affected by her queer desires, and her queerness drives the musical, if not the film. But re-arriving on Broadway in 2015 and playing through 2017, Doyle's revival of *The Color Purple* interacted with a new landscape of LGBTQ politics in the United States, one that had changed and refocused a great deal since 2005 – and certainly since the early 1980s.

Scholarly treatments of the musical, such as those by Deborah Paredez and Stacy Wolf, have seen it as a powerful feminist or "womanist" narrative, one that empowers women and connects women as sisters and divas.[6] In Wolf's analysis, "[Celie's] struggles are about gender; the musical thematizes male and female relationships, power between the sexes, and the importance of female self-knowledge, growth, and empowerment."[7] While this is certainly true, I am wary of taking for granted the queerness of *The Color Purple*. This is a text with a deeply queer approach to love and relationships,[8] and the implications of the musical's queer aspects have too easily been de-emphasized in analyses of the show.

Musical theatre scholars James Lovelock and Sarah Whitfield have both examined *The Color Purple* from the point of view of LGBTQ representation. After attending the Kimberley Rampersand-directed Canadian premiere of the musical, Whitfield writes that her experience watching Shug Avery, "is the first ever positive representation of my own sexuality that I have seen" in a piece of musical theatre, "the first time I have seen what it is to be bisexual on a stage."[9] For Lovelock, *The Color Purple* is a "womanist utopia," and he hears in Shug and Celie's love song "What about Love?" "a coming-out moment" for both women, referring to Celie's "lesbian identity" and "Shug's bisexuality."[10] As I argued in Chapter 1, though, *coming out* purports to tell a coherent story about sexual desires that are not, in fact, coherent. Neither Celie nor Shug "comes out" as lesbian or bisexual in this musical (or, indeed, in the novel on which it is based), but these characters' lack of a declared sexual identity, as with Hedwig in the previous chapter, does not prevent them from being available for the powerful work of audience identification. Whitfield describes her deeply complex emotional experience while watching Shug onstage as one in which "a space has been made." As Lovelock responds to *Purple*, he remarks that "new identities require musical theatre scholarship to move away from the binary . . . and to begin to consider bisexual, asexual, transgender and genderfluid identities."[11] My critically queer approach in this chapter is, instead, to move away from the consideration of identity positions as essential and toward an examination of the musical's intersections with the LGBTQ politics of its day. In other words, I'm less interested in what the musical might be doing in terms of representational politics and more interested in how *The Color Purple* – as both a musical and a novel – might offer us newer and queerer approaches to the world.

The focus of this chapter is the revival's engagement with LGBTQ politics in the period from 2015 to 2017, and I want explicitly to interrogate *The Color Purple* as both a feminist–womanist text *and* a queer text. As with the other case studies in this book, however, this chapter attempts to avoid assumptions about what queerness's engagements with politics will be. Certainly, *The Color Purple*'s appearance on Broadway was a landmark for LGBTQ representation in 2005, and it provided new opportunities for both identificatory and political practices. But the show's revival, a decade later, coincided with a newly invigorated Black Lives Matter movement, which had been founded in 2013 after the acquittal of George Zimmerman for the murder of Trayvon Martin. This shift in U.S. politics was fundamental to the show's reappearance. Between the original production of *Purple* and its revival on Broadway in 2015, the political force of the Black Lives Matter movement "had grown nationally in 2014 after the deaths of Michael Brown in Missouri and Eric Garner in New York."[12] *The Color Purple* greeted a very different audience in the United States in 2015 than it had in 2005.

Structuring this chapter are two differing performances by cast members of *The Color Purple* in response to anti-Black police violence in the United States, and these responses illuminate the central topics that this chapter interrogates: the 2015 revival's engagement with the Black church, *The Color Purple*'s treatment of god and religion, and LGBTQ participation in the Black Lives Matter movement. The chapter thinks through *The Color Purple*'s engagement with politics, responding to critiques of the novel by both bell hooks and Lauren Berlant, and I link Walker's politics to some of the fundamental goals of Black Lives Matter. The chapter closes by considering the political potential of Celie's anthem "I'm Here," both in context and out of context, looking, particularly, at two performances of the song – one by Jennifer Hudson at the Kennedy Center Honors and another by Cynthia Erivo at a conference for women's empowerment.

Writing Letters to God

One week after the Tony nominations were announced on May 3, 2016, Heather Headley joined the revival of *The Color Purple*. Her return to Broadway after more than a decade away was heralded by the *New York Times* with a headline declaring that to call in Heather Headley was "How to Keep a Musical Great."[13] This was a complicated time for *The Color Purple*, whose lead actress Cynthia Erivo and featured actress Danielle Brooks had been nominated for both the Tony and the Drama Desk Awards but whose headliner, Oscar winner Jennifer Hudson, had been snubbed by both groups. By the time the Tony Awards ceremony arrived on June 12, Headley had been in the role of Shug Avery for a full month, and it was she who would perform at the televised ceremony, singing "Mysterious Ways" before Erivo came downstage to wow the audience with an excerpt from *Purple*'s showstopping number "I'm Here."

As I noted in this book's introduction, the summer of 2016 was a truly complex period in the braided history of Broadway musicals and U.S. American politics, and the June 12 Tony Awards ceremony became a flashpoint for the politics of Broadway. This was the evening after the Pulse Massacre, and the Tony Awards seemed especially focused on attempting to heal the nation's divisions. 2016 was also an election year, and both the Republican and Democratic National Conventions would be held that July. U.S. Politics and Broadway were in the news together frequently, as Lin-Manuel Miranda, Julia Roberts, and many others raised money for Hillary Clinton's presidential campaign in a one-night-only Broadway engagement titled "Stronger Together," and Clinton herself quoted *Hamilton* in her acceptance speech at the DNC.[14] Indeed, Secretary Clinton saw Miranda's musical three times and used the show as a kind of object lesson on the campaign trail, reading *Hamilton* as an example of politicians putting aside their differences in order to work together.[15] Clinton, incidentally, would be in the audience for *The Color Purple*'s closing performance on January 8, 2017, "receiv[ing] several ovations from the sold-out audience as she arrived, and then another round of applause when she was acknowledged by the cast after the show."[16]

Less than a month after the Pulse shootings, however, violence in the United States erupted yet again when a 37-year-old Baton Rouge man named Alton Sterling was shot six times by police officers on July 5. Videos of the killing circulated widely on the Internet. The next day, on July 6, a policeman in a suburb of Minneapolis killed 32-year-old Philando Castile during a traffic stop, shooting him five times. Video of this shooting also circulated on the Internet, gaining international recognition. Then, on July 7, a man in Dallas shot and killed five police officers following what had been a large but peaceful demonstration protesting the murders of Sterling and Castile. The cast of *The Color Purple* responded to these deaths in several ways: on July 8, Heather Headley posted a statement on the social medium Facebook; on July 30, Cynthia Erivo, Kyle Scatliffe, and other members of the *Purple* ensemble appeared in a public performance piece called "Broadway Circle Up – This Is How We Shoot Back," and on July 31, Headley addressed the killings on National Public Radio in an interview with Michel Martin.

Headley's July 8 Facebook post begins as follows:

> My grief is not selective!
> My 'weeping' is not selective.
> My anger with injustice cannot be selective.
> I cried last night and I'm crying today.
> I mourn with Louisiana. Minnesota. Dallas. And too many others.
> If Love is Love . . . Then hate is hate! Evil is evil. Injustice is injustice.
> I can't dress it up and call it something else. I won't.
> So, this morning, my heart, which was already broken, has somehow found a few more pieces to break.
> I want EVERYONE to go home to their families. I want everyone to have justice. I want everyone, even if we disagree, to have the lives they work to have.[17]

Headley goes on to reference the biblical passage *Second Chronicles* 7.14 – "If my people, which are called by my name, shall humble themselves, and pray, and seek my face, and turn from their wicked ways; then will I hear from heaven, and will forgive their sin, and will heal their land." "I. Will. Pray!" Headley says in her Facebook status. "I will pray! / And I hope . . . I know that though He Weeps. . . . He will remember and keep His promise, and heal our land."

Headley was the most well-known performer in *The Color Purple* at the time, and she was continuing to do press for the show, so it is helpful to examine here how the performer's own politics leverage *The Color Purple* and its messages so that the musical's ideas intersect with the struggle for Black Life, abolitionist movements across the United States, and the politics of protest more generally. We should note, in addition, Headley's reference to the phrase "love is love," its links to the politics of marriage equality, and the way that it continues the "love is love is love is love is love is love" message offered by Lin-Manuel Miranda in his speech at the 2016 Tony Awards.[18] Headley's post repurposes Miranda's message of solidarity here, asking those on the side of a particular LGBTQ politics to mobilize those politics in another direction. I want to focus, however, on her reworking of the *spiritual* message of *The Color Purple* in this post, in particular, her quotation from the Old Testament scriptures and her use of the pronoun "He" with a capital *H*. Headley's post articulates a deeply complicated set of ideas about who and what god is, and these ideas exist in stark contrast to the most central theme of Alice Walker's book. Examining the distance between the novel and the musical in relation to the question of divinity, religion, and the church on the one hand and queer desire, pleasure, and nature on the other, helps us see the complexity of these questions for many LGBTQ-identified people in the twenty-first century.

Walker's original novel begins with the sentence "*You better not never tell nobody but God. It'd kill your mammy.*"[19] Over the first few letters in this epistolary novel, we come to realize that this sentence has been spoken by Celie's stepfather, but because the sentence sits there on the page, italicized, separate from the rest of the novel, it seems like an injunction from elsewhere or nowhere. This sentence is a demand for silence that is structural to society. The stepfather's patriarchal threat is a short preface to *The Color Purple* which will go on to comprise a series of letters, the first 51 of which are, as the injunction demands, addressed using the phrase "Dear God." Celie writes to her god *instead* of talking to anyone else, and in her first letter, she asks specifically for a sign that will explain what is happening to her as her stepfather violates her and orders her to remain silent. Celie imagines "God," in these first few letters, as a protector who will aid her as she tries to prevent her stepfather from raping her sister Nettie.

Celie writes "Dear God," and she means the very specific god whom she knows from the church she attends. As early as the book's first few pages, however, Walker associates the church with danger and violence. In letter 4, we learn that Mr. _____'s first wife was killed "by her boyfriend coming home from church," and in letter 5, Celie tells us that "He beat me today cause he say I winked at a boy in church."[20] This church continues to be a place where Celie struggles, and in letter 22, Celie notes that the other parishioners stood by silently while her stepfather raped her: "The women at church sometimes nice to me. Sometimes not. . . . They some of the same ones used to be here both times I was big." In this letter, Celie also articulates her frustration with the preacher, as she hopes that Mr. _____ will stand up to his attacks on Shug Avery:

> Even the preacher got his mouth on Shug Avery, now she down. He take her condition for his text. . . . He talk bout a strumpet in short skirts, smoking cigarettes, drinking gin. Singing for money and taking other women mens. Talk bout slut, hussy, heifer and streetcleaner.

The church ladies reappear in this letter, too. They flirt with Celie's husband, but that doesn't stop them from feeling superior to Shug Avery. As Celie tells us, "The same women smile at him, say amen gainst Shug."[21] Celie doesn't rebel against her god or Christianity here, but she does begin to understand the church more clearly as a place of toxicity and hypocrisy. Later, when Shug has come to live with Mr. _____ and Celie begins to help her get well, Shug hums a tune to herself as Celie combs her hair, and Celie asks about it: "What that song, I ast. Sound low down dirty to me. Like what the preacher tell you its sin to hear. Not to mention sing."[22] At this point in *The Color Purple,* the preacher's words seem still to be structuring Celie's thinking; Shug, of course, keeps right on humming.

Celie's ideas about the way things are, including the fixedness of her religion and her god, are challenged by the arrival of Shug Avery, but her questioning begins even earlier when Harpo's wife, Sofia, moves in. Celie goes against her own gut feelings when she tells Harpo to beat Sofia, and this troubles her so much that she can't sleep, knowing the harm she did to this strong woman. Confronted by Sofia, Celie uses the Bible as a justification for being obedient to her stepfather, and in many ways, this iconic confrontation between Sofia and Celie is actually a discussion about Celie's religious beliefs. Sofia asks Celie how she deals with her anger, but Celie says she doesn't get mad:

> Well, sometimes Mr. _____ git on me pretty hard. I have to talk to Old Maker. But he my husband. I shrug my shoulders. This life soon be over, I say. Heaven last all ways.
>
> You ought to bash Mr. _____ head open, [Sofia] say. Think bout heaven later.[23]

The women laugh together after this, and although Celie doesn't explicitly agree with Sofia here – she certainly doesn't bash her husband's head in – her worldview vis-à-vis religion has begun to alter.

The concept of god continues to be central to *The Color Purple.* Celie still begins her letters "Dear God," and the Bible and Heaven make regular appearances. A shift for Celie begins in letter 73, more than halfway through the novel, after she has discovered that Nettie is still alive, that her father was lynched, and that the man she thought was her father is her stepfather. Celie and Shug talk about God, but they have very different ideas about it. Their conversation is far reaching and fascinating. Celie says that "the God I been praying and writing to is a man. And act just like all the other mens I know. Trifling, forgetful and lowdown," but Shug argues that Celie's god is not only a male god but specifically *white* and male:

> If you wait to find God in church, Celie, she say, that's who is bound to show up, cause that's where he live. . . . Cause that's the one that's in the white folks' white bible.
> Shug! I say. God wrote the bible, white folks had nothing to do with it.
> How come he look just like them, then? she say. . . . How come the bible just like everything else they make, all about them doing one thing and another, and all the colored folks doing is gitting cursed?
> I never thought bout that.[24]

It is important to note here that Shug's critique is one that marks this god as specifically racialized, gendered, and aged by the white people who created him in their image.

Shug's personal theory about god is the one that Celie finally adopts, although it takes her a long time to arrive at this position – she struggles with it through several letters. In letter 73, though, Shug tells Celie that

> God is inside you and inside everybody else. You come into the world with God. But only them that search for it inside find it. . . . God ain't a he or a she, but a It. . . . I believe God is everything, say Shug. Everything that is or ever was or ever will be. And when you can feel that, and be happy to feel that, you've found it.[25]

It is in this same letter that Shug says the memorable phrase from which the book's title is taken, "it pisses God off if you walk by the color purple in a field somewhere and don't notice it."

Even more, Shug's theory of god is one deeply inflected by an ethos of sexual freedom and an emphasis on sexual pleasure. Shug understands desire and sex to be invented by her god, and she says that "God love all them feelings. That's some of the best stuff God did. And when you know God loves 'em you enjoys 'em a lot more. You can just relax, go with everything that's going, and praise God by liking what you like."[26] Shug's sexual ethic here emphasizes a free sexual choice that, significantly, doesn't emphasize a specific *sexuality* as much as it insists on sexual freedom and sexual pleasure – "go with everything that's going," Shug says, and "lik[e] what you like."

At the same time as her long talk with Shug, Celie stops writing letters to her god, writing instead to her sister Nettie, from whom she has been separated for the many years of the novel. Nettie has gone to Africa as a Christian missionary to a fictional ethnic group called the Olinka, but after their time in Africa, she and her husband Samuel come to see god in the same way that Celie does, as a spirit not tied to a particular image. Celie writes to Nettie until the moving final letter of the novel. By this time, Nettie and Celie's children have returned to Georgia and they have all been reunited, and so instead of writing to her sister, Celie addresses her final letter in this way: "Dear God. Dear stars, dear trees, dear sky, dear peoples. Dear Everything. Dear God. / Thank you for bringing my sister Nettie and our children home."[27] Celie has come to believe in a god that is everywhere and everything rather than a white patriarch who punishes sexual pleasure and demands obedience, and she is grateful.

Spielberg's 1985 adaptation of the novel significantly alters Celie and Shug's discussion, and screenwriter Meyjes completely omits the revision of god at which Celie and Nettie finally arrive. In the film's version of the sequence from letter 73, Shug and Celie walk in a field of purple flowers, but instead of talking about god as being present in the fields and in the trees, as they do in the novel, the movie skips ahead to the place where Shug says that everything wants to be loved: "You ever notice that trees do everything to git attention we do, except walk?"[28] In letter 73, this section is the very end of their conversation about god. The movie bypasses every one of the ideas that Celie, at this point in the book, thinks sound like "blasphemy."[29] None of Shug's ideas about god make it into the film.

The movie *does*, however, manage to be about religion quite a lot, but it does not use the ideas from Walker's book. Perhaps the most surprising thing about Spielberg's film is the addition of an entirely new plot that doesn't appear in the novel. This addition is especially curious because so much was cut from the novel in order for it to be adapted to film. The movie excises Shug and Celie's sexual relationship, Shug's betrayal of Celie with Germaine, the entire subplot of the family working together to get Sofia out of jail, Albert's redemption as he learns to care for Sofia and Buster's daughter Henrietta, and his new friendship with Celie after Shug leaves both of them. Yet Meyjes finds the space to *add* an entire plot that involves Shug trying to restore her relationship with her preacher father midway through the movie and then finally achieving this restoration into the Christian family by embracing her dad and singing gospel music. Near the end of the film, Shug stops singing "Sister (Miss Celie's Blues)," the song that represents the connection between her and Celie, and begins to sing the music from her father's church. Shug sings, "Speak, my Lord / I love you Lord / Save my soul," as she brings her audience away from the jook joint and into the church house. "See Daddy," she says when she gets there, "sinners have soul too." This plot addition is a very strange alteration to the text of the book: the novel fundamentally offers readers a radical reconceptualization of the idea of a white, male god in favor of a god that lives inside of all of us. The film does none of this.

In her liner notes to the movie soundtrack, Walker attempts to do some damage control for this sequence in the movie.[30] Objecting to the word "God" (which she puts in quotation marks), she says that:

> labels of any kind attached to the inner voice and the outer spirit are distracting. And loaded with racist, classist, sexist, ideological baggage. For instance, the word "Lord" is so man-derived, so oppressively classist, that its effect is to stifle the urge to worship, rather than stimulate it.

The word *Lord* can clearly be heard on the film's soundtrack, but Walker tells readers that

> whatever the inner voice is called – God, Jesus, Lord, or Goddess – the voices in this song direct us to a feeling recognition of the inner voice itself, refusing to let us get stuck outside ourselves, struggling over and fussing with names.[31]

Walker is being generous, here, with the changes made for the film, likely out of affection for Quincy Jones' music; nevertheless, she persists in making her principles – and those of the novel – quite clear, carefully noting the racist, sexist, and classist ideologies attached to the god inside the church.

Marsha Norman's libretto and Russell, Willis, and Bray's lyrics for the musical adhere much more closely to the ideas about god-as-inner-voice that run through Walker's book. On stage, Shug tells Celie to "look at all he give us – laughin', and singin' and sex. . . . Sky over our heads, birds singin' to us."[32] On stage, Shug doesn't make the anti-racist critique of Celie's god that she makes in the novel, but she declares that "God not some gloomy old man like the pictures you've seen of him. God not a man at all." The stage directions before the song then say that "Shug begins singing ['The Color Purple'], but easily, more like these are just her thoughts with a little music underneath." Shug sings that "God is inside you and everyone else," and she tells Celie that "We come into this world with God / But only them that look inside, find it."[33]

The lyrics of this song adhere very closely to *The Color Purple*'s letter 73. The songwriters carefully use their lyrics to replicate the novel as Shug slides from the pronoun *him* in the words she speaks to using the pronoun *it* once her voice moves into song. Further, Shug's ideas about god – as everywhere and in everyone – are rooted in Celie and Shug's queer desires, in learning to "love the way you feel," in "laughin', and singin' *and* sex." That the songwriters also managed to work the phrase "Like the color purple / Where do it come from?" into the song – directly from letter 73 – is extraordinary.[34]

Similarly, the musical's finale cleverly corresponds to the novel. The show's last song is a reprise of "The Color Purple," but first Celie sings the same words that open letter 90: "Dear God, dear stars, dear trees, dear sky / Dear peoples, dear everything, dear God." Onstage, Celie's entire family (including Mister) joins her to sing "Rising . . . / Like the sun / It's the hope that sets us free." The reprise includes the phrase "When we / Share love," which doesn't appear in Shug's version of the song but clearly expands on Shug's idea that love teaches us how to find god. The emphasis in the reprise is on love as multidirectional and communal. The song ends with Celie singing "I don't think us feel old at all / I think this is the youngest us ever felt" – the very last words of the novel – and then, in a sacred flourish, the show closes with the entire ensemble singing "A– / –men."[35] In this way, the musical's creators return to the novel's ideas about spirituality and reject the film's emphasis on Christianity, the church, and the white god of Celie's childhood.

Intriguingly, the 2015 revival seemingly attempted to split the difference between the novel and film a little more closely, returning us to the space of the church. Doyle's production began with the more participatory air of a Sunday morning service, cutting the overture that began the original production. As musical theatre scholar Laura MacDonald noted in a review of the production in London, "The ensemble, playing churchgoers, launched the performance by welcoming and blessing the audience, immediately establishing a warm atmosphere and a sense of community."[36] At the Tony Awards, the ensemble also entered through the audience, carrying the chairs that functioned as the show's primary scenery onstage, as they launched into "It's Sunday morning / So make a joyful noise / . . . Unto the / Lord."[37] Others have remarked on the church-like atmosphere of Doyle's production, with *Los Angeles Times* critic Charles McNulty referring to the show as "more like a church service than a traditional book musical" and Lea Salonga calling the show an "almost church-like experience."[38]

Of course, following the overture, *The Color Purple*'s original production also began with a church service; the song "Sunday Morning" was not added for the revival, and the musical always opened with the church ladies and the congregation praising the lord. Still, in an essay for the journal *Ecumenica*, Aaron Brown argued that in the revival, "worship functioned as a storytelling device that enhanced the story and avoided mere novelty."[39] Brown's comparison is with the original production, which he argues lacked authenticity and sold Black religious performance to voyeuristic tourists rather than encouraging participation. This is an odd argument when one considers the original production's popularity with Black audiences, but I take Brown's point that the Black church service was a structural element of Doyle's production.

In either case, what the musical does – and this is perhaps especially true for *The Color Purple*'s revival – is attempt to merge Shug's ideas about what god is and where god resides with the religious *feeling* of attending a church service filled with song and participation. This is an artistic choice bound to cause a great deal of slippage. In *her* version of the song "The Color Purple," for example, Heather Headley clearly and perceptibly changed the lyrics, refusing the pronoun for god in the script and singing instead, "We come into this world with God / But only them that look inside, find *him*."[40] Shug still said "God not a man at all," and she still clearly described her queer beliefs about god, but Headley's alteration is indicative of the challenges the musical's creators faced – and Walker continues to face – in communicating a different way of thinking about divinity.

It may be that I am being generous with the musical the way Walker was with the film, but it seems to me that – as Walker said about Jones's soundtrack for the movie – "once again the magic of music strikes." Even when the pronouns are not quite right, Shug's song encourages us to see god in ourselves, to see god in others, and to find, in Walker's words, that "there is no separation between us whatsoever."[41] This is an extremely powerful – and powerfully queer – theory of identity, one that finds the divine in each of us and sees that divinity as something that can bring us together.

Reimagining Masculinity

At the end of July 2016, Cynthia Erivo, Kyle Scatliffe, and other members of the *Purple* ensemble appeared in a performance piece called "Broadway Circle Up – This Is How We Shoot Back," and the Circle Up was recorded in a 360° video that was made available on the Internet. This performance protest was designed specifically to reference a 2014 gathering in Times Square, just two years prior, co-organized by Brandon Victor Dixon (the original Harpo) in response to the murder of Eric Garner, who was killed by police and whose last words *I can't breathe* became a political rallying cry. The Broadway Circle Up performance in the summer of 2016 echoed this protest, communicating outrage at the continued loss of Black life at the hands of police since Garner's death. Just to be very clear about the landscape of this country, during the 24 days between the death of Philando Castile on July 6 and the Circle Up performance on July 30, police officers in the United States shot and killed *eighteen* Black men, including Andre Johnson in Broken Bow, Oklahoma, Alva Burnett Braziel in Houston, Texas, Joseph Mann in Sacramento, California, Dayten Ernest Harper in Baltimore, Maryland, Jeff Cornell Tyson in Indianapolis, Indiana, Dalvin Hollins in Tempe, Arizona, Jeffrey Smith in La Quinta, California, and Paul O'Neal in Chicago, Illinois.[42] For the Broadway Circle Up performance at the end of July, members of the cast of *The Color Purple* joined cast members from *The Lion King, Shuffle Along, Motown*, and *Hamilton* to circle up, gathering and repurposing music from their shows in solidarity and "in protest of the continued loss of black lives due to prejudice."[43]

The Color Purple's relationship with Black men and their representation, however, is an especially contentious one that goes back primarily to Spielberg's 1985 film version – given its widespread visibility – but even further to Walker's novel. Responses to the film were vociferous and immediate, with protestors from the Coalition Against Black Exploitation picketing the film's premiere and numerous articles sounding off and taking various sides in relation to the film's alleged racist misandry in the *New York Times*, the *Washington Post, Frontline*, and *Coming Up*. The Spring 1986 issue of the journal *Black Film Review* devoted five separate columns to the film in a section titled "The Little Book (and Film) That Started the Big War." Attacks on Spielberg's *Color Purple* adaptation even rebounded to Alice Walker and onto the novel itself with, for example, the conservative critic Richard Grenier taking the opportunity to aim his usual racist and antifeminist rhetoric in Walker's direction, stating in *The Washington Times* that "It is well known, of course, that Miss Walker . . . hates black men with a passion."[44] Earl Walter Jr.'s much more reasonable summation of the critique in *Black Film Review* describes Spielberg's film as:

> relentlessly and thoroughly indict[ing] black men. Black men are the villains, the sources of pain, failure, and hopelessness for innocent women and children. So blatant are the male characters in their vile behavior that much of the first half of the film (supposedly a woman's story) is lost to a diatribe on negative black men.

One of the central issues in Walter's argument is that the Black men in the film exist in a world without context, and Spielberg's movie seems to frame misogynist violence as a problem caused by Black men, specifically.

Walter continues:

> Mr. _____ . . . and Pa . . . are both tragic figures who are thrust onto the screen without context or explanation for their behavior. They commit incest, child abuse, and attempt rape – all without qualification or consequence. The viewer is given nothing with which to understand these male characters. The implication is that these black men are inherently "no good" and change at the end of the movie only by an act of God.[45]

Indeed, the novel's depictions of sexual violence committed against Black women by *white* men are left out of the film, an elision that exonerates white men while demonizing Black men. As Rita Dandridge puts it:

> Spielberg's production of a Southern film which disregards the sexually exploitative white male in his relationship to women (both black and white) fails to articulate the method by which Southern female conformity has been enforced. . . . The white man's sexual subjugation of the black woman cannot be disregarded; *its consequences underscore and explain the insidiousness of racism and the contemptuousness of intra-racism.*[46]

To be clear, many Black critics were conflicted about the film's representations. Nearly all critics, male and female, were excited by the representations of Black women on screen and – across the board – praised the performances by Whoopi Goldberg and Danny Glover. But some, again both male and female, argued that the representations in *The Color Purple* were unfair and dehumanizing to Black men.[47]

From the perspective of the twenty-first century, there is a tendency in the received wisdom about *The Color Purple* to dismiss criticisms of the movie as simple reflections of the kind of antifeminist and racist critiques that someone like Richard Grenier might launch. Still, it is telling to note that the film's representations of Black men were a topic of debate almost exclusively among *Black* critics. Even the white critics who disliked Spielberg's adaptation of *The Color Purple* found little fault with his representations of Black men.[48] Critical debates about the novel and film's representations vis-à-vis gender and sexuality have proliferated, and I don't want to rehearse them here, but neither do I think they should be forgotten.[49] Accordingly, I want to take seriously the allegations of the film's misandry because – as I have argued throughout this book – identificatory operations that fail still have much to teach us, and these critiques of *The Color Purple* have the ability to illuminate some of the ethics central to Alice Walker's queer and antiracist politics and to illustrate how the musical has diverged from the politics of the film.

Spielberg's *Color Purple* adaptation appeared at the height of the Reagan era, and in 1985, incarceration rates, which continue disproportionately to affect the lives of Black men, were at an all-time high. Indeed, incarceration rates would continue to increase exponentially for the next 20 years, plateauing only around 2005 or 2006. The stakes of the representations of men in *The Color Purple*, in other words, were very high, and critics of Spielberg's portrayals of Black men in 1985 were responding to a real crisis in racist policing and incarceration in the United States that was deeply affecting Black men and Black families.

Representations, like those in the film version of *The Color Purple*, contribute to "the belief," in philosopher Tommy Curry's words, that Black men's

> intentions and motives can be adequately captured by generic theories of masculinity formulated on male children in colonial societies and upper-class settler culture. The asserted closeness that Black males, among the poorest, most uneducated, and most isolated (unassimilated) members of American society, are thought to have to hegemonic masculinity and white patriarchy is evidence not of their actual power or aspirations for (white) male domination, but of the extent to which theorists and scholars have internalized the negative stereotypes about Black males as hyper-masculine, violent, and dangerous.[50]

I want to argue here, along with Curry, that white critics found little fault with Spielberg's portrayals of Black men because they coincided with larger media campaigns in the 1980s around Black men and boys as dangerous, violent, and deserving of incarceration or death.[51] These media representations were ideologically designed to cover over the actual reality of the *vulnerability* of Black men and boys in U.S. American society and they, in fact, contributed to that vulnerability, which increased through the end of the century.[52]

Despite these criticisms, the film has come to be beloved. Indeed, the image the musical's producers used to sell the original Broadway production – two Black girls in straw hats playing patty-cake in a field – does not appear in the novel; it is an image taken directly from Spielberg's film. One of the reasons Sanders and his producing team expected *The Color Purple* to do so well on Broadway was because the film, by 2005, had become very popular with audiences. As a widely seen product of popular culture, Spielberg's film tends to take over in discussions of *The Color Purple*. To note just one example of the film's ability to dominate cultural memory of *The Color Purple* that *isn't* about masculinity, songwriter Allee Willis once shared that people constantly asked her if Quincy Jones's song "Sister (Miss Celie's Blues)" is sung in the musical.[53] Jones's song appears in at least two key moments during Spielberg's adaptation, and it was released by Jones's Qwest Records along with the film's soundtrack album in November 1986. "Miss Celie's Blues" does not appear in the stage adaptation; its position in the musical is taken by two songs – "Push da Button" and "Too Beautiful for Words." My point here is that the movie is well remembered and well liked, and this means that the musical *needed* to deal with the charges of misandry that were aimed at Spielberg's adaptation. A musical version of an award-winning novel and popular movie cannot escape – and must, in fact, respond to – the material it cites and references. This is precisely what the musical's creators attempted to do.

Marsha Norman, the musical's librettist, said that she "wanted to return to the book in its treatment of the men." The way she attempted this was to

> give Mister his full journey, which is all the way through to his redemption, to where he understands. . . . And so he's able to ask Celie to marry him at the end and also to do the work to bring her sister back. He really makes his amends. And she is able to accept them.[54]

By choice, then, the musical pays a different kind of attention to the men in Alice Walker's story than Spielberg's film did. We see Mister change and work hard to heal his relationship with Celie and his family.

Even more, we watch and listen to Mister wrestle with what he's done and how he came to think the way he thinks. After Celie leaves him, he sings "So tell me how a man do good when all he know is bad?" He begins, in other words, by simultaneously contextualizing his behavior and making excuses for it. But "Mister Song" is a musical theatre song with a narrative arc, one in which this character changes through singing. Albert comes to the realization *through the song* that he can only change the world and how the world sees him by changing his own behavior. "Nuthin' I say gon change people / Mind about me," he sings.

> Maybe all my good lie ahead of me.
> . . .
> Ain't gon be nothin' I say
> Gon be somethin' I do
> Maybe everything I do.[55]

And, as in the novel, Celie tells Nettie that Albert has finally decided that "it's time he was good to some little girl," as he begins to take care of Sofia and Buster's daughter Henrietta.[56] Indeed, at the moment in the musical when Celie is at her angriest at Albert – after she finds Nettie's letters – she doesn't threaten to kill him as she does in the novel or the film; Norman's libretto redirects Celie's anger at Albert (and the audience's too) toward the white policemen who have locked Sofia in jail.[57]

Perhaps just as important as the alteration to Albert's portrayal, the musical also fundamentally changes the movie's approach to Harpo. In the film, Harpo is a figure of comic fun, repeatedly falling through ceilings as if he's Harpo Marx; in the novel, too, he has his comedic moments, especially in letter 28 when he starts eating a lot more than usual and the women can't figure out why.[58] In the musical, however, Albert's path to change comes from *observing his son's different way of being in the world*. In fact, "Mister Song" is filled with questions about Harpo as Albert puzzles over his son's ability to be happy and wonders "How he keep findin' / So much good from so much bad?" Harpo's relationships with the world and with the women in his life are so much different than Albert's, yet "Everyone say Harpo shine."[59]

The musical's creators also give Sofia and Harpo, "Any Little Thing," a sexy love song late in act 2 in which we can see not only that their relationship is still sexually fulfilling but also that they're sharing responsibilities and divvying up household duties between them in an equitable way. "Is there anything else I can do for you? / Any little thing you might want me to?" they ask each other, and the song manages to be both erotically charged and reflective of an equitable distribution of domestic labor.[60] This sequence with Sofia and Harpo, in particular, communicates the novel's ideas about masculinity. It is fundamental to *The Color Purple*'s queer ethos that the masculinity preached by Old Mr. _____ and practiced by Mr. _____ is one that stifles men with its rigidity and strict rules about gendered behavior. We find out in letter 87, for example, that Albert tried sewing when he was young. He confesses to Celie that "I used to try to sew along with mama cause that's what she was always doing. But everybody laughed at me. But you know, I liked it."[61] And Sofia tells Celie in letter 28 that Harpo likes "cooking and cleaning and doing little things round the house" much more than Sofia does. She'd rather be "out in the fields or fooling with the animals."[62]

The fact that Albert eventually takes up sewing, content to sit with Celie on the porch chatting and smoking, has been difficult for some critics to reconcile.[63] Feminist scholar bell hooks, for example, describes Albert as "mov[ing] from male oppressor to enlightened being, willingly surrendering his attachment to the phallocentric social order reinforced by the sexual oppression of women." In hooks' reading of the change that Albert makes, she finds him "completely desexualized as part of the transformative process. / Unable to reconcile sexuality and power, Walker replaces the longing for sexual pleasure with an erotic metaphysic animated by a vision of the unity of all things, by the convergence of erotic and mystical experience."[64] Hooks' understanding of the way the book merges erotics and metaphysics makes sense, but this is not accompanied by desexualization in Walker's novel. Walker has not created, as hooks claims, "an ideal world of true love and commitment where there is no erotic tension – where there is no sexual desire or sexual pleasure."[65] On the contrary, near the end of *Purple*, when Shug comes back to Celie, the women talk about Albert. Shug is suspicious, imagining that Celie and Albert have been having sex. "I know Albert, and I bet he been up to *some*thing with you looking as fine as you look," Shug jealously tells Celie.[66] This little sentence points to the sexual desire that both Shug and Albert have for Celie, and it clearly indicates that all three of the characters are still sexually active and enjoying themselves.

One of the most fascinating aspects of Harpo and Sofia's song "Any Little Thing" is the way the duet offers audiences a portrait of masculinity with different notions of gendered activity while simultaneously retaining the sexiness of the man whose behavior no longer conforms to traditional masculine ideals and rules.

Underlining these connections, Norman has Albert *interrupt* Harpo and Sofia's song, coming in to tell them about his efforts to get Nettie and the kids back home from Africa, but then he notices that he's intruding on their sexual play, and he excuses himself. Sofia and Harpo resume their song and their lovemaking. Sex and being a good man go together in "Any Little Thing." The men in this musical change a great deal, and although the show is clear about its rethinking of strict gender roles, *The Color Purple* onstage presents these men as both sexually desirable and sexually fulfilled. In these ways and several others, the musical attempted to alter *The Color Purple*'s relationship to Black maleness. By most accounts, at least, the show succeeded.

The Politics of Forgiveness

I want to stay with the novel's revision of masculinity for just a little longer, because I think it's important to link Walker's ethical position with a particular twenty-first-century *political* position. In an interview with Justine Toms and Michael Toms in 1996, Walker reminded her audience that she loves Albert

> as much as I love anyone else in the book. . . . if I didn't love him so much I wouldn't have taken the trouble to put him through all of the changes that he goes through to become the kind of person who can be talked to and who can listen.[67]

Albert is a man who has repeatedly beaten Celie, violated her, and treated her as less than human, but Walker has Celie forgive him in the novel.[68] Albert is, in Walker's understanding, capable of changing, becoming a good person, and letting go of the enculturated masculinity that has previously structured his behavior.

But is forgiveness a political position? I ask this question because Walker has specifically said that her work is "grounded in spirituality rather than in politics," and critics have often noted that *The Color Purple* emphasizes personal transformation over collective political action.[69] In bell hooks' essay on the novel, for example, she argues, rather damningly that:

> Walker creates a fiction wherein an oppressed black woman can experience self-recovery without a dialectical process; without collective political effort; without radical change in society. To make Celie happy she creates a fiction where struggle – the arduous and painful process by which the oppressed work for liberation [–] has no place. This fantasy of change without effort is a dangerous one that keeps everyone in place and oppressive structures intact.[70]

Queer theorist Lauren Berlant mostly agrees, closing her essay on *The Color Purple* by noting that "[s]uch an emphasis on individual essence, in a false opposition to institutional history, seems inadequate to the construction of any national consciousness, especially one developing in a hostile, negating context."[71]

But if the novel fails in political terms, it's important to note that *avoiding* what is usually understood as "politics" is precisely one of the book's aims. As Berlant remarks at the beginning of her essay:

> *The Color Purple* deliberately fashions [a separation between the aesthetic and the political] in its attempt to represent a national culture that operates according to "womanist" values rather than patriarchal forms. While political language is laden with the historical values and associations of patriarchal power, aesthetic discourse here carries with it a utopian force that comes to be associated with the spirit of everyday life relations among women.[72]

Walker's novel creates somewhat of a utopian fantasy: she reimagines masculinity; she attempts to rethink familial structures from a queer perspective; she rejects the patriarchal white deity of Christianity in favor of the divine power of the natural world; she offers forgiveness instead of punishment; and she sets all of this in the racially segregated Southern United States of the 1930s and 1940s. These are not expressly apolitical positions but rather positions that begin first with individuals and our imaginations. These are political positions that attempt to imagine the world as it could be.[73] Walker finds that the first step to any change in the world is to rethink the limitations we have accepted in our own minds for what is possible.

If Walker's ideas here seem apolitical because of their apparent impracticality, perhaps this is because we have so frequently been unwilling to think *with* Walker, to attempt to recognize the limitations of our own imaginations when it comes to masculinity, queer families, the divine, and forgiveness. As one example of thinking that many people consider impractical, I'd like to return to the Broadway Circle Up performance organized to protest the continued loss of Black life at the hands of police forces nationwide. This performance, especially the contribution of *The Color Purple* cast, prompts us to consider the links between mainstream LGBTQ politics and the politics of the Black Lives Matter movement.

One allegedly impractical political goal that gained new popularity at the end of this decade was the movement to defund the police. Alex Vitale's book *The End of Policing* was published in 2017, and the slogan "defund the police" gained more widespread popularity after the murder of George Floyd in 2020.[74] As the *Economist* reported in the same year, however, "only a quarter of American adults are in favour of cutting funding for police departments outright," and only around half of U.S. Americans prefer an approach that sees a redistribution of police funds toward "alternative first responders, such as social workers, drug counsellors and mental-health experts."[75] Another allegedly impractical political position that many LGBTQ and antiracism activists have taken is the abolition of prisons in the United States. Criminologist and queer theorist Sarah Lamble, for example, has argued that

> It is more important than ever to reject strategies that allow queer, trans, and feminist politics to be used for war, imprisonment, state violence, and racism. We must put antiviolence, anti-racism, and anti-prison struggles at the center of queer, trans, and feminist organizing efforts.[76]

Lamble made this argument in 2015 in opposition to the much more popular organized politics around the passage of hate crime laws, LGBT inclusion in the U.S. military, and marriage equality. To many, the politics of police defunding and prison abolition have seemed impractical and even impossible; accordingly, organization around these issues has not seen widespread acceptance within LGBTQ political circles. It would seem that, for many, LGBTQ politics frequently begin to appear utopian or impossible precisely at the places where they overlap with antiracist politics.

I'm spending time, especially, with the politics of prison abolition and police defunding because Walker's novel takes up incarceration practices as a specific plot point when Sofia is imprisoned for defending herself in letters 37–41. Further, the novel explicitly links incarceration with sexual violence, corruption, and racism.[77] The politics of prison abolition and police defunding also seem to me very closely linked to Celie's forgiveness of Albert in *The Color Purple*. An ethics of forgiveness as opposed to an ethics of punishment would advocate for a decriminalization of sexwork, a decriminalization of poverty, and a more robust social safety net that treated people as possessing potential rather than risks.[78] In the musical, Albert says, "Maybe all my good lie ahead of me," and *The Color Purple* actually trusts that this is possible. Walker advocates a spiritual change rather than a political one, but the spiritual and ethical ideas embedded in the novel and musical are actually *structural* ideas that work to expand the field of possibilities open to us; Walker's allegedly impractical utopianism asks us to think with her to build a different, queerer, and more just world.

The Color Purple's representatives at the Broadway Circle Up performed just after those from the *Hamilton* cast, and I want to quote this entire segment of the performance because the Circle Up placed these lyrics, performers, and shows in conversation with one another, developing and insisting upon Black identity across the five Broadway shows and beyond – to audiences everywhere. As the organizers wrote, "The Circle Up reminds us how connected we are, not only as a Broadway community, but as a nation."[79]

Before the contingent from *The Color Purple* sang, Michael Luwoye repurposed Alexander Hamilton's lyrics from "The World Was Wide Enough," saying "I imagine death so much it feels more like a memory. / Is this where it gets me, on my feet, several feet ahead of me?" At this, Luwoye raised his hands in a gesture that has become a rallying cry of Black Lives Matter protests since the killing of Michael Brown by police in Ferguson, Missouri in 2014. "If I see it coming, do I run or fire my gun or let it be?" Luwoye continued. "If I throw away my shot, is this how you remember me? / What if this bullet is my legacy?"[80] Luwoye's chilling performance reworked the well-known sequence from *Hamilton* so that the lyrics challenged us to consider whether we'd remember this man for reasons other than for how he died.

Austin Smith then launched into the final section of Aaron Burr's song "Wait for It," singing, with the help of the rest of the company:

> Life doesn't discriminate
> Between the sinners and the saints.
> It takes and it takes and it takes
> And we keep living anyway

> We rise and we fall and we break
> And we make our mistakes
> And if there's a reason
> I'm still alive
> When so many have died
> Then I'm willin' to –
> Wait for it . . . / Wait for it . . . / Wait for it . . .[81]

It was at this point that Cynthia Erivo began to sing, *a capella*, a section from the reprise of "The Color Purple":

> It take a grain of love
> To make a mighty tree
> Even the smallest voice
> Can make a harmony
>
> Like a drop of water
> Keep the river high
> There are miracles
> For you and I[82]

The lyrics of these songs from *Hamilton* and *Purple* were unchanged from their libretti, but they took on new valences when sung in this space with a hundred Black activists.

The selection from "Wait for It" emphasized both mourning and militancy.[83] If so many have died but I'm still alive, these lyrics ask, then what is my reason for living? This is a question that emphasizes the persistence of Black activism in the United States and a renewed demand for justice. In the Circle Up performance, "Wait for it . . . / Wait for it . . . / Wait for it . . ." was dynamic and anticipatory; it was not an injunction to be patient. These lyrics were followed by the performance from the *Color Purple* group, who didn't articulate protest so much as they emphasized a rejection of hopelessness and an anticipation of miracles – in the usual spiritual fashion of *The Color Purple*. As a response to the lyrics from *Hamilton*, however, the words Erivo and the company sang seemed directly to answer the activist call put forward by "Wait for It." How do we "keep living anyway"? These final lyrics from "The Color Purple" respond to that question by saying that we keep living one small step at a time. Tiny grains can grow to make mighty trees, and drops of water can force a river to flood its banks.

To return, finally, to the consideration of *The Color Purple*'s preference for aesthetics over politics or its emphasis on spiritual awakening rather than collective organization, it may very well be true that Walker was writing from a spiritual perspective rather than a political one. It may also be true that the original novel of *The Color Purple* is not an activist text but one much more interested in expanding its readers' abilities to imagine queer worldmaking possibilities. But these cast members from *The Color Purple*'s revival on Broadway saw the show as deeply political. And even if the show (or the novel for that matter) is not political *on its own*, the cast's choice of lyrics for the Circle Up reminds us that *The Color Purple* doesn't need to do anything as a political tract *by itself*. It exists in conversation with other texts, other voices, other ideas. Like Celie – who gains strength and learns how to live better from the other women in her life – this story does not exist in a vacuum; the Circle Up emphasizes collective voices, identity across Broadway shows, and voices raised in protest and song. If critics, in other words, have found *The Color Purple* apolitical, audiences have found it politically energizing as well as emotionally powerful.

I'm Here

When the cast chose the lyrics "Even the smallest voice / Can make a harmony" for the Circle Up Broadway performance, they were illuminating one of the central themes of *The Color Purple* in all its forms – the importance of speaking up, speaking out, and finding and using one's voice. The power of the voice is, to be sure, a cliché in musical theatre, but themes of speaking up and singing out are also central to Walker's novel. Consider, for example, Harpo's mockery of his girlfriend Squeak's way of speaking and then Squeak's own declarations of a desire to sing in letters 42 and 74; or Albert saying he loves Shug because she speaks her mind like Sofia in letter 87; or Celie writing the very words of the novel because she doesn't have the voice to speak but can write instead. The voice and how we use the voice – in prayer, in song, in protest – is a central theme of Alice Walker's book and, as Daphne Brooks argues, a political position all its own. As Brooks puts it early on in *Liner Notes for the Revolution*, "Black women's musical practices are, in short, revolutionary because they are inextricably linked to the matter of Black life." For Brooks, "Black women's musical practices are revolutionary because of the ways in which said practices both forecast and execute the viability and potentiality of Black life."[84]

I noted in the introduction that the Celie who exists in the musical must, in fact, sing, even though it's almost impossible to imagine Celie singing in the novel or Whoopi Goldberg singing in the 1985 film. In a stage musical, however, there is no choice but for Celie to give voice to her desires and grievances through song; the form demands it. Celie's first song is a lullaby to her newborn, Adam. In many ways, this is an "I want" song. Celie sings to her son, "Somebody gonna love you / Yes, I'm always gonna love you," and she means it, of course, but she also sings for herself, telling us of her own need for love as a 14-year-old girl.[85] This is a young woman who needs someone to love her, who wants to be for her son what she has been needing in her own life. It's a small, brief, beautiful tune, and perfectly timed – Celie's first few letters in the novel are also very short missives. Celie's next song, which she sings with Nettie, articulates her desires more clearly. Nettie asks Celie what she wants, and Celie replies, "Wanna sit and do nothing / Make you a new dress / Hope my babies are happy / Some place God will bless," and again the musical articulates through song something the Celie of the novel is not able to do nearly as well.[86] The musical's Celie is filled with strong desires, and she tells us about them directly. When Mister sends Nettie away, Celie angrily tells her god that she never asks for anything. She begs for him to bring Nettie back and sings: "If I'm really a lily of the field / You will answer my prayers / Or you're no God at all!"[87] This would be an almost unthinkable phrase for Celie to speak in the novel. The Celie on the page is nearly silenced by grief at her sister's parting in letter 11, and she does not pray. She most certainly does not question the judgment of her god this early in the story.

I am noting these early moments of the musical in which Celie sings because this seems to me an overlooked aspect of the way the form of the musical changes Celie's story. Celie is a very different character in the musical because we know so much about – because she sings about – what she wants and who she is. I also want to draw attention to the way Celie demands identification through song, through singing the usual "I want" song in order to tell us about her desires early in the show.[88] In the novel, the second sentence Celie writes is crossed out: "I am I have always been a good girl," and this is significant, as Lauren Berlant notes, for the way that Celie figuratively strikes out her own subjectivity.[89]

In all versions of *The Color Purple*, Celie comes to articulate a self through her own voice – even more importantly than through her writing. This is especially evident at the moment in the story when she responds to Albert's insults and leaves him to move in with Shug. Celie describes her reply to Mr. _____ in letter 75 in the following way: "I'm pore, I'm black, I may be ugly and can't cook, a voice say to everything listening. But I'm here."[90] Celie refers to the voice that speaks these words *as if it is a voice that isn't quite her own,* another voice inside of her that she seems not to know that she possessed. As Berlant understands it, "This pure and disembodied voice speaks of its liberation from the disfigured body and enacts, through disembodiment, the utopian scene of self-expression from Celie's point of view."[91] In the musical, the composers have also designed this moment so that it feels disembodied. The entire scene that surrounds Celie's declaration is spoken; none of it is set to music. But Celie *bursts into song* in order to make her claim to selfhood: "I may be poor / I may be black / I may be ugly / But I'm here!"[92] These four lines of song are so short that the 2015 Broadway Revival Cast album doesn't even include them, skipping directly from "The Color Purple" to "Mister's Nightmare," but the musical's Celie cannot declare her subjectivity simply by speaking. Russell, Willis, Bray, and Norman knew that this moment had to be set to music and had to take up space in a different way than usual.

This second-act sequence in which Celie sings her subjectivity in response to Mister is sung in an even fuller way in the powerful 11 o'clock number for which Celie will repurpose the exact same phrase – *I'm here* – in the song that has become the musical's calling card. This song is important as the number that showcases Celie's new understanding of herself, but it is also a rallying cry for audiences, asking for identification, acknowledgment, and celebration. We should note from the outset that "I'm Here" is difficult to sing. As Stacy Wolf notes in her analysis of *Purple*, "the song almost feels like three different numbers, as if Celie is experimenting with a range of musical and linguistic self-expressions."[93] The song is difficult enough that Fantasia Barrino, perhaps the singer who has most frequently performed "I'm Here" in venues apart from the show (and will play Celie in Blitz Bazawule's 2023 movie musical), usually options down when she sings it. It might seem that the song's difficulty would display the singer's virtuosity at the expense of encouraging audience identification with the singer, but "I'm Here" actually manages to do both. This is no "I want" song; it's a rousing 11 o'clock number with a dance beat in the middle of it designed to hail audiences, to bring us to our feet in recognition and sympathy.

In 2007, "I'm Here" was used to advertise the continuing Broadway run to national television audiences: Barrino previewed her April debut in *The Color Purple* by performing the song on a February episode of *American Idol* season 6, and she sang it again less than a week later on *The Oprah Winfrey Show*. At the Tony Awards ceremony that June, she performed it yet again, and it appears as the final track on her 2010 studio album *Back to Me*. Since the 2015 revival, especially, the song has become a queer anthem, performed at LGBTQ Pride celebrations across the country. Take, for example, Bre Jackson's powerful rendition performed at the 2018 Broadway Sings for Pride Concert at the Cutting Room in New York.[94]

Jennifer Hudson's performance of "I'm Here" at the 2010 Kennedy Center Honors, however, remains the most widely viewed version on social media, and it marks a turning point in the song's history. For this powerhouse performance, Hudson altered the lyrics slightly so that she sang "You're beautiful" directly to honoree Oprah Winfrey before returning to the song's final "Yes, I'm beautiful / And I'm here."[95] One of the extraordinary elements of this performance is the appearance onstage of the Tennessee State University choir in the *middle* of the song. Hudson hits the seemingly impossible high notes in "I'm gonna sing out . . . / Sing out," and then the song nearly stops as Carl Kasell introduces the choir, who come in together, loud and fast, to join Hudson for "I believe I have inside of me / Everything that I need to live a bountiful life / With all the love alive in me / I'll stand as tall as the tallest tree." It's a compelling, emotionally charged moment that emphasizes the song's power as a call to audiences.

"I'm Here," with this performance, became bigger than a song the character Celie sings at the end of *The Color Purple*. These lyrics and this melody began to form a larger, more sweeping gesture in 2010, one designed to include others. In this performance, it is as if the nearly 50 students from Winfrey's alma mater, singing behind Hudson, have picked up her energy as it has been building over the course of "I'm gonna take a deep breath / Gonna hold my head up / Gonna put my shoulders back / And look you straight in the eye." The song literally comes to include the choir, the audience is asked to welcome them by the voice of the emcee, and after they join her, Hudson gestures to Winfrey to make sure to include her as well. This performance of "I'm Here" highlights what musical theatre songs are capable of doing in terms of their call for identification, their ability to inspire audiences, and the power they possess to catch their listeners and bring them along.

To promote *The Color Purple*'s Broadway revival, Cynthia Erivo appeared on national television a couple of times, singing "I'm Here" on *The Late Show with Stephen Colbert* and at the Tony Awards in 2016. At the April 2017 MAKERS conference, after the show had closed, Erivo further extended the song and its power, again displacing "I'm Here" from the show and asking her audience of predominantly women to understand the words of the song differently. Erivo's performance of this song was notable not especially for the different way that she sang "I'm Here" but for the way she separated her own voice as a performer from the character whose words she was singing. Erivo began her performance at MAKERS by *speaking*, reminding her audience that although she usually launches directly into singing when she performs, when she does this, "often people forget that the singing voice is attached to the person who has ideas."[96] Erivo sang two songs at this event, the first of which was Jazmine Sullivan's "Masterpiece (Mona Lisa)." She prefaced this song by exhorting the audience to identify with her voice:

> I want you to imagine that you are me singing these lyrics to yourself. So, for this song imagine that my voice is your voice, that these words are your words, and then when you get a moment to go back and listen to those lyrics again, say them to yourself again, 'cause they mean a lot, and we all need to say these things to ourselves.

After "Masterpiece," Erivo paused. She wasn't going to sing "this next song" because it's too hard to sing, she said. She has sung "I'm Here" some 500 times, and it takes a lot out of her to do it. Although at the beginning of this performance, Erivo asked audiences to remember that the voice that sings shares identity with the person who has ideas, she prefaced "I'm Here" by asking her audience to remember that even though others are calling the character Celie "ugly," she must hear those insults as a performer. Erivo's identificatory work as an actress means putting herself in the position of a character who has been abused and mistreated, a position in which her gender, sexuality, race, and class positions have all been violently turned against her by others and twisted from something beautiful into something "ugly." Here Erivo marked the identities she shares with her character, articulating the difficulty that a performer must go through in order to get to a place to be able to sing "I'm Here" well. "But . . ." she said, "I guess its message is more important than its circumstance," and so she sang it.

As Erivo described her identification with Celie as an actor, she modeled the identificatory process for the audience both in the room and on social media. That is, she made clear to her audience that this character is someone with whom they can identify, but that identification takes a certain amount of labor and care. As she noted before the Jazmine Sullivan song, *my voice can be your voice, these words can be your words*, if we do the work of identification. Erivo asked her audience to take in Celie's experiences and then to allow the song's "message [to be] more important than its circumstance." Erivo's performance of the song at MAKERS was as rousing and powerful as ever, and I want to note again that "I'm Here" has been effectively separated from the dramaturgy of *The Color Purple* so that the number has become a more generic anthem of survival and queer, female-identified power, hailing audiences of all kinds. Erivo didn't ask her audience in Palos Verdes, California, to sing along, but as with Hudson's performance at the Kennedy Center, "I'm Here" successfully carries us along with it, asking us to identify with Celie's ability to be "thankful for / Loving who I really am" and to find the power of our own voices.

Counterperformance

There have been two other important voices who have performed *The Color Purple* during the last decade. Alice Walker herself narrated an unabridged audio production of the novel for Recorded Books in 2010 – the audiobook's cover repurposed the poster art from the original Broadway production – and the actress Samira Wiley recorded a second audiobook version for Audible in the Spring of 2020.[97] I want to note these as additional *performances* of *The Color Purple*, that is, specific reinterpretations of the text – both by queer Black women – that highlight particular aspects of the novel.

One of the reasons the novel won the Pulitzer Prize was that it *gave* voice to topics and ideas that were not frequently discussed in 1982; accordingly, the novel has also been silenced by various conservative organizations attempting to ban the book. As early as May 1984, the Associated Press reported that the Oakland school board was enforcing a ban on the book, as some parents objected to their high school-age students reading the novel's frank portrayals of sexual violence, sexual pleasure, queer familial relations, and alternatives to Christian theology. The novel has weathered numerous attempts to ban it – mostly by local school boards and libraries – in the decades since its publication, and it ought perhaps to strike us as particularly ironic that an epistolary novel so invested in the themes of the silence of oppression, of the voice raised in protest, and of the voice raised in song should be so frequently attacked as too emphatic or too inappropriate or too distasteful.[98] That the lyrics of the *song* "The Color Purple," then, were repurposed to protest the loss of Black life at the Broadway Circle Up in 2016 is deeply in keeping with the spirit of the original novel.

In closing, I'd like to gesture once more to Heather Headley's citation of the phrase "love is love" and to say one final thing about the musical's reworking of the book and the film. The stage version attempts to rethink and restore the sexual relationship that Celie and Shug have in Alice Walker's novel but just barely have in Spielberg's film. The two women are given a love song in the show, and their sexual relationship is made clear. But *The Color Purple* onstage is queerer than a straightforward lesbian romance; the musical, rather, is more complicated in its portrayal of sexuality than a simple homonormative tale would be. It attempts, instead, to be as complexly queer as the novel, which emphasizes family networks and support systems and interconnected nodes of desire.

This chapter has not fully explored the very different ways the novel, film, musical, and revival represent queer desire. Indeed, although I have attempted to highlight the powerful influence of queerness on the politics discussed in this chapter, queer desire may, finally, seem only tenuously linked to the questions I've been exploring about *The Color Purple*'s relationship to white patriarchal religion, Black male vulnerability, and the power of the voice. Indeed, these queer ideas may differ widely from what we have understood or think we understand as issues facing LGBTQ-identified people. But I write this chapter as a resident of the Southern United States, where resolutions banning critical race theory in classrooms have already passed in some states and are being debated in the legislatures of many others. In Florida, where I work and live, the typical legislation that opposes critical race theory has been coupled with the so-called "don't say gay" bill.[99] That these two bills were signed into law by the governor of Florida at the same time is indicative of just how deeply interconnected the renewed forces of anti-Blackness and homophobia are in the South and elsewhere. It becomes much clearer how imperative it is that we identify with and listen to Celie, how important it is for young people (and the rest of us too) to hear the ensemble when they sing that there is power even in the smallest voice, and how significant it is to hear this resilient woman sing her own Black queer subjectivity: "I'm beautiful. / And I'm here."

Notes

1 Byrd, *The World Has Changed*, 20–21.
2 Only one other film (1977's *The Turning Point*) has ever been nominated for so many Oscars without winning a single one.
3 Russell, Willis, and Bray are invariably credited in this order; all three wrote both lyrics and music. Norman signed on much later after Regina Taylor, author of the widely produced play with music *Crowns*, departed the project.
4 Brantley, "*The Color Purple* on Broadway, Stripped to Its Essence."
5 For my use of the word *identity*, see "The Fiction of Identity" in this book's introduction.
6 See Paredez, "Diva Relations in *The Color Purple*, the 2015 Broadway Revival," 53. Alice Walker coined the term *womanist* in 1983. She explicitly contrasts *womanist* with the word *girlish*. That is, a womanist is not only "A black feminist or feminist of color," she is also, and importantly, neither frivolous nor irresponsible: "From the black folk expression of mothers to female children, 'You acting womanish,' i.e., like a woman. Usually referring to outrageous, audacious, courageous or *willful* behavior. Wanting to know more and in greater depth than is considered 'good' for one. Interested in grown-up doings. Acting grown up. Being grown up. Interchangeable with another black folk expression: 'You trying to be grown.' Responsible. In charge. *Serious*." See Walker, *In Search of Our Mothers' Gardens*, xi, emphasis in original. In her screenplay, Walker describes Sofia as "One of the first womanists. She can work and fight her own battles, enjoys men, the company of other women, sex, her children and her home." See Walker, *The Same River Twice*, 54.
7 Wolf, *Changed for Good*, 182.
8 See, for example, Mitchell, "How Reading Queer Authors Improved My Relationships."
9 Whitfield, "A Space Has Been Made."
10 Lovelock, "'What About Love?'" 195.
11 Lovelock, "'What About Love?'" 207.
12 See Howard University School of Law Library, "The Black Lives Matter Movement – A Brief History of Civil Rights in the United States."
13 Brantley, "How to Keep a Musical Great."

14 Cox, "Julia Roberts, Lin-Manuel Miranda and More to Stump for Hillary Clinton on Broadway"; McFarland, "Relax Haters. Hillary Clinton Knows *Hamilton* Better Than You."
15 "Hillary Clinton: I Saw Hamilton Three Times."
16 Paulson and Barbaro, "Clinton Attends Closing of *Color Purple*," C3.
17 Headley, "My Grief Is Not Selective!"
18 See "Equations of Love" in the introduction to this book.
19 Walker, *The Color Purple*, 3.
20 Walker, *The Color Purple*, 6, 7. In the novel, Celie calls her husband Mr. _____. She begins, after a long while, to refer to him as Albert. In both the film and the musical, he is called Mister. I tend to favor referring to him as Albert in this chapter, but I have tried, as with Crutchie and C.C. Baxter in other chapters of this book, to be specific to the medium.
21 Walker, *The Color Purple*, 40–41.
22 Walker, *The Color Purple*, 48.
23 Walker, *The Color Purple*, 39.
24 Walker, *The Color Purple*, 166.
25 Walker, *The Color Purple*, 166–167.
26 Walker, *The Color Purple*, 167.
27 Walker, *The Color Purple*, 242.
28 Spielberg, *The Color Purple*.
29 Walker, *The Color Purple*, 168, 165.
30 Cf. Brooks, *Liners Notes for the Revolution*, 6–8.
31 Walker, *The Same River Twice*, 148.
32 Russell, Willis, Bray, and Norman, *The Color Purple*, 93.
33 Russell, Willis, Bray, and Norman, "The Libretto," 161.
34 See Walker, *The Color Purple*, 168.
35 Russell, Willis, Bray, and Norman, "The Libretto," 177.
36 MacDonald, reviews of *The Color Purple* and *The Scottsboro Boys*, 444.
37 Russell, Willis, Bray, and Norman, *The Color Purple*, 5.
38 McNulty, "*Color Purple* Musical on Broadway Has a Divine, Moving Spirit"; Salonga, "*The Color Purple*"; see also Lemon, "The Color Purple, Bernard B. Jacobs Theatre, New York."
39 Brown, "Hallelujah and Amen," 66.
40 Color Purple Lover, "Heather Headley – The Color Purple," my emphasis.
41 Walker, *The Same River Twice*, 148.
42 Following the killing of Michael Brown by police in Ferguson, Missouri in 2014, the *Washington Post* has been gathering and publishing data related to fatal police shootings of civilians. You can see their data at "Fatal Force."
43 State Media 360, "Broadway Circle Up 360 – This is How We Shoot Back."
44 Grenier quoted in Nicholson, "From Coast to Coast, *Purple* Aroused Passions," 18.
45 Walter, "One Man's View," 16.
46 Dandridge, "In Adapting the Novel, Spielberg Left Out Too Much," 28, my emphasis.
47 In this way, the response echoed responses to those of the 1976 choreopoem *for colored girls who have considered suicide/when the rainbow is enuf*, written by Ntozake Shange. See Colbert, "A Woman's Trip," 233–234. The conception of the divine that we find in *for colored girls* ("i found god in myself / & i loved her / i loved her fiercely") is also echoed in Walker's novel. See Shange, *for colored girls who have considered suicide/when the rainbow is enuf*, 63. These connections are no coincidence; Walker and Shange were close friends. See Byrd, *The World Has Changed*, 23.
48 Take, for example, Maslin, "*The Color Purple,* From Steven Spielberg," C18; Sterritt, "Spielberg Scrubs and Softens *The Color Purple*," 23; and Canby, "From a Palette of Clichés Comes *The Color Purple*."
49 See the extensive bibliographical essays in Chapters 7, "*The Color Purple*: Feminist Text?," and 8, "Gender and Sexuality in *The Color Purple*," of Lister, *Alice Walker: The Color Purple – A Reader's Guide to Essential Criticism*.

50 Curry, *The Man-Not*, 18.
51 "Black males are often killed by police officers because the officers claim they fear for their lives – that Black men have life-threatening weapons or guns. This phobia is a normalized and institutional program used to justify police violence, ostracism, and incarceration; it is a fear that is given so much weight in individual cases precisely because it is a fear that both white America and many non-white Americans share. The vulnerability of Black men and boys lies in this consensus." See Curry, *The Man-Not*, 7.
52 See Cullen, "The History of Mass Incarceration."
53 Willis quoted in Funderberg, *The Color Purple: A Memory Book of the Broadway Musical*, 49. Jones's song was co-written with Rod Temperton and Lionel Richie.
54 Norman quoted in Funderberg, *The Color Purple: A Memory Book of the Broadway Musical*, 32.
55 Russell, Willis, Bray, and Norman, "The Libretto," 166.
56 Russell, Willis, Bray, and Norman, "The Libretto," 166, 169.
57 See Russell, Willis, Bray, and Norman, "The Libretto," 158.
58 See Walker, *The Same River Twice*, 35 and Walker, *The Color Purple*, 53–55.
59 Russell, Willis, Bray, and Norman, "The Libretto," 166.
60 Russell, Willis, Bray, and Norman, "The Libretto," 171.
61 Walker, *The Color Purple*, 230.
62 Walker, *The Color Purple*, 54.
63 In 1989, Walker said, "I wish that men could have more of an appreciation of gentleness in men and not find it so threatening. That's part of the problem of men who can read *The Color Purple* and only find negative things about men in it. Because once the men in my book change from being macho men, [the critics] just lose interest in them, they can't recognize them as men." Walker quoted in Byrd, *The World Has Changed*, 79.
64 hooks, "Reading and Resistance," 288.
65 hooks, "Reading and Resistance," 287.
66 Walker, *The Color Purple*, 240.
67 Walker quoted in Byrd, *The World Has Changed*, 186.
68 See Walker, *The Same River Twice*, 41, 51.
69 Walker quoted in Byrd, *The World Has Changed*, 227.
70 hooks, "Reading and Resistance," 295.
71 Berlant, "Race, Gender, and Nation in *The Color Purple*," 233.
72 Berlant, "Race, Gender, and Nation in *The Color Purple*," 211–212.
73 In this way, *The Color Purple* prefigures the work of playwright and poet Sharon Bridgforth, who describes her play *the bull-jean stories* as an act of "creating-remembering": "these are the stories they didn't tell me the ones i needed most. bull-jean is the butch/southern/poet/warrior wom'n hero i wish i'd known." See Sharon Bridgforth, *the bull-jean stories*, ix–x.
74 Vitale, *The End of Policing*.
75 Economist, "Most Americans Do Not Want to 'Defund' the Police."
76 Lamble, "Transforming Carceral Logistics," 271.
77 Walker, *The Color Purple*, 75–84.
78 See Lamble, "Transforming Carceral Logistics," 270. See, also, Rachel Marshall's argument in "I'm a Public Defender. What If My Clients Got the Same Treatment as Brock Turner?" in which she argues for the *opposite* of harsher sentencing laws: "Let me be clear: I am not advocating for harsher penalties for anyone. Instead, I want the humanity of all people, regardless of background, to be recognized in sentencing. . . . It is time for our system to treat all people with fairness, compassion, and humanity – not just the privileged."
79 See State Media 360, "Broadway Circle Up 360 – This is How We Shoot Back."
80 The lyrics are modified only minutely from Miranda and McCarter, *Hamilton*, 273.
81 Miranda and McCarter, *Hamilton*, 92.
82 Russell, Willis, Bray, and Norman, "The Libretto," 177.
83 Cf. Crimp, "Mourning and Militancy."

84 Brooks, *Liner Notes for the Revolution*, 3.
85 Russell, Willis, Bray, and Norman, "The Libretto," 117.
86 Russell, Willis, Bray, and Norman, "The Libretto," 119.
87 Russell, Willis, Bray, and Norman, "The Libretto," 125.
88 I'm disagreeing here with Stacy Wolf's analysis in *Changed for Good* that finds that Celie has no "I want" song until her 11 o'clock number. See 185, 187.
89 Walker, *The Color Purple*, 3; Berlant, "Race, Gender, and Nation in *The Color Purple*," 211.
90 Walker, *The Color Purple*, 176.
91 Berlant, "Race, Gender, and Nation in *The Color Purple*," 226.
92 Russell, Willis, Bray, and Norman, "The Libretto," 164.
93 Wolf, *Changed for Good*, 187.
94 Asaf Blasberg Videographer, "Bre Jackson Sings 'I'm Here' From The Color Purple."
95 The Kennedy Center, "Jennifer Hudson – 'I'm Here,' The Color Purple (Oprah Winfrey Tribute) | 2010 Kennedy Center Honors."
96 MAKERS, "Cynthia Erivo Performs 'I'm Here' From 'The Color Purple' | 2017 MAKERS Conference."
97 Walker, narrator, *The Color Purple* by Alice Walker; Wiley, narrator, *The Color Purple* by Alice Walker.
98 See Intellectual Freedom Committee – Young Adult Services Division, *Hit List*, 75–79.
99 Papaycik and Saunders, "Florida's Governor Signs Controversial Bill Banning Critical Race Theory in Schools"; Sczesny, "Medical Professionals Denounce 'Don't Say Gay' Law During Orlando Protest."

References for Chapter 4

Asaf Blasberg Videographer. "Bre Jackson Sings 'I'm Here' From The Color Purple." *YouTube*. 26 June 2018. www.youtube.com/watch?v=pmPogEbt4gA. Accessed 10 September 2022.

Berlant, Lauren. "Race, Gender, and Nation in *The Color Purple*." In *Alice Walker: Critical Perspectives Past and Present*. Edited by Henry Louis Gates, Jr., and Kwame Anthony Appiah. New York: Amistad, 211–238, 1993.

Brantley, Ben. "How to Keep a Musical Great: Call Heather Headley and Marin Mazzie." *New York Times*. 23 May 2016. www.nytimes.com/2016/05/23/theater/how-to-keep-a-musical-great-call-heather-headley-and-marin-mazzie.html. Accessed 14 February 2022.

Brantley, Ben. "*The Color Purple* on Broadway, Stripped to Its Essence." *New York Times*. 10 December 2015. www.nytimes.com/2015/12/11/theater/review-the-color-purple-on-broadway-stripped-to-its-essence.html. Accessed 23 June 2022.

Bridgforth, Sharon. *the bull-jean stories*. Austin: Red Bone Press, 1998.

Brooks, Daphne A. *Liner Notes for the Revolution: The Intellectual Life of Black Feminist Sound*. Cambridge: Harvard University Press, 2021.

Brown, Aaron. "Hallelujah and Amen: The Revival of *The Color Purple* as African-American Church." *Ecumenica* 11.1: 63–72, 2018.

Byrd, Rudolph P., (editor). *The World Has Changed: Conversations With Alice Walker*. New York: New Press, 2010.

Canby, Vincent. "From a Palette of Clichés Comes *The Color Purple*." *New York Times*. 5 January 1986. www.nytimes.com/1986/01/05/movies/moviesspecial/from-a-palette-of-clichs-comes-the-color-purple.html. Accessed 28 June 2022.

Colbert, Soyica Diggs. "A Woman's Trip: Domestic Violence and Black Feminist Healing in Ntozake Shange's *for colored girls*." In *Black Cultural Production After Civil Rights*. Edited by Robert J. Patterson. Champaign: University of Illinois Press, 225–247, 2019.

Color Purple Lover. "Heather Headley – The Color Purple." *YouTube*. 29 December 2016. www.youtube.com/watch?v=-irWoRkJF_g. Accessed 28 June 2022.

Cox, Gordon. "Julia Roberts, Lin-Manuel Miranda and More to Stump for Hillary Clinton on Broadway." *Variety*. 30 September 2016. variety.com/2016/legit/news/broadway-for-hillary-julia-roberts-lin-manuel-miranda-1201875089/. Accessed 14 February 2022.

Crimp, Douglas. "Mourning and Militancy." *October* 51: 3–18, 1989.

Cullen, James. "The History of Mass Incarceration." *Brennan Center for Justice*. www.brennancenter.org/our-work/analysis-opinion/history-mass-incarceration. Accessed 5 July 2022.

Curry, Tommy. *The Man-Not: Race, Class, Genre, and the Dilemmas of Black Manhood*. Philadelphia: Temple University Press, 2017.

Dandridge, Rita B. "In Adapting the Novel, Spielberg Left Out Too Much." *Black Film Review* 2.2: 16ff, 1986.

Economist. "Most Americans Do Not Want to 'Defund' the Police." *Economist*. 18 June 2020. www.economist.com/graphic-detail/2020/06/18/most-americans-do-not-want-to-defund-the-police. Accessed 30 June 2022.

"Fatal Force." *Washington Post*. www.washingtonpost.com/graphics/investigations/police-shootings-database/. Accessed 28 June 2022.

Funderberg, Lise. *The Color Purple: A Memory Book of the Broadway Musical*. New York: Carroll & Graf, 2006.

Headley, Heather. "My Grief Is Not Selective!" *Facebook*. 8 July 2016. www.facebook.com/permalink.php?story_fbid=10154051743972599&id=34333402598. Accessed 21 February 2022.

"Hillary Clinton: I Saw Hamilton Three Times." *Politico*. 14 July 2016. www.politico.com/video/2016/07/hillary-clinton-i-saw-hamilton-three-times-059913. Accessed 14 February 2022.

hooks, bell. "Reading and Resistance: *The Color Purple*." In *Alice Walker: Critical Perspectives Past and Present*. Edited by Henry Louis Gates, Jr., and Kwame Anthony Appiah. New York: Amistad, 284–295, 1993.

Howard University School of Law Library. "The Black Lives Matter Movement – A Brief History of Civil Rights in the United States." *Howard University School of Law Library*. library.law.howard.edu/civilrightshistory/BLM. Accessed 9 August 2022.

Intellectual Freedom Committee – Young Adult Services Division. *Hit List: Frequently Challenged Young Adult Titles; References to Defend Them*. Chicago: American Library Association, 1989.

Lamble, Sarah. "Transforming Carceral Logistics: 10 Reasons to Dismantle the Prison Industrial Complex Using a Queer/Trans Analysis." In *Captive Genders: Trans Embodiment and the Prison Industrial Complex*. Edited by Eric A. Stanley, and Nat Smith (2nd ed). Edinburgh: AK Press, 269–299, 2015.

Lemon, Brendan. "The Color Purple, Bernard B. Jacobs Theatre, New York – 'Poignant.'" *Financial Times*. 11 December 2015. www.ft.com/content/346880b8-9f2b-11e5-beba-5e33e2b79e46. Accessed 27 June 2022.

Lister, Rachel. *Alice Walker: The Color Purple – A Reader's Guide to Essential Criticism*. London: Palgrave Macmillan, 2010.

Lovelock, James. "'What About Love?': Claiming and Reclaiming LGBTQ+ Spaces in Twenty-First Century Musical Theatre." In *Reframing the Musical: Race, Culture, and Identity*. Edited by Sarah K. Whitfield. London: Red Globe Press, 187–209, 2019.

MacDonald, Laura. Reviews of *The Color Purple* and *The Scottsboro Boys*. *Theatre Journal* 66.3: 444–448, 2014.

MAKERS. "Cynthia Erivo Performs 'I'm Here' From 'The Color Purple' | 2017 MAKERS Conference." *YouTube*. 4 April 2017. www.youtube.com/watch?v=E-Flmo07ddk. Accessed 2 July 2022.

Marshall, Rachel. "I'm a Public Defender. What If My Clients Got the Same Treatment as Brock Turner?" *Vox*. 9 June 2016. www.vox.com/2016/6/9/11889472/stanford-sexual-assault-brock-turner. Accessed 1 July 2022

Maslin, Janet. "*The Color Purple,* From Steven Spielberg." *New York Times*. 18 December 1985. (C18).

McFarland, Kevin. "Relax Haters. Hillary Clinton Knows *Hamilton* Better Than You." *Wired*. 29 July 2016. www.wired.com/2016/07/hillary-clinton-really-does-love-hamilton/. Accessed 14 February 2022.

McNulty, Charles. "*Color Purple* Musical on Broadway Has a Divine, Moving Spirit." *Los Angeles Times*. 10 December 2015. www.latimes.com/entertainment/arts/la-et-cm-color-purple-broadway-review-20151211-column.html. Accessed 28 June 2022.

Miranda, Lin-Manuel, and Jeremy McCarter. *Hamilton: The Revolution*. New York: Grand Central Publishing, 2016.

Mitchell, Koritha. "How Reading Queer Authors Improved My Relationships." *Avidly*. 15 December 2021. avidly.lareviewofbooks.org/2021/12/15/how-reading-queer-authors-improved-my-relationships/. Accessed 25 June 2022.

Nicholson, David. "From Coast to Coast, *Purple* Aroused Passions." *Black Film Review* 2.2: 18–19, 1986.

Papaycik, Matt, and Forrest Saunders. "Florida's Governor Signs Controversial Bill Banning Critical Race Theory in Schools." *WPTV*. 22 April 2022. www.wptv.com/news/education/floridas-governor-to-sign-critical-race-theory-education-bill-into-law. Accessed 2 July 2022

Paredez, Deborah. "Diva Relations in *The Color Purple*, the 2015 Broadway Revival." *Studies in Musical Theatre* 12.1: 43–60, 2018.

Paulson, Michael, and Michael Barbaro. "Clinton Attends Closing of *Color Purple*." *New York Times*. 9 January 2017. (C3).

Russell, Brenda, Allee Willis, Stephen Bray, and Marsha Norman. *The Color Purple: 2015 Broadway Revival*. New York: Theatrical Rights Worldwide, 2016.

Russell, Brenda, Allee Willis, Stephen Bray, and Marsha Norman. "The Libretto." In *The Color Purple: A Memory Book of the Broadway Musical*. Edited by Lise Funderberg. New York: Carroll & Graf, 111–177, 2006.

Salonga, Lea. "*The Color Purple* – Almost Church-Like Experience." *Philippine Daily Inquirer*. 4 February 2016. entertainment.inquirer.net/189292/the-color-purple-almost-church-like-experience. Accessed 27 June 2022.

Sczesny, Matt. "Medical Professionals Denounce 'Don't Say Gay' Law During Orlando Protest." *WPTV*. 8 April 2022. www.wptv.com/news/lgbtq/pushback-grows-from-floridas-dont-say-gay-law. Accessed 2 July 2022.

Shange, Ntozake. *For Colored Girls Who Have Considered Suicide/When the Rainbow Is Enuf*. New York: Macmillan, 1976.

Spielberg, Steven, (director). *The Color Purple*. HBOmax. 18 December 1985.

State Media 360. "Broadway Circle Up 360 – This Is How We Shoot Back." *YouTube*. 17 August 2016. www.youtube.com/watch?v=zicgRnTruxA. Accessed 28 June 2022.

Sterritt, David. "Spielberg Scrubs and Softens *The Color Purple*." *Christian Science Monitor*. 20 December 1985. (23).

The Kennedy Center. "Jennifer Hudson – 'I'm Here,' The Color Purple (Oprah Winfrey Tribute) | 2010 Kennedy Center Honors." *YouTube*. 25 November 2016. www.youtube.com/watch?v=RUi2Ye6mN-w. Accessed 2 July 2022.

Vitale, Alex S. *The End of Policing* (2nd ed). New York: Verso, 2017.

Walker, Alice. *In Search of Our Mothers' Gardens*. New York: Harcourt Brace Jovanovich, 1983.

Walker, Alice, (narrator). *The Color Purple* by Alice Walker. Landover: Recorded Books, 2010.
Walker, Alice. *The Color Purple*. New York: Harcourt Brace Jovanovich, 1982.
Walker, Alice. *The Same River Twice: Honoring the Difficult*. New York: Scribner, 1996.
Walter, Earl, Jr. "One Man's View." *Black Film Review* 2.2: 16ff, 1986.
Whitfield, Sarah K. "A Space Has Been Made: Bisexual+ Stories in Musical Theatre." *Theatre Topics Online Content*. July 2020. jhuptheatre.org/theatre-topics/online-content/issue/volume-30-issue-2-july-2020/space-has-been-made-bisexual. Accessed 7 August 2022.
Wiley, Samira, (narrator). *The Color Purple* by Alice Walker. Newark: Audible Studios, 2020.
Wolf, Stacy. *Changed for Good: A Feminist History of the Broadway Musical*. New York: Oxford University Press, 2011.

5
FROZEN ELEGANZA

As *Frozen II* appeared on Blu-ray and VOD in February of 2020, *Saturday Night Live* poked fun at the sequel in a satirical commercial including "deleted scenes" from the movie. These include JJ Watt as Kristoff singing a song called "Big and Woke" that gently mocks *Frozen*'s more feminist approach to princes and princesses. The cast sings: "A new kind of prince that's not a creep / I won't kiss you while you're asleep. / He's not a bro, but he's not a cuck. / He's gentle at first, but he really can –." *Saturday Night Live* also mocked the presence of Mattias, the Black lieutenant of the King's Guard who first appeared in *Frozen II*. "You live . . . here?" Kate McKinnon as Elsa asks him. "Rural Norway. In 1840. That's correct," answers Kenan Thompson. The cast wonders how to solve a problem like Mattias, singing a riff on the famous song from *The Sound of Music*. There's also a sketch in which the snowman Olaf begins to hit puberty. Mikey Day enters wearing a snowman suit that resembles Olaf but with the addition of a suggestively placed second carrot. Olaf is growing up, and his friends no longer see his requests for warm hugs as innocent. Anna (Cecily Strong) looks at Olaf skeptically, and Kristoff runs away from him when he runs toward him with his stick arms wide open. The scene ends as Sven, the reindeer, says, "Uh oh. I *love* carrots!"[1]

The tentpole joke of the skit, of course, focuses on Elsa. McKinnon twirls into a forest landscape in full Elsa drag, asking, "Hello? Is anyone there? Anna? Kristoff? Olaf? I'm gay? Is anyone there?" When Anna finds Elsa, she wonders if she's heard her say *gay*. "No!" says Elsa in McKinnon's trademark mocking deadpan. "I'm not anything. You have a fulfilling heterosexual marriage at the age of eighteen, and I've just spent two whole movies playing with snow – both are equal and good. And then in *Frozen 3* I can just freeze my eggs." Anna answers by telling Elsa not to worry; she affirms the lesbianism Elsa has just denied – to the tune of "Let It Go":

DOI: 10.4324/9781003317470-6

> We all know
> We all know
> We've all known since you were a tween
> When you dressed as Brienne of Tarth
> On three separate Halloweens
> I don't care
> What Disney says
> The Twitter storm rages on . . .[2]

McKinnon's Elsa awkwardly finishes the song, saying, "The lack of any romantic interest never bothered me anyway."

This SNL skit touches obliquely on many of this chapter's topics, and although Elsa's lesbianism is the most obvious of these, SNL's treatment of *Frozen II* prompts inquiry in several directions. First, Cecily Strong's Anna mentions social media as the source of her information about Elsa's sexuality, despite Disney's (and Elsa's own) denials of her assumed lesbianism. Second, although the SNL sketch is ostensibly about *Frozen II*, its music mostly burlesques recognizable songs from the original *Frozen* film. In the sketch's exploration of *Frozen*'s overwhelming whiteness, however, it repurposes "Maria," one of the most memorable songs from Rodgers and Hammerstein's *Sound of Music*. The SNL sketch doesn't explicitly refer to *Frozen: The Broadway Musical*, which, in February 2020 was playing at the St. James Theatre on 44th Street, less than a 15-minute walk from where SNL was filmed. Still, this bit acknowledges that *Frozen* is musical theatre, and its reference to *The Sound of Music* assumes that its audience possesses at least a passing knowledge of the Broadway musical theatre repertoire.

Most importantly, the skit takes an adult approach to a film explicitly made for children; the performers on SNL perform for us as adult viewers, sharing in a series of jokes about which children are supposed to be ignorant. This comedic treatment entails a sexualization of the characters that is not readily apparent in the films (although we will see it in the *Frozen* shorts). Movies about Disney princesses are *normative*, certainly, but the great power of heteronormativity is that it does not present itself as *sexualized*. A Disney princess never chooses her prince based on sexual compatibility, even if many of the rest of us in the real world do precisely that. SNL's sexualization of these characters, then, introduces an adult reality that the film denies, reading eroticism into Disney's anodyne, mostly sexless figures. But the sketch does not sexualize Elsa alone: JJ Watt's himbo version of Kristoff is "gentle at first, but he really can [fuck]," the rhyme promises (and Cecily Strong mouths); and we are told that Olaf's additional orange appendage "is thicker than a Coke can." When Sven tells us he loves carrots at the end of the sketch, the joke even asks us to imagine a reindeer in a sexual position.[3]

Two months later, the hit VH1 show *RuPaul's Drag Race* contained a segment "inspired by the Broadway musical." RuPaul announced the runway category of the "Snatch Game" episode as *frozen eleganza*.[4] The contestants strutted down a stage unusually accoutered with six *Frozen*-inspired trees dripping in icicles, and the girls appeared in icy blue, silver, and white couture. A few took the *Frozen* theme literally, doing their best Elsa impersonations, but some opted for a less conventional look, appearing as, for example, a Good Humor girl or a hypothermic passenger from the Titanic. As always happens on the show, the two queens judged to be the bottom performers of the week lip-synced for their lives to – naturally enough – "Let It Go," and Brita Filter and Aiden Zhane did a dueling number while snow fell on the stage.

The trees and snow for this runway and lip-sync – additional theatrical elements that never appear on other episodes of *Drag Race* – were evidently the idea of the marketing team at Disney Theatricals, and they exerted other creative control as well.[5] Most notably, it was not Idina Menzel who belted out Elsa's signature anthem while the girls lip-synced; instead, it was Caissie Levy, the original star of the Broadway show. The episode's theme, then, was inspired not by *Frozen* but by its stage adaptation, and it was designed expressly to market *Frozen: The Broadway Musical* to viewers of a weekly drag program that features almost exclusively LGBTQ performers.[6] The presence of a Disney product on the *Drag Race* mainstage, however, did not curtail the judging panel's usual suggestive commentary as the queens strutted the runway. The old joke "How's your head?" made an appearance, "Alright, let's see someone Elsa," kidded Carson Kressley, and RuPaul (rather weakly) punned, "Let it ho, let it ho, let it ho." Like the SNL skit, *Frozen*'s appearance on *Drag Race* was aimed at an adult audience, and it sexualized *Frozen* in intriguing and challenging ways.

Both of these appearances on television in early 2020 demonstrated *Frozen*'s extraordinary ability to connect with LGBTQ audiences. Both *Drag Race* and SNL featured *Frozen* audience members performing creative riffs on the *Frozen* canon. In less than a decade, Elsa herself has become a queer icon, inspiring numerous hashtags (#lesbianelsa, #giveelsaagirlfriend, #lgbtprincess, #gayprincess, #gayelsa, #gayfrozen), countless memes, fan-fiction, fan art,[7] and a Change.org petition, as well as inspiring queer people, like Kate McKinnon and the queens of *Drag Race* season 12, to dress up and perform as Elsa.[8] *Frozen*'s remarkable heroine has appealed not only to lesbian audiences but also to asexual viewers, and *Frozen*'s appearance on *Drag Race* is a testament to further queer fandoms as well.[9]

This chapter explores Elsa's queerness by asking *how* Elsa's desires are represented in *Frozen* and its sequels. I am interested, too, in the way audiences have responded creatively to Elsa and her gang, working with the characters and elaborating on them via social media and other platforms. This chapter also examines the way further performances of Elsa and additional *Frozen* content manipulate and respond to audiences' intuitions about Elsa's fictional sexuality. I am interested, especially, in the distance between *Frozen* the 2013 film and *Frozen* the 2018 Broadway musical. Although each tells essentially the same narrative in a different medium, during the years between the two, Disney had the opportunity to respond to audiences' desires about Elsa's sexuality and shape the character – and the rest of the *Frozen* world – in new ways that reflect and refract those desires. The Broadway version of *Frozen* is especially intriguing for the way that it puts pressure on some of the exact same limits that the SNL sketch and the *Drag Race* episode seem newly to transgress. This chapter closes by discussing that most magical of Arendelle's denizens, Olaf. I argue that thinking through the little snowman as a queer child illuminates *Frozen*'s emphasis on childhood as a queer space and offers new identificatory possibilities for queer audiences.

Elsa as Queer Icon

Frozen is much more than a movie and its sequel; it is a behemoth mass-media product, a franchise much larger than *Frozen* and *Frozen II*, its two flagship films. Visit your local toy store or Target and you can find *Frozen*-themed swimming pools and *Frozen*-themed desks; there are smartwatches and Bluetooth-enabled karaoke microphones, bubble wands, nightlights, duvets, drapes, *Frozen* tea sets, *Frozen* party supplies, and battery-powered *Frozen*-themed four-wheel vehicles. Of course, there are dolls as well, including tiny LEGO Annas and Elsas and larger soft ones for snuggling and taking to bed. The streaming network Disney+ even shows sing-along versions of the two *Frozen* films so that children at home can perform along with the characters. Girls are also encouraged to dress up as Elsa and Anna: Disney sells *Frozen* makeup collections, nail polish, and jewelry-building kits, in addition to Halloween costumes, tiaras, and child-sized scepters that allow young people to identify with Elsa and Anna and to perform as these princesses in practical and physical ways.

None of this would work without the steady stream of *Frozen* narratives emerging from the studio. The first film appeared in movie theatres in November 2013. Its enormous popularity prompted *Frozen Fever*, a short film that accompanied Disney's *Cinderella* to movie theatres in March 2015, as well as a four-episode animated series called *Frozen: Northern Lights* (2016) designed to advertise *Frozen*-themed LEGO sets. Next, the holiday-themed short film *Olaf's Frozen Adventure* was released theatrically (for two weeks) in October 2017 accompanying the feature-length *Coco*.[10] Two Novembers later, in 2019, *Frozen II* arrived in theatres. Then in early 2020, as the SARS-COV-2 pandemic consigned many children to attending school from home, Disney began to release very short videos featuring Olaf, ostensibly in quarantine, doing mostly solo activities such as fishing, dancing ballet, and playing music. Titled *At Home with Olaf*, the series appeared on YouTube beginning in April 2020; the credits for the series prominently displayed that animators were working from home. Yet another short film, *Once upon a Snowman*, also featuring Olaf, was released via Disney+ in October 2020, and in November 2021, five more shorts appeared under the series title *Olaf Presents*.

Most of these films and shorts feature Anna, Elsa, Kristoff, Olaf, and Sven – the central players in *Frozen*'s family. Oaken, the tall, burly shopkeeper who runs Wandering Oaken's Trading Post and Sauna, also appears in all of these narratives (more on him later), and Grand Pabbie, the friendly and wise old troll, appears in most of them. *Frozen II* introduces several new characters and an epic and convoluted new narrative, but none of the new people we meet is the future *king* of

Arendelle, and though marriage is central to the plots of both *Frozen* and *Frozen II*, no one proposes to Elsa.¹¹ She spends no time with either of the two obviously eligible men who appear in the second feature, and none of the shorts introduces anything remotely approaching a romantic interest. Still, as far as canonical information about *Frozen* goes, Elsa is not a lesbian. She certainly has no *female* romantic interests; she shares no kisses with other women (Anna has *two* male love interests in *Frozen*). Neither is Elsa stereotypically a lesbian. Her gender presentation is extremely high femme, her chief hobby would appear to be hosting lavish parties – an activity she does in *Frozen Fever*, *Olaf's Frozen Adventure*, and *Frozen II* – and aside from using her cryokinetic powers for various activities, most of Elsa's energies are directed toward caretaking, motherhood, and keeping other people happy.

Still, if Elsa is not supposed to be a lesbian, she is certainly supposed to be *different*, and this can most obviously be seen in contrast with her younger sister. In their first shared song in *Frozen*, for example, Anna sings about finding "the one"; she fantasizes about "suddenly see[ing] him standing there / A beautiful stranger tall and fair," while imagining herself inside a series of different paintings, interacting with various men in each.¹² At exactly the same time, Elsa is singing "Don't let them in / Don't let them see / Be the good girl you always have to be" – lyrics that will repeat in her big anthem "Let It Go" – and "Conceal, don't feel / Put on a show / Make one wrong move and everyone will know." Elsa's desires are to be well behaved and to keep herself from putting anyone in danger. These aren't particularly queer desires; the point, however, is not that Elsa experiences same-sex desire but rather that *Frozen* deliberately contrasts Elsa's desires with heterosexual desire. One girl sings about falling in love and getting married, and the other one sings about *something else*. Both Anna's second and third songs are about heterosexual love ("For the First Time in Forever" and "Love Is an Open Door"); Elsa never mentions it. *Frozen II* makes this even more explicit. In the first few minutes of the film as the young girls play in a pretend enchanted forest, Anna performs romantic heterosexual fantasies, making her toy prince and princess kiss on the lips. "Ew, Anna, ugh," chides little Elsa. "Kissing won't save the forest."¹³ Anna, we are told, is invested in marriage even at this very young age. Elsa does not share this interest; Elsa is *different*.

Elsa also possesses magical cryokinetic abilities that she is asked to keep hidden from everyone she knows, and – at least since Bryan Singer's 2000 film *X-men* – audiences are also practiced at reading hidden superpowers as an allegory for sexuality in general and queer sexuality in particular.¹⁴ She is told by her parents that her powers are dangerous and that she must hide them from the entire kingdom, including her beloved sister. Even more importantly, Elsa fulfills a queer *narrative* function in *Frozen*. She explicitly refuses to give her blessing to Anna's marriage to Hans, the prince she has known for less than one day, and as Elsa fumblingly attempts to advise Anna against a hasty wedding, she steps into the role of the queer villain, the *sinthomo*sexual so carefully described by Lee Edelman in *No Future*.¹⁵ Elsa actively disrupts the heterosexual couple's imagined future (the one Anna has been singing about for most of the movie), and in this way, she functions narratively as the negative force that must be defeated, the Disney villain, like Ursula or Scar or Jafar.

Audiences have often noted that villains in Disney animation, such as *Peter Pan*'s Captain Hook or *Pocahontas*'s Governor Ratcliffe, are frequently coded as queer, or, rather, they *read* as queer, whether coded this way or not.[16] These characters desire the destruction of happy, heterosexual romance, but whether they want this because they are evil or because they are queer is a confusing question in Disney animation because the two are so frequently tied together. Queerness is in relationship with villainy. Indeed, for Disney's animated features, villainy and queerness seem to be identical. Ursula, Scar, and Jafar are obvious examples, but consider Cinderella's stepmother or *Alice in Wonderland*'s Queen of Hearts or *Hercules*'s Hades; all three are queerly coded despite the fact that we know they've been in heterosexual marriages.[17] As Edelman argues, these villains — Elsa included — don't need to *be* queer: in their function as attempted destroyers of happiness they represent queerness *as such*.

Snow Queens

As we consider villainy, it is worth meditating, briefly, on *Frozen*'s source material, Hans Christian Andersen's 1844 story "The Snow Queen." *Frozen* is adapted *very* loosely from the original tale. There is, for example, no Arendelle in "The Snow Queen"; there are no sisters and no parents; no one is a princess; there is no Olaf; and there are no trolls. There is, however, a talking reindeer in Anderson's story, and, as in *Frozen*, a heart that has almost been overtaken by ice is rescued by an act of true love. In "The Snow Queen," however, the villain is an evil hobgoblin who manufactures a sinister mirror that distorts everything one sees in it. This mirror shatters into millions of pieces and is magically distributed around the world, getting into the eyes of unsuspecting people and disturbing their vision so that everything they see seems terrible. This happens to a young boy named Kai in Andersen's story. He becomes stubborn and negative when the sliver of mirror gets lodged in his eye, and he transforms from an innocent child into someone bitter and unkind. It is at this point in the tale that he is kidnapped by the Snow Queen. Kai's adopted sister, who loves him unconditionally, goes on an odyssey to the arctic to find him, encountering numerous characters on the way. Finally finding him in the Snow Queen's castle of ice, she weeps pure-hearted tears, which wash away the piece of mirror from Kai's eye and warm his nearly frozen heart. Andersen describes the queen as scary, clever, and very beautiful, but she — like the other numerous kidnappers of children in "The Snow Queen" — is not particularly evil in the tale, and we never meet her again after she takes Kai off to her castle of ice in Lapland.[18] The Snow Queen is a mysterious and powerful figure with inscrutable motives, but she barely appears in Andresen's story despite her prominent position in its title. It is worth noting, too, that the Snow Queen has no apparent sexuality, and her motive for kidnapping Kai is, at least on the surface, neither romantic nor sexual.

In feminist scholar Pauline Greenhill's analysis of "Snow Queen" adaptations, she finds that the eponymous figure is often interpreted, especially by male readers, as a figure for the refusal of heterosexual desire.[19] In these readings of Andersen's tale, the snow queen represents an unattainable or hostile heterosexual love object for the author himself, who creates her as a figure for sexual refusal or unrequited love. Greenhill notes that the snow queen has also frequently been identified with Andersen himself, and her essay's exploration of Andersen's sexuality deeply enriches the possibilities for queer readings of "The Snow Queen."[20] Greenhill surveys the evidence related to Andersen's sexuality, finding that his biographers refuse to acknowledge the possibility of his homosexual desires. "Indeed," she argues, "the fervency of protests and the rampant speculation in demurrals bolster rather than debunk readings of Andersen as queer."[21] *Queer* describes Andersen perfectly, if vaguely: his biographer Wolfgang Lederer states flatly that he "never engaged in any overt sexual acts, heterosexual or otherwise" before adding evocatively

> that he was capable of strong erotic (sensual, not sexual) feelings toward either sex, including children; and that therefore, without sexual or sensual outlet of any kind, he was left with the feeling of being incarcerated in an icy, depressing, eventually deadly jail made of his own frustration.[22]

Greenhill cites this passage in Lederer for the way it explicitly identifies Andersen with his Snow Queen, representing him as imprisoned, like his character, in a frozen queer sexual solitude.[23] As a way to explain the inscrutable motives of the Snow Queen, then, critics have frequently looked to Andersen's sexual interests but found them, too, inscrutable. I include this speculation here because it is so comparable to readings of Elsa that have, in the absence of evident sexual activity, attempted to fix her sexuality. To put it another way, queer readings of *Frozen* go all the way back to its source material in nineteenth-century Denmark.

The characters in *Frozen* remix the plot and characters of "The Snow Queen." Instead of a boy who is kidnapped by the queen and rescued by his sister, we have two sisters, one of whom takes the role of both queen and kidnapper, and one, pure of heart, as in the original, who takes the journey and does the rescuing. The partially frozen heart in "The Snow Queen" is transferred from the boy to Anna, and in a twist that is legitimately confusing in magical terms, Anna's act of true love in *Frozen* saves her *own* heart from freezing. Both "The Snow Queen" and *Frozen* are fundamentally about coming of age; the characters must decide between growing up bitter and unkind or happy and loving. Villainy in both stories consists of being self-serving and mean, but in "The Snow Queen," these qualities are impermanent, the result of an accident or an error that can be rectified.

Elsa was initially imagined as an evil snow queen by Disney artists, and early conceptual drawings of her character represent her as a sinister and sardonic figure. As the story of *Frozen* took shape, however, and after co-director Jennifer Lee was brought on board, things began to shift. "They kept calling her the 'villain,'" Lee says in *The Art of Frozen*,

> But there came a point when we said, "We can't use that word anymore." You care about someone who's been forced to hide who they are. Elsa's not a villain, she just makes some bad choices because she's in a very difficult situation.

Like Kai in "The Snow Queen," Elsa sees things in a flawed way, and this can be altered by the love of a sister, just as it is in Andersen's tale. What is *unalterable* is something else, what Lee gets at when she describes Elsa as "someone who's been forced to hide *who they are*."[24]

The animators and other artists behind *Frozen* consistently discuss Elsa using essentialist terms. "I love Elsa," says story artist Chris Williams,

> because we can make her cold and distant, but our hearts will still go out to her. We'll know she's living in a prison she can't share with anybody. There are some pretty deep themes that come from not being able to admit *who you are* for fear of how people will react.[25]

As Charles Solomon sums it up, "Elsa begins as a *repressed* character, forced to conceal *who she really is*."[26] This is how Disney's snow queen describes herself, as well. As Anna tries to convince her to leave her ice fortress and come back to Arendelle, Elsa says, "I belong here, alone. Where I can be who I am without hurting anybody." It is not important to make the argument here that Elsa is a lesbian or even to decide between describing Elsa as homosexual or asexual; her availability to be read as a figure for queerness is patently obvious. What is more important to note is that Elsa's sexuality in *Frozen* is figured as essential. In other words, *Frozen* does not represent queerness as a set of desires, practices, or pleasures. Her queerness isn't even figured in terms of identity – she has no role models or anyone with which she might queerly identify.[27] *Frozen*, instead, figures queerness as who one is.

Who Elsa is seems to manifest most palpably as loneliness, secrecy, and a desire for solitude – the classic Hollywood attributes of the lesbian.[28] Elsa consistently hides information, as well as her ideas and feelings, from her sister and the rest of her gang. Her most pronounced gesture is pushing people away and closing doors. This is made explicit in the lyrics of "Let It Go" when she sings "Turn away and slam the door," but it is a move that is later repeated in *Olaf's Frozen Adventure*. Elsa gets upset about ruining Christmas, and she literally slams the door on Anna, who wants to process the issue.[29] This same gesture happens many times in *Frozen II*, so that Anna is continually forced to beg Elsa to let her accompany her, to tell her about the voice she is hearing, and to communicate with her. In perhaps the film's most shocking, violent moment, Elsa responds to Anna's pleas by fashioning a boat out of ice and magically pushing her sister and Olaf away (and into mortal danger). For Anna, love is an open door; Elsa habitually slams them closed.

In contrast to this chilly behavior, in the short film *Frozen Fever*, Elsa attempts to throw Anna a birthday party, but she is hampered by a very bad cold.[30] She is constantly sneezing, but she also repeatedly denies her experience of illness when Anna and Kristoff ask how she is doing. The plot of *Frozen Fever*, in other words, involves Anna, Kristoff, and the audience knowing something about Elsa that she, too, knows but insists on denying. That Elsa has a cold in *Frozen Fever* is an open secret – all the more obvious because each of her sneezes produces a dozen tiny snowgies who immediately skitter away to cause trouble. The plot of this short is resolved when Elsa admits what we all already know and Anna puts her to bed. When Cecily Strong, then, sings "We all know / We all know" on *Saturday Night Live*, she gets at something fundamental to the way *Frozen* functions. Not only is Elsa's queerness figured as essential to who she is, *Frozen* represents Elsa as a lesbian *who is denying precisely this fact*. Elsa is not merely a lesbian; she is a lesbian in the closet.

Show Queens

Frozen II teases viewers with the possibility of something else. Elsa has two big numbers in this sequel, and both are duets with other female voices. In "Into the Unknown," Elsa sings with a second voice, Norwegian singer AURORA. For the first two verses, Elsa repeats her usual (closeted) denial of her own desires, saying, "I can hear you / But I won't" and "I'm sorry secret siren / But I'm blocking out your calls." As the song progresses, however, we move into new relational territory for this snow queen. Her questions for the other voice reveal desires we have not yet heard her articulate:

> Are you here to distract me
> So I make a big mistake?
> Or are you someone out there
> Who's a little bit like me
> Who knows deep down
> I'm not where I'm meant to be?
> . . .
> Don't you know there's part of me
> That longs to go
> Into the unknown?

We hear in this song that Elsa is looking for "someone out there" with whom she shares some "little bit" of identity. We learn, too, that she wishes – as her sister does in "For the First Time in Forever" – to open the doors and come out from "within these walls."

More importantly, in "Into the Unknown," Elsa sings about herself as more than one essential thing. She seems to understand herself here as composed of "part[s]," which may have contrasting or conflicting desires. She is pulled in more than one direction in this song, simultaneously out toward the voice into the unknown and back home with the people she loves. She seems, in this song, to be more than the "who I am" who built a castle of ice in order to protect other people from her power; instead, we meet an Elsa who begins to articulate longing – for the first time in the *Frozen* franchise.

Elsa's second song in the film is a spectacular third-act number in which she, again, sings to a second female voice, telling her to "Show Yourself!" By this point in the narrative of *Frozen II*, Elsa has followed the voice far north in the Arctic to a glacier called Ahtohallan to find answers to the mysteries of the film's plot. "I can sense you there," she tells the voice, "Like a friend I've always known." Elsa, we learn in this song, has someone she has "been looking for all of [her] life," and she asks the voice:

> All my life I've been torn
> But I'm here for a reason
> Could it be the reason I was born?
> . . .
> Is this the day
> Are you the way
> I finally find out why?

Elsa has not been looking for some *thing* all of her life but, as in "Into the Unknown," for some *one*.

As the plot resolves, however, only ghosts wait for Elsa when she gets to the center of the glacier. The song ends as Elsa sings with the ghost of her mother, who appears to have been the other voice all along. "Come, my darling, homeward bound," her mother intones, reprising an earlier song, and Elsa finishes the rhyme with "I am found!" She and her mother then sing together:

> Show yourself
> Step into your power
> Grow yourself
> Into something new
> You are the one you've been waiting for
> All of my life! / All of your life!

In a twist that could not help but disappoint supporters of the hashtag #giveelsaagirlfriend, Elsa learns in *Frozen II* that she has been waiting for *herself* all of her life. Aside from the narrative confusion of this plot development, what *Frozen II* does here is contain and control Elsa's search for identity. In "Into the Unknown," Elsa looks for someone *a little bit like her*, and in her second song, she demands that this person show herself, but although she travels to the northernmost part of the world, she finds no one with whom she can identify. She finds, instead, herself, and her mother says that it is *Elsa* who needs to show herself. We return, in other words, from the possibility of the snow queen finding identity with somebody (or with "the one," as the song has it) to the much less complex facticity of *who Elsa is* that we encountered in *Frozen*, as well as the demand that she show the truth of herself to others.

Less queerly still, what Elsa locates in the arctic is her own family history. Her quest results in access to the memories of the enchanted forest, her grandfather's betrayal of the Northuldra, her parents' first meeting, her own childhood, and more of her family's history as violent colonizers. She arrives at Ahtohallan seeking explanations; she is attempting to discover why "[she has] always been so different," but the answer the film offers is to be found in her genetic material. She finds identity with her biological family unit. "Show Yourself" defines Elsa *genetically*, familially, rather than practically or affectively.[31] The end of this song is an overt betrayal of Elsa's queerness. If Elsa has "always been so different," that difference has been articulated repeatedly as a difference *from* the rest of her family and – as I have demonstrated – from the heterosexual desires common to Disney princesses. While *Frozen II* begins by promisingly articulating the possibility of finding identity elsewhere, in the unknown, with a voice that is separate from "everyone [she's] ever loved," the final section of "Show Yourself" tells Elsa that it is actually her family that she needed to discover, that the difference she experienced from her family was identity after all. Although Disney narratives from the early part of the decade emphasized chosen family over genetics, as I demonstrated with the It Gets Better campaign and *Newsies the Musical* in Chapter 2, 2019's *Frozen II* works hard to reincorporate feelings of difference from heterosexuality *back into* family history.

In *Tinker Belles and Evil Queens*, Disney historian Sean Griffin describes "gay culture's appreciation of Disney villains [as] a humorous cheering on of those forces within the narrative that disrupt and frustrate heterosexuality's dominance."[32] As the *Frozen* franchise tells the Snow Queen's story, however, it refashions the classic queer Disney villain who is a threat to heterosexuality into a queer Disney superheroine-cum-Fifth-Spirit.[33] To be queer the way Elsa is queer is to possess magical powers but to use them for good, to perceive and experience difference from the family unit but to be told that your experience is merely imaginary, to long for someone else but to have your vision constrained. Elsa is told (by her mother) to show herself, to grow herself, to *be* herself, and these suggestions incite Elsa to *perform*, to "step into her power," to reach her potential as a queer being, one who feels different from her family but belongs within it. The songs Idina Menzel belts in *Frozen II* are about self-actualization and self-love, but both songs repeat the big dramaturgical moves of the original film: they tell us that when Elsa leaves her family, she finds herself alone. The promises queerness offers in *Frozen* are promises of aloneness, and *Frozen II* sings a celebration of a self that rejects all relationships external to the family – including any possibility of romantic or sexual relationships. This narrative demands that Elsa leave her desires and come back to the family. At the end of *Frozen II*, Elsa is transformed into a magical being – the Fifth Spirit of the world. Her longing is contained, and her desire is fulfilled not by finding identity with someone else or even *relationship* with someone else but by her own benevolence. She will build a new life as a caretaker of the natural world. The conflicting parts of Elsa's self are integrated fully at the end of *Frozen II*, and her family and community no longer perceive her as a threat.

Dangerous Dreaming

Frozen on Broadway is a much queerer cultural object, and this is not only because it retells the plot of the original film in a new medium without the addition of the plot of *Frozen II* but also because Michael Grandage's directorial choices and the form of the Broadway musical itself make more queer responses available to audiences. As I hinted earlier, the stage musical's more intriguing queerness is also partially related to the fact that the audience for *Frozen: The Broadway Musical* is largely the same as the audience for *Saturday Night Live* – adults. Their attitudes toward and ideas about *Frozen*'s characters are quite different than those of the majority audience of the films.

The plot of the stage musical is nearly identical to the first movie, with a few key alterations. Olaf's construction by the two girls takes a good deal more time in the show, and little Anna and Elsa sing a new song, "A Little Bit of You," while they build him. Onstage, the trolls from the film are transformed into "the hidden folk of the mountain," although they come to help the royal family just as the trolls would. Pabbie and the other trolls trade in their smooth, round, stone-shapes for long hairy tails, dreadlocks, and washboard stomachs (the trolls' real muscles are on display in their scenes; no bodystockings for these rock-hard abs). Functionally, the hidden folk *are* the trolls, but this way the characters become humanoid, and the change obviates the need for giant puppets or cartoony bodysuits like the ones we might see at a Disney theme park. Another alteration for the musical is that in a bit of clever rewriting designed to anticipate the plot of *Frozen II*, the girls' mother tells the hidden folk that she is "a child of the northern nomads."[34] It is she who calls the hidden folk to the castle and not her husband. There is one other important plot alteration: in the musical, Anna explicitly *hires* Kristoff to take her to find her sister. They do not meet in Oaken's shop. In fact, Kristoff already has most of the supplies Anna will need to reach the north mountain. Unfortunately, Marshmallow, the giant ice golem Elsa creates in the film, does not appear on Broadway, and neither do the film's multiple hungry wolves.

All of the songs from the movie make appearances on Broadway: Anna sings "Do You Want to Build a Snowman?," "For the First Time in Forever," and (with Hans) "Love is an Open Door"; Olaf sings "In Summer"; Kristoff sings "Reindeer(s) Are Better Than People"; Grand Pabbie and his chorus sing "Fixer Upper"; and, of course, Elsa belts out "Let It Go." But *Frozen: The Broadway Musical* is no mere jukebox show stringing together the movie's songs with a plot. A Broadway musical demands many more songs than an animated feature. This has important consequences for audiences and our relationships with the characters. As I noted in the introduction, the effect of a song in a musical works to "double characterization," in Scott McMillin's words.[35] Characters become multiple by singing; they show us parts of the characters that don't exist for those who don't sing. The additional songs, in other words, have the ability to enlarge and shift the characters who sing them, making them accessible to us in new ways. This is notable for Kristoff, Oaken, and Hans, who sing so little (or not at all) in the film, but it is especially important for Elsa, who is given two new songs and whose character is thereby considerably enriched.

Structurally, the position of "Let It Go" is replaced on Broadway by a new song, "Dangerous to Dream." (Obviously, "Let It Go" belongs in the show's climactic position, and so it needed to be moved to the end of act 1.) Elsa's new song doubles down on the imagery of solitude with which we are so familiar from the films; "Dangerous to Dream" is filled with images of walls closing, pulling inside, and putting up guards. But Elsa onstage *is aware of the hiding she's doing*, and we see her attempt to connect with her sister. She sings "Dangerous to Dream" *to* Anna, who cannot hear her. "I wish I could tell the truth / Show you who's behind the door," she tells her sister. "I wish you knew what all this / Pantomime and pageantry was for." In the theatre, these feelings are expressed explicitly, and so the audience has access to a very different Elsa than the one in the film. This Elsa sings about more than hiding or repressing. "Dangerous to Dream" articulates a series of desires, even more than the wishes I've mentioned already. Elsa sings, I "wish / I could make choices of my own," and she laments to an unhearing Anna that "I can't show you / I'm not as cold as I seem." This song offers the audience an insight into the feelings of the character that we cannot see either in the libretto or in "Let It Go." Although the central metaphor for Elsa and Anna's relationship – the closed door – is still at work in "Dangerous to Dream," the difference this song gives us is Elsa's desire for things to be different, to "open up that door / And finally see you face to face." Even more, we are able to glimpse not only the possibility of freedom and openness that Elsa articulates but also her emotional response to that freedom. Elsa tells us at the end of the song that she "can't stop smiling," and she says to Anna that she "would love to know you." We see, just briefly, within the lyric time of "Dangerous to Dream," an uncloseted Elsa, one who knows she made her parents proud and wants to get to know her sister. We must return to book time, of course, and, as in the plot of the film, Elsa opposes Anna and Hans's engagement, frightens all of the courtiers, and then flees into the mountains.

"Let It Go" on Broadway is a fabulous number, even if it is nearly identical to the film's version of this song. It is, in fact, lyrically indistinguishable, but the Broadway show's stage technologies make this "Let It Go" something special. The number's high point is a theatrical dress-reveal that arrives after the bridge at *exactly* the perfect moment. In the film, Elsa builds her new dress over the course of two repetitions of "let it go" and the phrase "I'll rise like the break of dawn." Onstage, the change happens in one satisfyingly spectacular instant. It's a stunning onstage quick-change that happens so fast that it – unlike the construction of Elsa's ice castle and the snow flurries that issue from her hands – actually *looks* like magic. The gown Elsa reveals is covered in crystals and stones, and the fact that the drag queens on *Drag Race* season 12 were asked to riff on this look reminds us that this aspect of *Frozen* on Broadway belongs to the context of drag performance. Elsa's gown – at least on stage – was modeled on gowns from the world of drag pageantry. Further, Elsa's onstage quick-change resembles nothing so much as the talent portion of a pageant competition like Miss Continental, Miss Gay USofA, or Entertainer of the Year. Dress reveals like Elsa's have been part of drag acts like those of Aurora Sexton, Asia O'Hara, and Nina West for years and were brought to television viewers most notably in 2015 by Violet Chachki on *RuPaul's Drag Race* season 7.[36] Caissie Levy's vocal performance of "Let It Go" reaches higher and does so more easily than Idina Menzel's version in the film, but in many ways "Let It Go" on Broadway gets a standing ovation for its drag-pageant combination of gown/talent.

Elsa's big song in act 2 is called "Monster," and its approach to the snow queen is totally different from the essentialist versions of Elsa in the original film and its sequel.[37] In this song, Elsa describes to us how *others* read her. She recognizes that it is the perceptions of others that label her as monstrous, and rather than singing about shutting doors and closing walls, she wonders if she is trapped "in a cage" that is not of her own making. The shift of this song is fundamentally about Elsa's own agency, and her powers here are not contrasted with heterosexuality so much as they are contrasted with hostility and normativity. In "Monster," Elsa poses a question critical theory might ask, wondering if monstrosity has a history, if it is something created by the forces of normativity. "Is the thing they see / The thing I have to be?" she asks. What is fascinating about "Monster" is that although it returns us to the familiar question of *Who Elsa Is*, it shifts the perspective so that Elsa begins to ask not about who she is inside but if she is what other people say she is, and even more importantly than that, to ask *who she wants to be*: "I cannot be a monster," she sings to herself, "I will not be a monster / Not tonight." It is a song in which the snow queen refuses others' labels for her and charts her own way into the future. "Monster" is an enormous departure from the film's Elsa; we know next to nothing of her thought process in the film's version of this part of the story. Broadway's Elsa recognizes the labels she has been given by others, and she refuses them.

Happy Coming Out Day

Frozen on Broadway engaged even more explicitly with queer sexualities on National Coming Out Day, October 11, 2019. In short videos shared by *Good Morning America*, *Frozen* cast members Noah J. Ricketts (who replaced Jelani Alladin in the role of Kristoff), and Adam Jepsen (who played Sven) both shared coming-out messages. Ricketts encouraged those struggling with coming out and told them he knew it was difficult but that there are folks on the other side cheering them on.[38] Jepsen's message encouraged more bisexual people to come out.[39] Other performers in *Frozen* in 2019 certainly *could* have come out, and I do not wish to make too much of the specific selection of the actors playing Kristoff and Sven as the two performers from *Frozen* to come out on a national platform, but in "Fixer Upper," the trolls have always described "His thing with the reindeer" as "a little outside of nature's laws." This hint at a queer relationship between Kristoff and his reindeer companion, which appears both in the original film and in the Broadway show, is a joke, a sexualized and normative one, to be sure, but also one that is more or less good-natured. Indeed, the trolls sing this line while quickly planning a wedding for Anna and Kristoff, and the joke, in its sexualization of the relationship between Kristoff and Sven, is designed, precisely, to *prevent* queer readings of their relationship through acknowledgment and dismissal.

Another character available for queer readings is, of course, the story's actual villain – Prince Hans of the Southern Isles with his "line of mean big brothers / That goes on for miles." Neither the film nor the Broadway show codes Hans as particularly gay, but although Elsa functions as the queer villain by refusing to sanction Hans and Anna's wedding, Hans himself surely steps into this role by the story's end. That is, he takes the narrative position of the *sinthom*osexual, representing queer villainy as such. He refuses even to *attempt* the fabled true love's kiss and instead tells Anna he never loved her, abandons her to hypothermia, and then attempts to murder Elsa. Hans's betrayal of Anna and Elsa – and the entire kingdom – reveals him as a pretender to heterosexual romance who functions in opposition to the "true love" that Anna sings about while nearly freezing to death.

There is yet another character from the original film whose queerness has been seized upon by fans: Oaken, the very tall, very brawny proprietor of Wandering Oaken's Trading Post and Sauna. Many viewers have wondered if, when Oaken says "Hi family" and waves to a group of naked people in his sauna, he is waving to *his* family or simply waving to *a* family. Sarah Whitfield goes so far as to call *Frozen* "the first Disney film to openly present a gay family (albeit only for seconds)."[40] It is, however, by no means clear that Oaken is in a romantic relationship with the man in the sauna; neither is it obvious that the three women and girls in the sauna are Oaken's daughters. Later appearances by Oaken – he appears in every one of the *Frozen* films and shorts – do not bear out this theory. Following his first appearance, Disney seems to have disavowed the alleged family with two gay dads. He appears unaccompanied at a family event in *Frozen II*, and in *Olaf's Frozen Adventure*, although Sven and Olaf go looking explicitly for "family" traditions for the holidays, and although we spend a large amount of time with Oaken, we do not meet his family. Instead, Olaf and a nearly naked Oaken sit in his sauna and Olaf melts. The absence of Oaken's family in this short film is especially notable because Olaf and Sven visit dozens of other families on their adventure, all of whom appear to be traditionally heterosexual.

On Broadway, Oaken is given his own gigantic musical number. It opens *Frozen*'s second act, and it is called "Hygge." Oaken explains: "Hygge means comfortable / Hygge means cozy." The entire song, in fact, is designed as a definition of the word, and Oaken is backed up by the musical's male and female ensemble, who appear, wearing next to nothing, from out of Oaken's apparently voluminous sauna, to form a kick line and sing "hygge, hygge, hygge, hygge, hygge." As he does in the film, Oaken says, "Hi, family," to this enormous chorus, but this group of patrons is decidedly not his family in any biological sense. As he addresses this phrase to the chorus, the musical shifts the original interpretation so many had of Oaken's queer "family," transforming this familial feeling (hygge) into a feeling many businesses claim to have toward their customers. Indeed, Oaken sings about what he is selling, and his customers sing about what they are buying, which, in both cases is hygge, family.

By its end, the "Hygge" number transforms into a camp version of the kind of classical Broadway number that we might have seen in the follies. These burlesque dancers would all have been women under Florenz Ziegfeld's direction, but here, queerly enough, the kick line is gender neutral. The men and women from the sauna sing, dance, and perform a tantalizing striptease, in which they cover themselves and then each other with the birch branches they carry from the sauna. Both the male and female dancers in the chorus are naked, or rather, none of them is naked: unlike Grandpabbie and his visible abs, the members of this naked chorus wear bodystockings that from a distance give the appearance of – but remove the possibility of actual – nudity. Oaken's possible queerness is dispensed with in the musical in favor of a more generalized feeling of familial belonging that is for sale.[41] On Broadway, Oaken is contained by capital and his family repositioned; the eroticism teased by the "Hygge" chorus girls and boys is made family friendly by nude illusion.

Intriguingly, Oaken is most persistently sexualized in the *Frozen* short films. In *Frozen Fever*, Oaken is running a kiosk in Arendelle's town square, and he appears shirtless or naked in the kiosk's attached sauna. In *Once upon a Snowman*, Olaf arrives at Oaken's for the first time and immediately says to the proprietor, "Wandering Oaken's? Do you know that if you scramble up those letters it's an anagram for Naked Norwegian's? And I can't even read. I genuinely don't know how I just did that."[42] Later, Olaf refers to Oaken as "fuzzy man-bear" and when he leaves the shop he says, "Thank you big, lovable, pink-faced, bear-man." I've already mentioned Oaken and Olaf's trip to the sauna in *Olaf's Frozen Adventure*, but this visit ends with Oaken giving Olaf a portable sauna he can take with him on Sven's sleigh. Olaf then makes a request: "Would it be possible to get one of those awkwardly revealing yet tastefully traditional towels your family's so fond of wearing?" Oaken, clad only in this tiny garment, replies "Take mine, *ja*?" and tosses the towel to Olaf, where it covers his face. "It's still warm!" Olaf exclaims, delighted. The camera cuts away just before we would have seen the fuzzy man-bear naked. If Oaken is not gay *per se* – and he appears not to be – audiences are certainly asked to *think* about him queerly. The *Frozen* team seems fascinated by this naked Norwegian, and he is consistently presented to us as overly friendly, hulking but benign, and comfortable with his body but socially awkward. Because he most frequently interacts with Olaf, rather than any of the other human characters, Oaken becomes a *de facto* family man, even though his family all appear to be customers. Oaken's naked chorus on Broadway is made family friendly through the introduction of bodystockings; Oaken's nudity in the short films is made family friendly through the juvenile innocence of Olaf's gaze. Potential queerness is again *contained by family* in the *Frozen* franchise, this time by transforming "family" into a feeling customers can buy.

Do You Want to Build a Snowchild?

Although the girls ask, "Do You Want to Build a Snowman?" and although Olaf's gender is apparently male (he suggests Fernando and Trevor as possible other names in *Once upon a Snowman*), he is manifestly not a *man*. The girls do not imagine an adult playmate, as the kids do in *Frosty the Snowman* (1969); instead, they build themselves a child. Olaf is a hilariously naive little kid, a fact most spectacularly in evidence in his signature tune, in which he imagines himself doing "whatever snow does in summer." Olaf speaks and behaves like a child. He always wants to play. He is desperately impatient. He is delighted by everything, including things like wolves and explosions that might be very dangerous. He is intensely talkative, to the point where the adults need to trick him into being quiet, and he takes instructions literally, like a miniature sub-zero Amelia Bedelia.

For Hyrum Osmond, Olaf's supervising animator and the man who designed the series *At Home with Olaf*, "Olaf, is my five-year-old boy at home: loving and trusting and pure and very naive."[43] Story artist Jeff Ranjo puts it this way: "He's almost like a baby: He's just been created. He doesn't know that much about the world, so you have to explain things to him you take for granted, just as you would to a little kid."[44] This naivety allows Olaf to make jokes, observations, and innocent mistakes that an adult wouldn't normally make. These are usually inane but occasionally very wise, and Olaf's alleged purity sometimes gives his wisdom an especial gravity, as when he tells Anna in the first film that "some people are worth melting for."

Key to the way Olaf functions is that audiences have the ability to fill in gaps that Olaf himself cannot. This is used cleverly by Kristen Anderson-Lopez and Robert Lopez in "In Summer" when Olaf sings "Winter's a good time to stay in and cuddle / But put me in summer and I'll be a . . . happy snowman." In the Broadway show, after Olaf has been dismembered, he uses this comic technique a second time, singing, to a recognizable tune:

OLAF. Do you want to build a snowman?
    I would help you but, alas
    Right now I'm rather incomplete
    Without my twigs and feet
    And most importantly my aaaaaaaaaaaaaaaaaabdomen
ANNA. Though everything's in pieces
    We've got your back
KRISTOFF. Even better, we've got your butt!

In the case of both *puddle*, in the movie as well as the show, and *ass*, only in the show, audiences can finish the rhyme even if Olaf has trouble. Both children and adults are the intended audience of the first joke and, as with the unfinished rhyme in the *Saturday Night Live* skit I described earlier, adults are the intended audience of the second. The technique I'm describing here renders Olaf innocent because the joke is crafted in such a way that Olaf doesn't know he's making it. The adult audience must finish the joke ourselves, and Olaf remains ignorant of the humor of which he is apparently the author. This also renders innocent Olaf's encounters with content that might otherwise be troubling such as Oaken's nudity. But although Olaf frequently appears to be innocently hitting on some bit of wisdom or hilarious bit of inanity, his behavior – and please forgive the obviousness of this statement – has been scripted exclusively by adults. Olaf is not a child at all; he is an adult's projection of a child. He can occasionally speak like an adult because adults carefully choose every word he says. Olaf in this way recalls one of the central tenets of queer theorist Kathryn Bond Stockton's work in *The Queer Child*. Stockton reminds us very early in the book that "The child is precisely who we are not and, in fact, never were. It is the act of adults looking back. It is a ghostly, unreachable fancy."[45]

I will return to Olaf presently, but I emphasize this snowchild's minority – and the adults behind him – because, in fact, a majority of the characters in *Frozen* are children. We meet Anna, Elsa, and Kristoff when they are very little; we even first meet Sven as an adorable baby reindeer. For much of the films, these characters appear to be adults, but in truth, they are still very young – Elsa has just "come of age" on her coronation day in *Frozen*; Anna is younger still. More importantly, the film consistently links both young women's behavior with their childhood habits. Anna, now a teenager, repeats the same actions in "For the First Time in Forever" that she did as a child in her first song, "Do You Want to Build a Snowman?," while Elsa repeats the same mantra she was told as a child, "Conceal, don't feel." Elsa's consistent act of running away and slamming doors is, fundamentally, the behavior of a teenager who doesn't have words for what she's experiencing, and Anna's big act of foolishness in *Frozen*, in which she falls in love with a man she's only just met, is a child's mistake. Even Kristoff comes in for continuous mockery for doing a voice for Sven – he's transformed his childhood companion into a kind of imaginary friend. When *Elsa* has the chance to create a companion for herself, she does not create an adult, she creates the snowchild Olaf, a giant golem made of snow, and the numerous tiny snowgies she manufactures with her sneezes in *Frozen Fever*.

The sequels continue to treat the girls as children. *Frozen Fever* is about producing a childhood birthday party for Anna, and *Olaf's Frozen Adventure* is about attempting to remember Anna and Elsa's childhood holiday traditions. Although most of the action of *Frozen II* takes place a few years after *Frozen*, this film begins as the first one does, with Anna and Elsa as very little children – even younger than they were in *Frozen* – playing in the snow.[46] Doubling down on the characters as children, *Frozen II* not only takes us back to Anna and Elsa's childhood, but it also takes us back to their *parents'* childhood. We see scenes of them falling in love as children, reading fairy tales, swinging in trees, and doing other childhood activities. And when Queen Anna and General Mattias unveil the monument to Anna and Elsa's parents at the end of *Frozen II*, it is, rather strangely, a statue of the pair *as children*. Rather than monumentalizing the statesmanlike behavior or military prowess of the king and queen – or even their parenting skills – as a statue of them as adults might have, the ideological purpose of this statue is to remind Arendelle of the importance of innocent connection, friendship, and play uncomplicated by economic concerns, racial animus, or interstate politics. There is, in other words, a great deal attached to the concept of the child in *Frozen* and its sequels.[47] The child is asked to do an enormous amount of symbolic work – which is, perhaps, why children in the world of *Frozen* proliferate like snowgies.

If we consider Stockton's work in *The Queer Child*, we can go a long way toward explaining Elsa's extraordinary popularity with children as well as her insistent pull on queer adults. One of the queer children Stockton discusses in *The Queer Child* is "the grown homosexual." Stockton argues that queer people are frequently represented as children or as not-quite adults. The adult homosexual is "fastened," in Stockton's words,

> to the figure of the child – both in the form of a ghostly self and in the form of "arrested development." This latter phrase has been the official-sounding diagnosis that has often appeared to describe the supposed sexual immaturity of homosexuals: their presumed status as dangerous children who remain children in part by failing to have their own.[48]

As I have discussed, Elsa is consistently represented as frustrated or unhealthily attached to a childhood desire to hide or to be alone. And adult viewers are positioned so that we can see the solutions to Elsa's problems even if Elsa herself cannot. One of the reasons Elsa cannot *come out* as queer – as lesbian or as asexual – in the world of *Frozen* is that to do so would transform her into an adult; her arrival into sexuality would mark the death of her childhood.[49]

Stockton's attention to the "gay" child, though, becomes "the means, the fine-grained lens, by which to see any and *every* child as queer, even though the troubles of this specific child [the 'gay' child] seem to be unique."[50] For Stockton, as the gay child "emerges as an idea it begins to outline, in shadowy form, the pain, closets, emotional labors, sexual motives, and sideways movements that attend all children, however we deny it. A gay child illuminates the darkness of the child."[51] *Frozen* and its sequels, in this sense, take part in a larger (adult) discourse within contemporary animated films – about children whose choices cannot be explained, who "act out," whose behavior is antisocial or mysterious or queer. Films such as *Song of the Sea* (2014), *When Marnie Was There* (2014), *Inside Out* (2015), *My Life as a Courgette* (2016), *Your Name* (2016), *The Boss Baby* (2017), *Bao* (2018), *Over the Moon* (2020), *Soul* (2020), *Wolfwalkers* (2020), *Belle* (2021), *Poupelle of Chimney Town* (2021), *Luca* (2021), *Encanto* (2021), and *The Mitchells vs the Machines* (2021) represent the child as frustratingly obtuse and distant, its desires inscrutable, its thought processes impossible (for the adult) to access. These are, in other words, *all* films about the queer child, the child who resists growing up according to the approved path laid out by adults or, as Stockton puts it, the child who *grows sideways*. Unlike many of these films, *Frozen* appears to celebrate the idea of Elsa leaning into this sideways growth, even if the film's narrative still insists that she *illuminate* – "show herself" – so that her darkness no longer remains a mystery. Calls for Elsa to be given a girlfriend, then, work similarly to the film's narrative demand that she show herself. For Elsa to come out would in some ways affirm her queerness, but it would also, finally, clear things up, making *sense* of Elsa's weirdness and domesticating that strange longing for the unknown for which she herself cannot quite find the words – even in song.

Olaf's Queer Quest

I want to close this chapter by returning to Olaf. Of all the (queer) children in *Frozen*, he is the most unpredictable, the most magically pliable, and although he is, perhaps, the most annoying, he is also the most fun. As I noted earlier, I also consider Olaf to be a fascinating projection of the child – an intriguing adult fantasy of the possibilities and mystery a child contains. Accordingly, Olaf has been given more solo narratives than any other character in the world of *Frozen*. Olaf and Sven get their own short film in *Olaf's Frozen Adventure*; the other characters appear, but we spend the most time with Olaf. And Olaf's origin story is told in *Once upon a Snowman*. He is the main character in both of these shorts, in the YouTube series *At Home with Olaf*, in the Disney+ series *Olaf Presents*, and in his own video game, *Frozen: Olaf's Quest*. No other character in the *Frozen* world appears so often without the others.

I noted earlier that Olaf's ignorance about almost everything gives him a power to transform scenarios that might otherwise seem creepy or strange into innocent situations. This has not prevented audiences from reading these scenarios as sexually suggestive – as with the additional carrot in the *Saturday Night Live* skit – but Olaf's ignorance about matters concerning adults makes any scenario in which he's involved charming or silly rather than troubling. Olaf's strange position in this world also allows him a kind of meta-awareness of the twenty-first century, and perhaps even of the film itself. He *performs* the plot of the first movie for the residents of the enchanted forest in *Frozen II* as if he (like us) had watched it, and he makes himself laugh with jokes that don't belong in *Frozen*'s world, like being grossed out by "yellow snow" or yelling "I'm defying gravity!" while sailing through the air on a sleigh. In *Olaf Presents*, the snowchild retells the plots of other Disney films, performing amateur theatrical versions of movies he couldn't possibly have seen with Sven, the snowgies, and Marshmallow. Olaf is the quintessential musical theatre kid in these short episodes, trying on Rapunzel's wig, singing "A Whole New World," and wearing Ariel's seashell bra while belting "Part of Your World."[52] In these and other ways, Olaf functions as an onscreen substitute for twenty-first-century children in the audience, although he is, of course, played by an adult, actor Josh Gad.

On Broadway, Olaf might be an even queerer subject than on film. He is explicitly the "child" of the two girls who sing "A little bit of you / A little bit of me" as they create him – a song he reprises upon his first appearance. We even watch him being built in his exact shape by his two mothers, with two blocks for legs, a ball for his belly, a snare-shaped drum for his torso, and a little boat for his head. And unlike the other characters onstage, Olaf is played by a puppeteer who stands behind him and speaks his lines. Olaf is the only aspect of *Frozen: The Broadway Musical* that uses this theatrical convention from *The Lion King* – Sven's puppeteer wears a Sven suit, and we never see him. This is, perhaps, fitting, since Olaf is the only character who has been created by magic, but the fact that Olaf is a puppet makes him an especially theatrical figure.

I've addressed a few of *Frozen*'s formal choices already, but there is one very important additional convention that must be discussed. The cast of *Frozen* on Broadway takes part in the theatrical convention of so-called colorblind casting, though, of course, it isn't blind at all. Kristoff, represented as white in the film, was originally played by Black actor Jelani Alladin onstage, and Elsa and Anna's family has, in every onstage iteration, combined actors of different racial make-ups. Producers have taken a colorblind approach to the lead roles, as well. Indeed, when *Frozen* closed in March 2020, Elsa was being played by multiracial actress Ciara Renée. Olaf, however, is the only character whose performer has switched *gender*: Ryann Redmond debuted as Olaf in February 2019 and was playing Olaf when the show closed in 2020. Because Olaf is a puppet, though, he had in fact always been played by more than one actor onstage. During a scene in which he is dismembered, his head is manipulated by the actor playing Anna, while a different, offstage performer speaks his lines. In this way, Olaf's body – constructed in pieces by Anna and Elsa and performed by more than one actor (of any gender) *outside* of that body – becomes an intriguing figure for thinking subjectivity in pieces and for how those different pieces come to be thought of as sharing identity.

Who better than Olaf, then, to ask some of the important questions about subjectivity? This is exactly what Dan Abraham and Trent Correy do in the short film *Once upon a Snowman*. As soon as Olaf comes to life, created by Elsa during "Let It Go," he begins asking questions about his own existence: "I'm alive! Who said that? I said that! I can talk! I can think!" he exclaims. "I appear to be some sort of snowman. . . . Who am I? Hello?! Anybody there? I'm having a bit of a crisis of identity . . . I think. . . . I think I'm lost and confused. I'm definitely confused." Olaf doesn't find answers to the hard problem of consciousness in this short film, but he does keep asking questions about animacy. He wonders, for example, about his difference from his natural environment: "So, I'm made of snow, and I'm walking on snow. That's kind of weird," he says to himself. Disney artists, in fact, wondered this exact thing while they were drawing Olaf. Charles Solomon reports that "In addition to his vague anatomy [!], Olaf posed another difficult problem: how to make a snowman stand out in a snowy environment."[53] Olaf is having an "identity" crisis, he says, and he attempts to make sense of this problem through differentiation. How is Olaf different than the snow on which he walks, indeed? We might also ask – depending on what Lacanian mirrors are available to us – how we are different from our mothers or brothers, or how we differ from the grass or dirt or sand on which *we* walk or the air that we breathe.[54]

Later, in Oaken's shop, Olaf uses identity instead of difference as a way to make sense of his subjectivity. He cycles through various identificatory possibilities by trying out different names and by *trying on*, or, rather, incorporating into his anatomy, different noses – a flag, a paddle ball, etc. – before Oaken finally gifts him a not-at-all-sexually-suggestive summer sausage. In this sequence, Olaf stays recognizably Olaf, even if his appearance varies quite a bit. Olaf is able to change this way in *At Home with Olaf*, as well. In "Pink Lemonade," one of the best of these shorts, Olaf drinks a large glass of lemonade and turns himself pink. He is delighted and jumps up and down, running off and calling, "Hey Anna! I'm a sno-cone."[55] He's a wonderfully alterable subject, delighted by the changes in his own body as well as by the external substances and objects his body can incorporate.

If Olaf is able to shift his body and still retain his sense of subjectivity, there is one identity about which he feels very strongly, and this arrives for him in *Once upon a Snowman*. He is immediately smitten by a slideshow of summery images that Oaken shows him using a child's toy. "I've never identified with anything so much in my whole life," he says in awe. "It's like snowmen and summer just belong together." Oaken, understandably, looks troubled, but, like the kids in Jules Gill-Peterson's *Histories of the Transgender Child*, Olaf knows for himself that he is the same as this warmth that appears to be his opposite.[56] It is significant, too, that Olaf's love for sun and sand is acquired from a *visual* identification with summer. Olaf – like, perhaps, some young people watching *Frozen* – sees a series of images and *knows that's him*.

Most important, though, is Olaf's uncanny ability to break apart and come back together. Olaf is a subject who exists in pieces. This is initially troubling to the snowchild – "I'm falling apart!" he screams in *Once upon a Snowman* – and he wonders if this aspect of his anatomy is a skill or a design flaw, but he is exultant when he finds that his parts come together again. This aspect of Olaf appears in all of his storylines, including the game *Frozen: Olaf's Quest*, in which he can toss his own head in order to collect the points he needs to win the game and transform into a snowball that heaves itself down icy slopes and crashes through barriers and spikes. For the artists drawing him, Olaf's pliability is exciting: "You can rip his arms off, you can cut his head off, you can make a hole in him. He doesn't care."[57] And it's true. He can "fall apart, reassemble in any conceivable way, melt and move like snow."[58] He is easily the best of his friends at charades, and he can transform completely into a puddle but be reconstituted by being tossed into the freezing cold. Even when Olaf "flurr[ies] away" completely in the third act of *Frozen II*, he comes back just the same to tell his story and proclaim, "I live!"

I dwell on Olaf's magical ability to live life in pieces because so many of the narratives in the world of *Frozen* are focused on complementarity (searching for the one, resenting being alone) or are desperately essentialist (drilling down into the genetic past, attempting to define and perform who one is, rejecting the parts of oneself that don't seem to fit). Olaf does none of this. He incorporates whatever anyone throws at him. He tries it out or tries it on, at least for a while. He plays with hungry wolves. He asks a million questions. And he, unlike *Frozen*'s other characters, *knows he is composed of separate parts*; sometimes those parts fit together well and other times not so well. Olaf changes shape and rearranges himself, and if he falls apart, his parts go looking for each other, even over long distances. He is resilient and capacious and willing to change. He is a magical figure, to be sure, a fantasy of a queer child created by adults. But Olaf understands better than most of us that our subjectivities are composed of multiple aspects and desires, that our bodies and the bodies of others will change and rearrange, and that we can experience a feeling of identification inside ourselves even if everyone around us thinks it might be too hot for us to handle.

In many ways, *Frozen* is an ideal show for taking stock of the relationship between Broadway musicals and LGBTQ politics at the end of the second decade of the twenty-first century. It's an excellent example of a show that explicitly refuses the LGBTQ identity politics requested by its audiences, and yet it is available for queer identification at every turn. *Frozen*'s version of queerness jettisons the chosen-family politics of *Newsies* and *The Color Purple* in favor of an essentialized sexuality reincorporated into the biological family and a capitalization of family as product for sale. At the same time, *Frozen* desexualizes queerness, representing its central queer character as someone whose desires are different but not erotic. Elsa longs for something other than the heterosexual romance her sister wants, but she neither desires nor gets a queer relationship of her own. In fact, she seems to acquiesce to Fran Kubelik's demand in *Promises, Promises* to "shut up and deal." And yet the snowchild Olaf, who switches genders onstage, or perhaps whose gender (like Hedwig's or those of the mythical figures in the *Symposium*) was always multiple in the first place, is a perfect figure for the queer, trans, or nonbinary child trying out and trying on new identificatory possibilities until finding one that feels right, no matter how terrifying that may be for the child's caretakers. A child onstage, as anyone from Lee Edelman to Cherríe Moraga could tell you, represents the future. And in this way, Olaf's plasticity represents possibilities: for the creativity of audiences as they approach their identificatory relationships with musical theatre characters and for the new possibilities and strategies that queer people in the world will devise as we learn to describe ourselves.

Notes

1. Saturday Night Live, "Frozen 2 – SNL."
2. Brienne of Tarth is a character from George R.R. Martin's *A Clash of Kings* and other books. The skit references the character as played by Gwendoline Christie in the series on HBO. Neither the character nor the actress is a lesbian, but then, neither is Elsa.
3. Perhaps, it is worth mentioning that Sven and Kristoff always *share* carrots in *Frozen*. Kristoff always gives Sven the first bite before taking one himself.
4. "Snatch Game."
5. The contestant Sherry Pie, who made it to the final four during the show's filming, was disqualified before the show aired and largely edited out of the season. The reason for her disqualification was related to catfishing allegations and alleged deviant sexual practices. Sherry's runway looks appeared on all other episodes of the season, but her *Frozen eleganza* runway was edited out. See Mack, "*Drag Race* Star Sherry Pie Apologized after Five Actors Said She Catfished Them."
6. The strangeness of this was especially palpable on this episode of *Drag Race* because the SARS-COV-2 pandemic had shuttered all of Broadway, closing *Frozen* on March 11.
7. See kaiyame, "IDK Anything . . ."; lgbtq_repost, "Have Y'all Seen Frozen 2 Yet?"; Taylor, "It's Getting Nippy Out There . . ."; rainderxu_1106, "Untitled."
8. Drag queens have been performing as Elsa in bars and clubs for years. A simple YouTube search will reveal dozens of queens doing excellent Elsa numbers.
9. See "Disney's Frozen – Elsa and Asexuality (MAJOR Spoilers Follow)."
10. *Olaf's Frozen Adventure* frustrated viewers a great deal; audiences thought it was much too long to play as a short before *Coco*, and the movie was pulled from theatres after two weeks. See Wilkinson, "Why the Frozen Short That Played before Pixar's Coco Kicked Up So Much Controversy."
11. Indeed, in *Frozen II*, the romantic plot of Anna and Kristoff is nonsensically extended by making the narrative about whether or not the young man will propose marriage to the young woman.
12. Buck and Lee, *Frozen*.
13. Buck and Lee, *Frozen II*.

14. See Vary, "Mutant Is the New Gay." See also Schrodt, "*First Class*: The Latest Chapter in the *X-Men* Gay-Rights Parable."
15. Edelman, *No Future*, 33–66.
16. Griffin, *Tinker Belles and Evil Queens*, 75.
17. Try to name a Disney villain who *is not* coded as queer. Prince John from *Robin Hood*, Cruella De Vil from *101 Dalmatians*, Professor Ratigan from *The Great Mouse Detective*, Maleficent from *Sleeping Beauty*: they all seem to be villainous and queer simultaneously. Even when there is no heterosexual romance to destroy, as in *Dumbo*, the troublesome gossipy elephants and the theatrically swishy ringmaster still fulfill queer functions and exceed gender norms.
18. Andersen, "The Snow Queen," 11. The castle of ice, the frozen warriors, and the scene in which the Snow Queen invites Kai to sit with her in her sledge under her bearskin were all reworked by C.S. Lewis for *The Lion, the Witch, and the Wardrobe* (1950). The Snow Queen is decidedly villainous in Lewis's novel.
19. Greenhill, "'The Snow Queen': Queer Coding in Male Directors' Films," 119–120.
20. Greenhill, "'The Snow Queen': Queer Coding in Male Directors' Films," 116.
21. Greenhill, "'The Snow Queen': Queer Coding in Male Directors' Films," 116.
22. Lederer, *The Kiss of the Snow Queen*, 153.
23. Greenhill, "'The Snow Queen': Queer Coding in Male Directors' Films," 119.
24. Lee quoted in Solomon, *The Art of Frozen*, 14, my emphasis.
25. Williams quoted in Solomon, *The Art of Frozen*, 137, my emphasis.
26. Solomon, *The Art of Frozen*, 62, my emphasis.
27. See my discussion of "The Fiction of Identity" in this book's introduction.
28. See White, *Uninvited*, 24
29. Deters and Wermers, *Olaf's Frozen Adventure*.
30. Buck and Lee, *Frozen Fever*.
31. This emphasis on genetic history is fundamental to how *Frozen II* deals with race as well. Elsa and Anna discover that they are *biologically* Northuldra in the course of the film, and this genetic identity grants them instant acceptance by the Northuldra in the forest.
32. Griffin, *Tinker Belles and Evil Queens*, 75
33. Apologies to Luc Besson are unnecessary here, apparently, since earth, fire, air, and water are not *elements* in this film; they are *spirits*.
34. This is a plot point we don't learn until the third act of the *Frozen II* film. In another anticipatory easter egg, the girls onstage play with Elsa's toy puffin, Sir Jorgenbjorgen, whom we do not meet in either *Frozen* feature but whom Elsa finds in an attic in *Olaf's Frozen Adventure*.
35. McMillin, *The Musical as Drama*, 21.
36. Chachki, "Born Naked." See also Sexton, "US of Aurora Episode 2: Miss Gay USofA"; see also West, "Nina West – Entertainer of the Year 2008 – Evening Gown."
37. Here I am in disagreement with Hannah Robbins' reading of this number, which sees "Monster" as "reinforc[ing] the implication that Elsa is deviant from the majority and will be unable to find peace or accept her power without causing harmful disruption to the people she loves." To my mind, Robbins' reading of this moment ignores the fact that the audience already loves Elsa and is rooting for her. See Robbins, "'I Can't Be What You Expect of Me,'" 5.
38. Good Morning America, "Coming Out Day Messages from Disney on Broadway: Noah Ricketts."
39. Good Morning America, "Coming Out Day Messages From Disney on Broadway: Adam Jepsen."
40. Whitfield, "For the First Time in Forever," 232.
41. On Broadway, Oaken is the extortionist Kristoff accuses him of being in the film. He charges 10,000 Norwegian kroner for the items he sells the pair, an exorbitant sum by today's exchange rate, even before adjusting for inflation from the 1840s.
42. Abraham and Correy, *Once upon a Snowman*.
43. Osmond quoted in Solomon, *The Art of Frozen*, 108.

44 Ranjo quoted in Solomon, *The Art of Frozen*, 109.
45 Stockton, *The Queer Child*, 5.
46 Even when we do spend time with them as adults, Elsa plays with the children at the big party they throw in Arendelle, and then later the characters play charades in the castle.
47 Cf. Nyong'o, *The Amalgamation Waltz*.
48 Stockton, *The Queer Child*, 22. The bisexual is also consistently framed in popular culture as needing to grow out of bisexuality and into an either homo- or hetero- adult sexuality.
49 Stockton, *The Queer Child*, 6–7.
50 Stockton, *The Queer Child*, 2.
51 Stockton, *The Queer Child*, 3.
52 Osmond, *Olaf Presents*.
53 Solomon, *The Art of Frozen*, 110.
54 My questions here are indebted to those asked by New Materialism, and Mel Y. Chen's work in *Animacies* also prompts us to consider the significance of Olaf's whiteness, perhaps especially in contrast to the physicalized water, wind, earth, and fire in *Frozen II*.
55 Walt Disney Animation Studios, "'Pink Lemonade' | At Home with Olaf."
56 Gill-Peterson, *Histories of the Transgender Child*.
57 Solomon, *The Art of Frozen*, 109.
58 Schiller quoted in Solomon, *The Art of Frozen*, 108.

References for Chapter 5

Abraham, Dan, and Trent Correy, (directors). *Once upon a Snowman*. Disney+. 23 October 2020.

Andersen, Hans Christian. *The Snow Queen*. *The Snow Queen and Other Fairy Tales*. London: Edward Arnold, 1894. (1–51).

Buck, Chris, and Jennifer Lee, (directors). *Frozen*. Disney+. 22 November 2013.

Buck, Chris, and Jennifer Lee, (directors). *Frozen II*. Disney+. 22 November 2019.

Buck, Chris, and Jennifer Lee, (directors). *Frozen Fever*. Amazon Prime Video. 13 March 2015.

Chachki, Violet, (performer). "Born Naked." *RuPaul's Drag Race* 7.1. 2 March 2015.

Chen, Mel Y. *Animacies: Biopolitics, Racial Mattering, and Queer Affect*. Durham: Duke University Press, 2012.

Deters, Kevin, and Stevie Wermers, (directors). *Olaf's Frozen Adventure*. Disney+. 27 October 2017.

"Disney's Frozen – Elsa and Asexuality (MAJOR Spoilers Follow)." Asexuality.org. 25 January 2014. www.asexuality.org/en/topic/97999-disneys-frozen-elsa-and-asexuality-major-spoilers-follow/. Accessed 6 January 2022.

Edelman, Lee. *No Future: Queer Theory and the Death Drive*. Durham: Duke University Press, 2004.

Gill-Peterson, Jules. *Histories of the Transgender Child*. Minneapolis: University of Minnesota Press, 2018.

Good Morning America. "Coming Out Day Messages From Disney on Broadway: Adam Jepsen." *Facebook*. 11 October 2019. www.facebook.com/watch/?v=556204468494145. Accessed 6 January 2022.

Good Morning America. "Coming Out Day Messages From Disney on Broadway: Noah Ricketts." *Facebook*. 11 October 2019. www.facebook.com/watch/?v=727982257671092. Accessed 6 January 2022.

Greenhill, Pauline. "'The Snow Queen': Queer Coding in Male Directors' Films." *Marvels & Tales* 29.1: 110–134, 2015.

Griffin, Sean. *Tinker Belles and Evil Queens: The Walt Disney Company From the Inside Out*. New York: New York University Press, 2000.

kaiyame, "IDK anything . . ." *Instagram*. 20 November 2019. www.instagram.com/p/B5HK-TFph0Ok/. accessed 5 July 2022.

Lederer, Wolfgang. *The Kiss of the Snow Queen: Hans Christian Andersen and Man's Redemption by Woman*. Berkeley: University of California Press, 1986.

lgbtq_repost. "Have Y'all Seen Frozen 2 Yet?" *Instagram*. 7 December 2019. www.instagram.com/p/B5ydrcJnmR7/. Accessed 5 July 2022.

Mack, David. "*Drag Race* Star Sherry Pie Apologized After Five Actors Said She Catfished Them." *BuzzFeed News*. 5 March 2020. www.buzzfeednews.com/article/davidmack/rupaul-drag-race-sherry-pie-catfish-joey-gugliemelli. Accessed 6 January 2022.

McMillin, Scott. *The Musical as Drama: A Study of the Principles and Conventions Behind Musical Shows From Kern to Sondheim*. Princeton: Princeton University Press, 2006.

Nyong'o, Tavia. *The Amalgamation Waltz: Race, Performance, and the Ruses of Memory*. Minneapolis: University of Minnesota Press, 2009.

Osmond, Hyrum, (artist). *Olaf Presents*. Disney+. 12 November 2021.

Rainderxu_1106. "Untitled." *Instagram*. 8 July 2020. www.instagram.com/p/CCZb-Jonp8Nb/. Accessed 5 July 2022.

Robbins, Hannah. "'I Can't Be What You Expect of Me': Power, Palatability, and Shame in *Frozen: The Broadway Musical*." *Arts* 9.1.39: 1–13. 2020.

Saturday Night Live. "Frozen 2 – SNL." *YouTube*, 2 February 2020, www.youtube.com/watch?v=tKvDw6cfR3c, accessed 6 January 2022.

Schrodt, Paul. "First Class: The Latest Chapter in the *X-Men* Gay-Rights Parable." *Atlantic*. 6 June 2011. www.theatlantic.com/entertainment/archive/2011/06/first-class-the-latest-chapter-in-the-x-men-gay-rights-parable/239959/. Accessed 6 January 2022.

Sexton, Aurora "US of Aurora Episode 2: Miss Gay USofA." *YouTube*. 18 October 2016. youtu.be/7-dv200–10s. Accessed 6 January 2022.

"Snatch Game." *RuPaul's Drag Race* 12.6. 3 April 2020.

Solomon, Charles. *The Art of Frozen*. San Francisco: Chronicle Books, 2013.

Stockton, Kathryn Bond. *The Queer Child, or Growing Up Sideways in the Twentieth Century*. Durham: Duke University Press, 2009.

Taylor, Tommy. "It's Getting Nippy Out There . . ." *Instagram*. 3 December 2019. www.instagram.com/p/B5oAUMJAjaQ/. Accessed 5 July 2022.

Vary, Adam B. "Mutant Is the New Gay." *Advocate*. 23 May 2006. (44–45).

Walt Disney Animation Studios. "'Pink Lemonade' | At Home with Olaf." *YouTube*. 28 April 2020. www.youtube.com/watch?v=6LpF0ZHTkqs. Accessed 6 January 2022.

West, Nina. "Nina West – Entertainer of the Year 2008 – Evening Gown." *YouTube*. 10 October 2014. youtu.be/45SZVE86HkY. Accessed 6 January 2022.

White, Patricia. *Uninvited: Classical Hollywood Cinema and Lesbian Representability*. Bloomington: Indiana University Press, 1999.

Whitfield, Sarah K. "'For the First Time in Forever': Locating *Frozen* as a Feminist Musical." In *The Disney Musical on Stage and Screen: Critical Approaches from 'Snow White' to 'Frozen'*. Edited by George Rodosthenous. London: Bloomsbury, 221–238, 2017.

Wilkinson, Alissa. "Why the Frozen Short That Played Before Pixar's Coco Kicked Up So Much Controversy." *Vox*. 14 December 2017. www.vox.com/culture/2017/12/4/16709884/olafs-frozen-adventure-coco-disney-pixar-explained. Accessed 15 August 2022.

INDEX

Addams Family, The 12
Advocate, The 49–51, 110
Ain't Too Proud: The Life and Times of the Temptations 25
Aladdin 157–158, 172
Alice in Wonderland 158
Alladin, Jelani 166, 172
Allegiance 2
American Idiot 12
Andersen, Hans Christian 25, 29, 158–160
Anderson-Lopez, Kristen 29, 169
Andrews, Julie 21
Annie 12, 76–77
Apartment, The 27–28, 40, 43–46, 48, 54, 56
Ashford, Rob 40, 46
Ashmanskas, Brooks 46, 55, 60n40
Astaire, Fred 42
At Home with Olaf 156, 169, 172–173
AURORA 161

Bacharach, Burt 27, 46
Bale, Christian 65, 67, 77
Barrino, Fantasia 143
bathroom bills 7, 93
Be More Chill 74
Billy Elliot 83
Billy's Hollywood Screen Kiss 49
bisexual 8, 10, 23–25, 33n82, 41, 57, 68, 96, 100, 111, 123, 166, 177n48
Black, Dustin Lance 39, 51
Black Lives Matter 124, 132, 138–139
blood ban *see* Food and Drug Administration

Brando, Marlon 77
Brantley, Ben 53–54, 66–67, 83, 122, 124
Bray, Stephen 29, 122, 130, 142, 146n3
Bridgforth, Sharon 148n73
Bright Star 2
Broadway Cares/Equity Fights AIDS 73–74
Broadway Circle Up 125, 132, 138–141, 145
Buck, Chris 29
burlesque 80–82, 167

Cabaret 19, 106
Cage aux Folles, La 11
Calhoun, Jeff 65, 68, 77, 82
Carousel 20
Castile, Philando 125, 132
casting 2, 39, 48, 56–58, 86–87, 102–108, 116n57, 172
Cats 55
Chachki, Violet 165
Chenoweth, Kristin 27, 39, 41, 50–51, 54, 61n82
chosen family 68, 72, 74–75, 88, 163, 175
Christianity 6–7, 29, 127–131, 138, 145
Cinderella 12, 105, 156, 158
Clinton, Hillary 3, 73, 125
closet 6, 24, 28, 30, 40–41, 43–51, 55–58, 161, 165, 171, 175
Coalition Against Black Exploitation 132
Color Purple, The (film) 20, 29, 121–123, 129–131, 132–135, 141, 145; "Sister (Miss Celie's Blues)" 129, 134

Color Purple, The (musical) 2, 5, 11, 13, 20, 24, 27, 29, 121–146, 175; "Any Little Thing" 136–137; "The Color Purple" (song) 130–131, 140–141, 142, 145–146; "I'm Here" 124, 142–146; "Lily of the Field" 142; "Mister Song" 135–136, 139; "Mister's Nightmare" 142; "Mysterious Ways" 124, 131; "Our Prayer" 141; "Push da Button" 134; "Somebody Gonna Love You" 141; "Sunday Morning" 131; "Too Beautiful for Words" 134; "What about Love?" 123, 145
Color Purple, The (novel) 20, 24, 29, 121–131, 132–142, 145
Come from Away 12
Company 19, 52
concept musical 19
Corden, James 3–5, 10–11, 13, 28, 39–40, 55–59
Covid-19 *see* SARS-COV-2
Criss, Darren 58, 103, 106–108, 111
cryokinesis *see* magic powers

Darling Lili 52
dating apps 6, 54–55
David, Hal 27, 46
Dear Evan Hansen 12, 74
DeBose, Ariana 13, 55, 57
Democratic Party 11, 125
Design for Living 42–43, 46–47
Diamond, I.A.L. 27, 43–44, 60n43
Diana: The Musical 12
Diggs, Taye 95, 103, 107–108
disability critiques 28, 84–85, 88, 110, 113–114
Disney Theatrical Productions 76–77, 86–87, 155
Disney villains 78, 88, 157–159, 163, 166–167, 176n17
Domingo, Colman 73
Don't Ask Don't Tell 12
down low 48–49
Doyle, John 122, 131
drag 81–82, 96, 97, 99, 100, 103, 107, 109, 154–156, 165, 175n8

Eltinge, Julian 82
Encanto 12, 171
Erivo, Cynthia 29, 122, 124–125, 132, 140, 144–145
essentialism 33n82, 51–52, 123, 160–161, 166, 174–175
Everett, Rupert 27
Everybody's Talking about Jamie 12

fairy 28, 68, 81–82
Falsettos 11
Fankhauser, Ben 77
Federal Bureau of Investigation 44
Feldman, Jack 28, 65, 67–68, 71, 81–82
femininity 28, 39, 42, 51, 52–57, 75–76, 78–80, 82–85, 97, 100, 105, 107
Fiddler on the Roof 2
Fierstein, Harvey 28, 65, 68, 71, 74–75, 78, 81–82, 89n17
Floyd, George 138
Food and Drug Administration 6
Franklin, Aretha 27, 100
Frozen (film) 23, 27, 29–30, 153–163, 165–167, 170–172; "Do You Want to Build a Snowman?" 170; "Fixer Upper" 166; "For the First Time in Forever" 157, 161, 170; "In Summer" 169; "Let It Go" 154–157, 165; "Love Is an Open Door" 157
Frozen (musical) 5, 13, 25, 27, 29–30, 153–175; "Dangerous to Dream" 164–165; "Do You Want to Build a Snowman?" 164, 168; "Fixer Upper" 164, 166; "For the First Time in Forever" 164; "Hans of the Southern Isles" 166; "Hygge" 167–168; "In Summer" 164, 168–169; "Let It Go" 164–165; "A Little Bit of You" 164, 172; "Love Is an Open Door" 164; "Monster" 166; "Reindeer(s) Are Better Than People" 164; "True Love" 167
Frozen Fever 156, 157, 160–161, 168, 170
Frozen II 29, 153–154, 156–157, 160, 161–164, 167, 170–172, 174; "All Is Found" 162; "Into the Unknown" 161–162; "Show Yourself" 161–163
Fun Home 1–2, 11, 12, 30n4

Gad, Josh 172
Gattelli, Christopher 66–67, 68, 80, 82, 83
Gay & Lesbian Alliance Against Defamation 9, 39, 41, 51, 110
gender-reveal party 94
Glee 53, 73, 106, 111
Goldberg, Whoopi 121, 133, 141
Grandage, Michael 163
Greatest Showman, The 80
Greeley, Horace 69, 79
Griffin, Gary 122
Grindr *see* dating apps
Groff, Jonathan 38, 51, 53
gun violence 2–3, 6, 8–9, 139, 148n51

Hall, Lena 103, 108
Hall, Michael C. 103, 106, 108, 114
Hamilton 2–4, 10–11, 103, 107, 125, 132, 139–140
Harris, Neil Patrick 29, 41, 51, 52, 73, 93, 103–106, 108, 114, 116n62
Hart, Lorenz 47
Hayes, Sean 27–28, 38–39, 41–43, 45, 47, 49–52, 54–55, 60n63, 61n82
Headley, Heather 29, 124–126, 131, 145
Head over Heels 11, 103
Hedwig and the Angry Inch (film) 28, 95–97
Hedwig and the Angry Inch (musical) 5, 13, 24, 28–29, 93–114, 123, 175; "The Angry Inch" 101; "Exquisite Corpse" 101; "Midnight Radio" 99–100, 114; "The Origin of Love" 98–99, 112–113, 114; "Tear Me Down" 101; "Wicked Little Town" 99
Hercules 158
HIV/AIDS 48, 73–74
homophobia 7, 10–11, 39, 41–42, 48, 51, 55–56, 58, 72–74, 146
Horton, Edward Everett 42–43
House Un-American Activities Committee 44
How I Met Your Mother 41, 105
Hudson, Jennifer 29, 122, 124, 143, 145
Human Rights Campaign 8, 9, 94, 110

In Dahomey 82
integrated musicals 19–21, 32n65, 45
In the Heights 12, 20
Islam 6–7, 8
It Gets Better 12, 28, 72–75, 84–85, 87–88, 163

Jagged Little Pill 25
Jenner, Caitlyn 93
Jepsen, Adam 166
Jesús, Robin de 73
Johansson, Scarlett 103
Jones, Cherry 73
Jordan, Jeremy 77
jukebox musical 25, 164

Keenan-Bolger, Andrew 77
Kelly, Gene 66
Kennedy Center Honors 124, 143, 145
Kidd, Michael 66
Kidman, Nicole 55
Kilroys List 93
King and I, The 2
Kron, Lisa 1–2, 12

Lane, Nathan 73
Latinidad 2, 4, 6–7, 9–10, 31n32
Lawson, Richard 39–40, 56
Leavel, Beth 55
Lee, Jennifer 29, 159–160
Levy, Caissie 155, 165
Lewis, C.S. 29–30, 176n18
Lion King, The 67, 132, 172
Little Mermaid, The 172
Lopez, Robert 29, 169
Luwoye, Michael 139

Madonna 53
magic powers 156, 157, 159–160, 163, 165, 171–174
Manning, Chelsea 12, 94
marriage 7, 9–10, 12, 26, 31n30, 72, 98, 109–110, 113, 126, 139, 153, 157–158, 175n11
masculinity 27, 28, 40, 42–43, 46–47, 53–57, 69, 75–78, 80–84, 86, 105, 114, 115n37, 132–138
McDonald, Audra 73
McKinnon, Kate 153–154, 155
Mean Girls 12
Menken, Alan 28, 65, 71, 77, 82
Menzel, Idina 53, 155, 163, 165
Miranda, Lin-Manuel 4–5, 9–10, 31n32, 73, 125, 126
Mitchell, John Cameron 28–29, 95–97, 100–102, 103–104, 106, 108, 112, 114
Morton, Euan 103, 107
Motown 132
Murphy, Ryan 24, 39, 41, 51, 55–57
Music Man, The 44, 52

Natasha, Pierre & the Great Comet of 1812 103
National Football League 74
National Rifle Association 8
Newsies (film) 27–28, 65, 67–72, 78, 80–81, 88; "High Times, Hard Times" 80; "King of New York" 82; "My Lovey-Dovey Baby" 80–81; "Santa Fe" 69, 71; "Seize the Day" 71; "The World Will Know" 75
Newsies (musical) 5, 13, 24, 27–28, 65–88, 163, 175; "Carrying the Banner" 77, 78; "King of New York" 78, 79–80, 82; "Letter from The Refuge" 72, 87; "Once and for All" 71, 84; "Santa Fe" 71–72, 75, 76; "Seize the Day" 67, 71–72; "Something to Believe In" 75; "That's Rich" 81, 87; "Watch What Happens" 75, 79

Newsies jr. 28, 66, 86–88; "Just a Pretty Face" 87–88; "Letter from The Refuge" 87
No, No, Nanette 52
nonbinary 8, 57, 58, 86, 93–94, 98, 103, 111–112, 175
Norman, Marsha 29, 122, 130, 135, 137, 142, 146n3

Obama, Barack 12, 73, 93
Obama, Michelle! 67
O'Hara, Asia 165
Oklahoma! 25, 52
Olaf's Frozen Adventure 156, 157, 160, 167–168, 170, 172, 175n10, 176n34
Oliver! 76–77
Once upon a Snowman 156, 168, 172–174
On Your Feet! 2
Orbach, Jerry 27, 54
orphanhood 65, 69–71, 77
Ortega, Kenny 65, 66, 68, 70–71, 80

Pellman, Jo Ellen 55, 57–58
Pence, Mike 4, 11
Penn, Sean 58
performativity 8, 18, 23, 42, 46–48, 107, 166
Peter Pan 158
Pink Pistols 8–9
Plato 24, 28, 95, 98–99, 113
Pocahontas 158
Porgy and Bess 20, 25
Porter, Billy 73
Porter, Cole 47
Priscilla, Queen of the Desert 11, 73
prison 8, 12, 29, 70, 138–139, 159–160
Prom, The 13, 24, 28, 39–40, 55–58, 59
Promises, Promises 5, 13, 24, 27–28, 38–59, 175; "A Fact Can Be a Beautiful Thing" 44; "Half as Big as Life" 46; "A House Is Not a Home" 27; "I Say a Little Prayer" 27; "Our Little Secret" 44–45; "She Likes Basketball" 44; "Where Can You Take a Girl?" 45
Pulse Massacre 2–10, 12, 31n32, 125; *see also* gun violence

Rannells, Andrew 55, 103, 105–106, 108, 114
Reach Out 74
Redmond, Ryann 173
Renée, Ciara 173
Republican Party 6, 125
Respect 12
Rich, Frank 52
Ricketts, Noah 166

Riedel, Michael 54, 66
Roberts, Julia 125
Roosevelt, Theodore 70, 78–79, 81
RuPaul's Drag Race 30, 154–156, 165, 175n5
Russell, Brenda 29, 122, 130, 142, 146n3

Salonga, Lea 2, 131
Sanders, Scott 122, 134
SARS-COV-2 12, 156, 175n6
Saturday Night Live 25, 30, 153–156, 161, 164, 169, 172
Savage, Dan 28, 72–73, 85; *see also* It Gets Better
Scatliffe, Kyle 125, 132
School of Rock 2
Scottsboro Boys, The 12
Setoodeh, Ramin 38–41, 45, 47, 51–55, 56, 59n2, 59n11
Sexton, Aurora 165
Shange, Ntozake 147n47
Show Boat 25
Shuffle Along 2, 132
Simon, Neil 27, 40, 43–46, 53, 60n36, 60n43
sissy 41–43, 46–47, 54, 56–57, 82; *see also* fairy
Smash 77
Smith, Austin 139
social media 3–6, 10, 14–15, 17, 25, 30, 54, 67, 75, 125, 143–144, 154–155, 175n8
Sound of Music, The 153–154
South Pacific 20
Spielberg, Steven 20, 55, 121–123, 129, 132–135, 145
Spring Awakening 2, 83
Sterling, Alton 125
Stonewall 24, 42, 47, 52, 109
Strange Loop, A 11, 18
Streep, Meryl 55
Strong, Cecily 153–154, 161
Sullivan, Jazmine 144
Symposium 24, 28, 95, 98–99, 112–114, 115n31, 175

Taylor, Regina 146n3
terrorism 2, 5–6, 125
Tesori, Jeanine 1
Tick, Tick . . . Boom! 12
Tinder *see* dating apps
Tony Awards 2010 39
Tony Awards 2011 52
Tony Awards 2012 65, 67

Tony Awards 2014 95, 103
Tony Awards 2015 1–2, 12
Tony Awards 2016 2–5, 9–12, 121–122, 124–126, 131, 143–144
Tootsie 12
transphobia 7, 48, 93, 109–110
Trask, Stephen 28, 101, 103–104, 108, 112
Trevor Project 74
Trump, Donald 3, 4, 6–7, 11, 12

Vandross, Luther 27
villains *see* Disney villains

Waitress 25
Walker, Aida Overton 28, 81–82
Walker, Alice 20, 29, 121–122, 124, 126, 129–132, 135–141, 145, 146n6, 147n47, 148n63
Walker, George 82
Warwick, Dionne 27

West, Mae 28, 81–82
West, Nina 165
West Side Story 12, 20, 55, 77, 89n45
Wicked 13, 53, 172
Wilder, Billy 27, 43–44, 60n43
Wiley, Samira 29, 145
Will & Grace 28, 38, 41–42, 49, 59n22
Williams, Bert 82
Williams, Michelle 122
Willis, Allee 29, 122, 130, 134, 142, 146n3
Winfrey, Oprah 121, 143
womanist 123–124, 138, 146n6
Women on the Verge of a Nervous Breakdown 12

X-men 41, 157

Yentl 103

Zadan, Craig 50

For Product Safety Concerns and Information please contact our EU
representative GPSR@taylorandfrancis.com
Taylor & Francis Verlag GmbH, Kaufingerstraße 24, 80331 München, Germany

www.ingramcontent.com/pod-product-compliance
Lightning Source LLC
Chambersburg PA
CBHW050302010526
44108CB00040B/2080